'Alan and Jackie Gear have been congratulated by supporters of the organic gardening movement, including the Prince of Wales, for their 25 years at the helm of the Henry Doubleday Research Association. Over the years, the couple's dedication and efforts have transformed the association and helped to gain the organic movement the mainstream respect that it enjoys today.'
– *BBC Gardeners' World* magazine, January, 1999

'A compelling insight into the organic movement, from the global issues to the microbes in your compost heap, from the couple who were near the heart, then at the helm, of the UK's largest organic organization for 30 years.'
– Joy Larkcom author of *Grow Your Own Vegetables*. *The Independent* referred to Joy as 'the most influential British writer on vegetables today.'

'Jackie and Alan Gear have been the driving force behind campaigns to get us growing without chemicals in our gardens. It is thanks to the couple's unflagging dedication that organic gardening has blossomed in this country.'
– *Mail on Sunday*, 26 October, 2003

'For 30 years Jackie and Alan have been the driving force behind HDRA, the largest organic organization in Europe. They educated, informed and inspired a growing army of organic gardeners. They are an extraordinary couple who gave up everything to spread the word of organic gardening.'
– Monty Don, Presenter of *Gardening Heroes* August 2005

In 2006 the Royal Horticultural Society conferred Honorary Fellowships on them citing, 'Since 1975 Alan and Jackie have helped organic gardening develop from being a fringe activity into what is now the major influence on 21st-century gardens and gardening.'

'Somehow they've managed to persist; it's determination, keeping repeating the message, doing good science, good research; it's just been amazing; one of the great stories of horticulture in the last couple of decades.'
– Rosie Atkins, Director of the Chelsea Physic Garden, speaking on *Gardening Heroes*

'Alan and Jackie made growing your own organic fruit and vegetables popular, and reconnected us with both our soil and our food.'
– Raymond Blanc OBE, February 2009

Alan and Jackie Gear both gave up science careers in their early years to take up full-time organic gardening. Appointed directors of the Henry Double-day Research Association in the 1980s they subsequently became household names as presenters of the first television series devoted to their subject, *All Muck and Magic?* They have continued to spread the word about organic gardening through countless TV and radio programmes such as the BBC's *Gardeners' World*, *The Food Programme* and *Farming Today*. Between them they have written numerous books, and articles for most of the quality national newspapers as well as the gardening press.

Alan and Jackie resigned from the HDRA in 2003 and set up their own consultancy, working on a range of organic gardening, farming and food projects. Clients to date include chef Raymond Blanc, the national fruit centre at Brogdale in Kent and The Jerusalem Trust. The couple were each awarded an MBE for services to organic horticulture in 2003.

oRGANIc GARDENING: THE WHOLE STORY

Foreword by

HRH The Prince of Wales

ALAN & JACKIE GEAR

PUBLISHING

)NDON

This edition published in the UK in 2009 by
Watkins Publishing, Sixth Floor, Castle House,
75–76 Wells Street, London W1T 3QH

1 3 5 7 9 10 8 6 4 2

Edited by Diana Loxley
Designed and typeset by Paul Saunders

Printed and bound in Great Britain by Athenaeum Press Ltd

British Library Cataloguing-in-Publication Data Available

ISBN: 978-1- 906787-24-0

www.watkinspublishing.co.uk

This book is dedicated to Graham Parker and his wife Sue,
and to Betty Albon and her husband David.

CONTENTS

LIST OF PLATES

PLATES 1 and 2 Jackie and Alan arriving at Braintree railway station in the early days of working for HDRA. © Alan and Jackie Gear

PLATE 3 Lawrence D Hills, HDRA founder and director from 1958 to 1986. © Alan and Jackie Gear

PLATE 4 Jackie receives instruction from Lawrence D Hills on the Bocking trialground, 1975. © HDRA

PLATE 5 Alan and Jackie Gear at Ryton, not long after the gardens opened, 1987. Reproduced with the kind permission of ITV West

PLATE 6 The Prince of Wales chats to Alan Gear during his first visit to Ryton Gardens, July 1989. Reproduced with the kind permission of *The Rugby Advertiser*

PLATE 7 Jackie Gear with organic wine producer, Dr Huw Tripp, and Joanna Simon, *Sunday Times* Wine correspondent, at the first National Organic Wine Fair, July 1988. Reproduced with the kind permission of The Rugby Advertiser

PLATE 8 Joy Larkcom at Ryton in the late-1980s. © HDRA

PLATE 9 Keen organic gardener, Thelma Barlow, the popular actress from ITV's *Coronation Street*, 1998. © David Lawson

PLATE 10 Channel 4's *All Muck and Magic?* Britain's first organic gardening television series. Pauline Pears, Alan and Jackie Gear, Sue Stickland and Bob Sherman. Reproduced with the kind permission of ITV West

PLATE 11 The ever-popular composting display at Ryton, 1990. © HDRA

PLATE 12 The Cook's Garden at Ryton, 1998. © David Lawson

PLATE 13 Dr Bill Blyth, HDRA Chairman from 1992 to 2004. © Kit Brooke-Harris

PLATE 14 Commercial vegetable variety trial at Ryton. © HDRA

PLATE 15 Community intensive vegetable growing in Cuba, 1997. © Phil Harris

PLATE 16 The National Trust's Plot to Plate vegetable growing display at the Chelsea Flower Show, 2002. © Mike Calnan, courtesy of The National Trust

PLATE 17 Potato variety display at Ryton Garden's national Potato Day event, 2002. © David Lawson

PLATE 18 Actress Susan Hampshire at the 2002 Chelsea Flower Show with HDRA gardener Rebecca Costello on the Alitex stand. Reproduced with the kind permission of Alitex Ltd., specialists in Greenhouses and Conservatories

PLATE 19 Children at Howarth Primary School demonstrate their vegetable-growing credentials. Reproduced with the kind permission of Howarth Primary School

PLATE 20 Garden Organic Vice President and keen organic enthusiast, celebrity chef Raymond Blanc. Reproduced with the kind permission of Raymond Blanc

PLATE 21 Geoff Hamilton – one of the country's most popular TV gardeners of all time. Reproduced with the kind permission of Barnsdale Gardens

PLATE 22 Bird's-eye view of the Vegetable Kingdom, HDRA headquarters and part of the gardens at Ryton, 2008. © Andy Sadler

ACKNOWLEDGEMENTS

Alan and I have written books before, but none has been as multi-disciplinary as this one, covering, as it does, aspects of history, science, philosophy and practical horticulture, so we are especially grateful to the many people who have helped us. First, we are indebted to our agent, Jane Graham Maw, for her tenacity, and to Michael Mann, our publisher, for his faith in us, his sheer exuberance and, last but not least, his own knowledge of organic gardening. We'd also like to thank his colleagues at Watkins, including Penny Stopa and Diana Loxley, our eagle-eyed editor.

We couldn't have amassed all the information in this story without spending many years in the organic movement, where we, and HDRA (Henry Doubleday Research Association), were given truly outstanding support. The organization's founder, Lawrence Hills, that organic gardening giant, was our mentor and an infinitely interesting and informative companion. Where we have included narrative involving Lawrence it is usually based on the many conversations he had with us. However, dialogue that relates to the period prior to our joining the organization has been adapted from written reports in HDRA's members' bulletins.

We were also fortunate to work with Pauline Pears, one of today's organic gardening giants, who joined the organization early on at Braintree, and we thank her for casting a friendly eye over chapter five.

Sue Stickland, Bob Sherman and Margi Lennartsson joined us at Ryton – all experts in their fields, whom we depended on consistently over our working lives there. Likewise, HDRA's Council, which underpinned our work as directors, was blessed with some outstanding figures. Dr Bill Blyth, its long-time Chairman, was one such – a source of great intelligence, stability and commonsense. His calming presence meant the world to us, and he helped to make organic gardening what it is today. Lord Kitchener, too, served the organization steadfastly and with great dignity as its President. He and Bill provided the continuity at HDRA that was necessary for the smooth evolution of the organic philosophy in this country. Similarly, Graham Dodd, the organization's one-time Honorary Treasurer, saw the organization safely through many financial ups and downs over the years.

On our staff there have been many stars – too numerous to describe, but Alan's wonderful PA, Chris Bailey, acted with perfect professionalism at all times; just as I depended on Angela Bull during her shorter, but always supportive, career with the organization. We were blessed with many other hard-working team members, some of whom could have earned a lot more money elsewhere – webmaster Simon Levermore springs to mind – and those who were simply special characters, including handyman Mike Campisi who is, sadly, no longer with us. He would turn his hand to any practical task at a moment's notice and, in doing so, saved the organization many thousands of pounds over the years.

Myles Bremner is now the Chief Executive of Garden Organic and we thank him for giving us access to HDRA's archives, including the extensive picture library, and also for the generous assistance provided by his members of staff.

The most important organic gardening projects mentioned in this book could not have gone ahead without generous donations from major supporters, who truly believed in what we were trying to achieve. Leslie Marr, Amy Goldman and Charlotte Albuquerque have been outstanding in this respect. Likewise David Morrell, whose legacy to the organization was also his personal legacy to organic gardening. We have also been fortunate in enlisting help from contributors who are known to the world at large: actresses Thelma Barlow and Susan Hampshire, culinary supremos Raymond Blanc and Sophie Grigson, and professional horticulturalists, such as Monty Don and the late Geoff Hamilton, head a star-studded list of personalities who have assisted HDRA over the years.

A word should also be said in recognition of the countless ordinary organic gardeners up and down the UK – HDRA's, and now Garden Organic's, members and local groups. All these people have helped us to push organic gardening forward, although perhaps none more so than the organization's patron, The Prince of Wales. His Royal Highness has been instrumental in promoting organic growing over decades, and we also thank him profoundly for contributing the Foreword to this book.

On a more personal note, I would like to thank Heather Gerrard, my aunt, for passing on to me her love of the English language; and, finally, our parents, whom we miss dearly. They gave us much love, support and encouragement, and we thank them from the bottom of our hearts.

Jackie Gear, Snettisham, Norfolk, Christmas 2008

I was delighted to be asked by Alan and Jackie to contribute a Foreword to this book which charts the astonishing rise in popularity of organic gardening over the past sixty, or so, years.

When I began to garden at Highgrove in the early 1980's I was determined to do so in ways that avoided using artificial fertilizers and pesticides. I need hardly say that, at the time, a multitude of eyebrows were raised at what was viewed as a highly retrograde and unfashionable step. However, I had been deeply moved when I was young by the dreadful destruction wrought on the British countryside by two decades of chemically-driven agri-industrial intensification and, in my own small way, I wanted to redress the balance on the farm at Highgrove and in the garden by re-establishing a rapport with Nature.

For most of my adult life I have believed strongly that we abuse the environment at our peril, and that this chemical agri-industrial 'experiment', for that is what it is, whilst being undoubtedly successful in increasing food production in the short term, has been at the expense of the long-term sustainability of the land. The very survival of the human race, I believe, depends on us revisiting the accumulated wisdom of our ancestors and grafting onto it the latest scientific developments in ecological growing.

I first met Alan and Jackie not long after they had taken over running Garden Organic, or the Henry Doubleday Research Association as it was known then, from its founder, Lawrence Hills. I became Patron of the organization in 1989 and, over the years, I have had the pleasure of visiting its headquarters at Ryton Gardens on a number of occasions, each time observing the gradual transformation of what had been a bare field into an inspirational and productive showcase for organic methods – the first of its kind anywhere.

I wonder if Lawrence Hills ever imagined that Alan and Jackie, and their group of dedicated and determined staff, would develop his organization into one of the foremost organic institutions, respected the world over for its scientific research and educational work which has, I am sure, contributed in no little way to the huge change in public consciousness towards organic gardening and food that we see today? Equally important, in my view, has been Garden Organic's championing of traditional varieties of vegetables in the face of European legislation which, had it not been for its efforts, would have led to many hundreds of varieties becoming extinct.

I do know that this work, however worthy, would not have changed hearts and minds in the way that it did without the professionalism and bubbling enthusiasm shown by Jackie in her particular areas of responsibility – the commercial, promotional and fundraising activities of the organization. For, in my opinion, it was the gardeners who led the organic revolution in the country and now, as I say, even more people are growing their own organic fruit and vegetables and look to Garden Organic for help and advice.

I particularly commend other organic gardening practitioners and supporters, whether unsung growers up and down the land or the more well-known media gardeners, for their continuing endeavours to cultivate this precious land of ours in a way that will nurture it, and therefore successive generations to come.

I wholeheartedly recommend organic growing to anyone who has never done it before – and I mean anyone – wherever you live and however small your own particular plot of land. It is an activity that will repay you many times over for your efforts, with a bounty that includes healthy, tasty food, real enjoyment and spiritual well-being.

INTRODUCTION

WHAT IS ORGANIC GARDENING? Most people would probably say that it means growing plants without the use of chemical sprays and fertilizers. But this is only part of the story. The real secret of environmentally friendly organic gardening lies in looking after that most underrated, and yet most precious, of resources – the soil. Lady Eve Balfour, a pioneering organic farmer in the 1940s, described it as the 'living earth'. And indeed, far from being inanimate dirt, soil is literally teeming with life – not just with the worms and other magnificent creatures that are revealed when you turn over a clod of earth, but also with the billions of infinitesimally tiny bacteria, fungi and other organisms that are invisible to the naked eye, of which there are more in a single, heaped teaspoonful than there are people on the planet. It's these organisms that convert complex organic matter in the soil into the simpler chemicals of life upon which plants depend. The job of the organic gardener is to supply the soil with the organic matter it needs. Feed the soil and this, in turn, feeds the plants. And the more fertile it becomes, the stronger and healthier are the plants that grow there. But this won't happen overnight, so we must find some interim means of controlling potentially harmful pests and diseases without resorting to pesticides. As it happens, there are lots of non-chemical ways of keeping damage to the minimum, such as covering crops with netting and other physical barriers, planting disease-resisting varieties, operating a crop rotation, and encouraging beneficial creatures like ladybird beetles and frogs into the garden.

This natural approach to growing is nothing unusual these days. Imagine, for example, that it's a Friday evening and you're watching the gardening programme on television. The camera pans lazily over a crop of ripening broad beans and comes to rest on the presenter, who is busy forking compost into the soil. As he turns towards you he notices that several of the bean plants are infested with scores of tiny black insects, each no bigger than a grain of rice, that are feeding on the fresh, young growth. 'Blackfly!' he exclaims, and hastily pinches out the top few inches. 'That's the end of them! The ladybirds can eat what's left.' As he walks slowly along the narrow path through the vegetable garden a dragonfly hovers over a pond to his left, seemingly motionless, its iridescent wings shimmering in the bright sunlight. A couple of frogs peer out, goggle-eyed, from below the water's surface. 'It's a pleasure to see them, isn't it?' he says, as he passes. 'We wanted to attract frogs to the garden so we'd have fewer slugs.' Next in shot are a couple of rows of carrots, just visible under a protective covering of fine, white net, which will stay on all season as a defence against carrot-root flies that might otherwise seriously damage the crop. Many of the vegetables are covered with netting of one type or another: some to ward off cabbage white butterflies whose caterpillars can reduce cabbage leaves to shreds; others, with larger mesh, to prevent attack by birds.

At the far end of the plot the presenter pauses for a moment by what look like compost bins and explains that the fruit tree he is about to plant will need plenty of compost and a good dressing of bonemeal, which is a great source of nutrients for the roots. With a well-practised hand he sprinkles a generous fistful of gritty, grey powder onto the soil and deftly back-fills the hole with soil, mixed half and half with rich, dark compost. 'And that's it – job done,' he remarks contentedly, as he hands over to his co-presenter.

Although the cameo I've just described is entirely fictitious, you could see something similar on any gardening programme nowadays. It's only when you compare it with the situation several decades ago that you can appreciate how dramatically the approach to gardening has altered. If this programme had been made in the early-1960s, for example, the scene would have been very different. For a start, the blackfly on the beans would have been drenched with DDT, which back then was being hailed as a miracle spray. And while it did indeed kill blackfly, it also killed ladybirds and many other innocent creatures. Few gardeners would have dug a pond in their vegetable plot to attract beneficial wildlife for the purposes of pest control. The idea would have seemed incredible to them. Fine woven mesh had yet to be invented, so the carrots would also have been sprayed, as would most of the other crops in the garden. In fact, it was standard practice to spray on a regular basis, just as a precaution. And as for compost and manure, TV presenters and most gardeners were convinced that these bulky organic wastes had had their day and that artificial fertilizers, which were clean, compact and scientifically formulated, were the thing of the future. This vision of gardening held sway for much of the last century. How, then, did it come to be so comprehensively eclipsed by organic growing? What is it about a more natural way of gardening that has captured people's imagination?

Answering these questions is what this book is all about. It's told as a story that has its beginnings in the early part of the last century, when chemical fertilizers replaced farmyard manure that had for so long been the foundation of farming fertility. In the 1950s, powerful new pesticides appeared on the farming scene, offering a seductive vision of a world free from the scourge of pests, diseases and weeds. Gardeners were also quick to embrace the new sprays and fertilizers. At long last, it seemed, humans had triumphed over nature.

But not everyone was caught up in the euphoria. A few far-sighted individuals expressed concern that the widespread use of chemicals would cause unacceptable damage to the environment and that food wouldn't be as nourishing. Agriculture and horticulture, they believed, should be firmly rooted in a respect for natural systems. They coined the term 'organic growing' for this method of working with nature. But few were listening.

Throughout the 1960s the vast majority of farmers and gardeners continued their love affair with chemicals, but the tide started to turn in the mid-1970s, as the ensuing environmental damage became too great to ignore. Rivers and lakes were polluted by fertilizers and pesticides, which 'ran off' the fields. Hundreds of thousands of acres of priceless habitats were destroyed, wildlife was decimated as a result of pesticide poisoning, and some species were brought to the brink of extinction.

This is where Jackie and I entered the story. We were part of the 'back to the land' generation of young people who quit their jobs and left the cities to begin a 'self-sufficient' life in the countryside. In our case, we started working for Lawrence Hills, one of the organic pioneers, who had gone on to set up an organic gardening research organization on a couple of acres of land in Essex. A decade later he retired and we took over as directors of the Henry Doubleday Research Association, or HDRA as it was known then. We relocated the organization to the Midlands, setting up the national centre for organic gardening at Ryton Gardens, near Coventry.

Over the next 20 years organic gardening was rarely out of the spotlight – a constant stream of HDRA projects, campaigns and media appearances kept it firmly in the public eye. Combined with public concern about the way in which government and big business consistently relegated issues affecting the environment, food and health to the sidelines, the popularity of organic gardening exploded.

All sorts of people became involved. The Prince of Wales cultivated his garden at Highgrove organically, television gardening presenters and other 'personalities' went organic, and more and more individuals began to grow their own organic fruit and vegetables. The consequence of all this is that today, children in school gardens, young people saving on the housekeeping, inner-city community gardeners and countless others are reconnecting with the land and discovering the joys of organic growing. Sales of vegetable seeds have exceeded those of flowers for the first time since the Second World War, and in some places you may have to wait ten years for an allotment. And this trend is not confined to Britain. Organic gardening is on the increase across the world – in Europe, America, Australia and New Zealand. It's a global phenomenon. Even in the Third World, where hunger is an ever-present threat for millions of people, small-scale organic farming (organic gardening, essentially), which is cheap, easy and safe, is increasingly being seen as the best way of insuring against future food shortages.

This book offers a clear and comprehensive understanding of the background, principles and practices involved in organic gardening. At its heart is a respect for the incredible sophistication of natural systems. Nature doesn't use artificial fertilizers and pesticides, so why should we? If you haven't grown organically before, or even if you haven't gardened at all, it will offer you some invaluable insights before you get started. You don't need a huge garden – you can be organic on the tiniest of plots. So go on, it's great fun! Not only that, but you'll be eating the most delicious, healthy produce you've ever tasted.

This story of organic gardening is written from an unashamedly personal perspective. Jackie and I have been at the heart of the organic world for more than 30 years, most of them at HDRA, which recently changed its name to Garden Organic. Its inspirational team of people has led the way in developing organic gardening practice into what it is today, and we are privileged to have been a part of it. It's perhaps inevitable, therefore, that the story should be seen through our eyes. Many of the facts, observations and opinions expressed in the book are a result of theoretical and practical knowledge gained over a lifetime of learning and working in the organic movement, including countless conversations with its pioneers, HDRA's staff and members, as well as with other gardeners, farmers and scientists across the world. We've made a conscious decision not to write it as a textbook, with every statement annotated; however, the reading list at the end has been carefully compiled to offer sources of additional information for those who may wish to delve into the subject in more detail.

In the same spirit of readability, we've used the first person singular throughout the book. Jackie and I have been equal partners during our working lives and share the same philosophy; so working in the organic movement has been a truly joint experience. We have embraced our triumphs and our low moments, our joys and heartaches, and our trials and tribulations together. We hope you enjoy the tale, and will turn the final page feeling that you have gained a real understanding of what organic gardening is all about.

Chapter One

ORIGINS

LIKE MANY PEOPLE, there's nothing I like better than pottering about in the garden. Pruning an old apple tree, digging a patch of weedy ground or watching life unfold as tiny seeds grow into sturdy young plants is somehow deeply satisfying. As organic gardeners, Jackie and I also enjoy observing the magical transformation of a pile of rotting garden and kitchen waste into rich garden compost. And we feel privileged to share our plot with local wildlife, from beetles to butterflies, tadpoles to toads and worms to wagtails – it's heady stuff!

We also feel a strong sense of responsibility for our tiny patch of earth and believe that our plants should be grown as naturally and sustainably as possible. We therefore don't use chemical fertilizers – partly because their manufacture uses inordinate quantities of fuel, but mainly because they destroy living organisms in the soil and pollute streams and groundwater. Nor do we use chemical sprays, which kill indiscriminately – garden foes and friends alike. Also, like other organic gardeners, we try our best to recycle and re-use, provide habitats for wildlife and do all we can to keep pollution and our use of finite resources to a minimum. In our gardens, at least, we can take a stand on some of the most pressing issues of our times. And with more and more of us gardening organically, we believe that, together, we can make a real difference to our lives and, in some way, to the planet.

Many people seem to think that before the advent of chemical fertilizers in the 19th century everyone gardened organically. But this simply isn't the case. The Romans introduced vegetables such as onions, parsnips and carrots into Britain, but their gardens, along with everything else, were abandoned when the Roman Empire in the West collapsed in the fifth century. Moving forward a few hundred years to medieval times, the great English monasteries maintained flourishing walled gardens, where herbs and other culinary and medicinal plants were grown. But these islands of horticultural excellence were the exception. The nobility were too busy fighting each other at home or in foreign conquest to give gardening a thought – not, at any rate, until life regained a semblance of normality at the end of the Wars of the Roses in the late-15th century. Only then did the formal ornamental and kitchen gardens start to appear that would reach their apogee in the magnificent walled kitchen gardens and estates of the Victorian aristocracy in the second half of the 19th century.

Our knowledge of how ordinary people in England gardened is much sketchier, but it's probably not too fanciful to assume that from around the mid-16th to the mid-18th centuries they had access to enough land to be able to enjoy something of a self-sufficient life, producing most of their own fruit and vegetables, along with some meat. But all this changed for the worse between the late-18th and early-19th centuries with the introduction of the Enclosure Acts in England and Wales, which led to the commandeering of common land in the interests of agricultural efficiency, thus enriching a minority of landowners at the expense of everyone else. William Cobbett, who travelled the country on horseback in the 1820s, described vividly the wretched conditions of the labouring poor in his book *Rural Rides*. So desperate were many of them that they left the land for good and moved to the new industrial cities that were springing up like mushrooms in the north and Midlands of England. Gardening was impossible in the crowded and frequently slum conditions that pre-vailed in these regions. The government was eventually forced to tackle the grinding poverty of many of the landless urban and country dwellers and passed the Allotment Acts of 1819 and 1845, which obliged local councils to set aside land for people to grow food for their families. However, they weren't given enough land to be tempted to neglect their daytime jobs – a point expressed forcefully in several official reports of the time.

Until the late-19th century, farmyard manure and other animal-based products were used to improve the soil, and I imagine that most people simply took their chances with plant diseases, with some of the more enterprising souls concocting homemade sprays derived from plant extracts in an attempt to repel pests. However, they didn't practise crop rotation and would probably have burned or otherwise disposed of garden waste as rubbish. It's undoubted that nobody at that time would have made what we think of today as 'compost'. So perhaps the best way of describing how people gardened then is 'almost organic'.

From the late-19th century onwards we know that many gardeners, whether in the great walled kitchen gardens of England's stately homes, in the gardens of the swelling city suburbs or in market towns and villages throughout the land, took advantage of the chemical fertilizers that were used by farmers – superphosphate, nitrate of soda, sulphate of ammonia, and so on. The Victorians also invented a number of particularly nasty pesticides, such as the innocuous-sounding Paris Green, made from arsenic, or preparations distilled from tar oil, none of which any self-respecting organic gardener today would wish to use. So how did organic gardening, as we understand it now, come about? To answer this, we need to go back much further in time and make a detour into the world of agriculture.

For most of the million or so years that human beings have lived on the Earth their impact on the environment has been minimal. Roaming around in small bands, gathering fruits and leaves and occasionally eating meat and fish, our earliest ancestors were just another species adapting to its environment. Then, around 10,000 years ago, people in the Middle East started to develop agriculture. Land was cleared of trees and other vegetation, the soil was tilled and villages began to be established. As numbers increased, these small communities expanded into towns and some eventually became cities. Soils that had sustained the crops that fed these ever-growing populations became steadily less productive as the demands on them increased, until ultimately they were no longer worth cultivating. At this point, a new patch of ground would be brought under the plough and the old land would be abandoned, frequently turning into desert. It was only in places like Egypt, in which the annual flooding of the River Nile brought fresh soil down from the mountains to replenish the earth, that farmers were able to avoid the perennial problem of declining fertility. This is one reason why the great Egyptian civilization survived for as long as it did.

In Britain and northern Europe the soils are more forgiving than those in many regions of the Middle East and, over the centuries, our ancestors were able to obtain crops season after season by resting the land and adding manure and other animal by-products, such as bonemeal and 'hoof and horn' powder. Although it was probably not recognized at the time, these materials boosted the organic content of the soil, and helped to stabilize it, and provided an extra, external source of nutrients. In addition, crop residues and other plant wastes would be burnt, and the ashes returned to the soil or, alternatively, people might leave them to rot down naturally where they lay – practices that were also beneficial to the soil.

Understandably, these generations had little real knowledge of how plants feed. According to the Greek philosopher Aristotle in his *De Partibus Animalium* (*On the Parts of Animals*), written in 350 BC, plants use their roots to suck up all the goodness they need from the dead and decomposing matter in the top layer of soil (what we call humus), in much the same way as we take food in through our mouths. Although Aristotle realized the importance of organic matter in the soil, he had an incomplete appreciation of the precise role it plays. His 'humus theory' remained unchallenged until the early-19th century, when a real breakthrough took place in the understanding of what came to be known as photosynthesis – the process by which plants acquire some of their goodness, in the form of carbohydrates, by making it in their leaves, using water, carbon dioxide and energy from the sun.

Aristotle's humus theory of plant nutrition was discredited by this discovery, but it wasn't completely destroyed until 1840, when a German chemist, Baron Justus von Liebig, published his book *Chemistry in its Application to Agriculture and Physiology*. His laboratory experiments had shown that when a plant is burnt the weight of the minerals that remain in the ash corresponds exactly to a reduction in the weight of the soil in which it had been grown. He concluded that a plant needs mineral nutrients from the soil, and nothing else. He believed, incorrectly, that humus is irrelevant. There was a deal of truth in what he said, even if he only saw part of the picture. But, a great publicist, this didn't stop Liebig from telling farmers that in order to feed their crops all they needed to do was to replace the minerals that are lost from the soil when plants are harvested. Unfortunately this marked the beginning of the chemical mentality that has dogged agricultural science ever since: the erroneous belief that any shortcomings in a soil's fertility can be overcome merely by adding soluble fertilizers.

Other scientists picked up where Liebig left off, and within a couple of decades it was commonly thought that plants only needed three major nutrients – nitrogen, phosphorus and potassium (the 'N, P & K' found on fertilizer bags), plus lesser amounts of calcium, magnesium, iron and sulphur. But they still hadn't deciphered the entire puzzle, and it was left to scientists from then on, until the late-20th century, to discover all the tiny amounts of trace minerals, or micronutrients, such as boron, selenium, molybdenum and zinc, that are now known to be essential elements of plant nutrition.

Two years after Liebig's discoveries, the world's first soluble 'chemical' fertilizer was invented by John Bennet Lawes and Henry Gilbert. These two Englishmen took bonemeal, a rich source of the mineral phosphorus, and treated it with sulphuric acid, to produce superphosphate. Other natural sources of phosphorus were also given the same treatment, one of the more unusual being fossilized dinosaur droppings called coprolite (which literally means 'dung stone'). This was excavated and transported from the fields of Cambridgeshire to a site near the port of Ipswich, where a superphosphate processing factory had been set up by Edward Packard. His business was eventually taken over by Fisons, which became one of the biggest chemical fertilizer manufacturers in the country. Superphosphate was an immediate commercial success: farmers discovered that plants took up the new soluble mineral readily and grew more quickly than they had done when fed with bonemeal.

In 1908, another German scientist, Fritz Haber, produced the first chemical nitrogen fertilizer. He had designed an innovative piece of apparatus that was able to produce ammonia gas from hydrogen and nitrogen. From there, it was a relatively simple chemical step for him to create nitrogen fertilizers, although he only ever produced small quantities. Five years later, on the eve of the First World War, his compatriot, Carl Bosch, found a way of scaling up the process to make commercial quantities of ammonia, in what became known as the Haber-Bosch process. Ammonia is still made in the same way today. But it wasn't fertilizers that Bosch was interested in: with war looming, the nitrate was needed because it is a critical ingredient of dynamite.

In 1918, following the First World War, the German chemical industry stopped making explosives and switched to the commercial production of nitrogen fertilizers. At this time, farmers in Britain happily used superphosphate but viewed the new chemical nitrate fertilizers with deep suspicion. Most of them believed, intuitively, that soil would lose its 'heart' without manure. It would take another world war to establish the total dominance of the culture of chemicals, because, throughout the hostilities, the War Agricultural Committees were given draconian powers by the government to compel farmers and market gardeners to use chemical fertilizers in order to maximize food production. Few resisted.

By the end of the Second World War there was no going back, and in 1947 the Agriculture Act enshrined the goal of increased food production in Britain, backing it up with generous fertilizer subsidies. The entire government-run agricultural research establishment, its advisory services, universities and agricultural colleges, along with the fertilizer and pesticide industry, were hell-bent on persuading farmers to adopt the new chemical approach. Almost all of them did – and indeed, many farmers still do.

It is impossible to deny that chemical fertilizers boost crop yields in the short term, but their results over the long term are frequently no better than those of crops grown on organically managed farms. Ultimately, soils need organic matter for their very stability. History has shown that civilizations that neglect to maintain the humus content of their soils eventually perish. After all, the community of life in the soil has evolved over the millennia to be self-sustaining. The complex molecules of decomposing matter and minerals in the earth, which contain the essential goodness that plants need, exist in an insoluble form that the plants are unable to absorb. But types of fungi called mycorrhizae have evolved, which live in close association with plant roots. The plant's roots release sugar for the mycorrhizae to feed on and they, in turn, break down complex matter in the soil into simple minerals like phosphate, which the roots then absorb. There are also soil bacteria that are able to convert nitrogen in the atmosphere into soluble nitrate that plants can utilize. All these beneficial organisms, and many more, are present in soils that are rich in humus. Artificial fertilizers are unnecessary.

This was certainly the view of a small but vocal group of people in England who, from as early as the 1930s, stood up against the chemical onslaught. A key figure at the time was Sir Albert Howard, a remarkable man and a gifted scientist. He had spent most of his career at the Agricultural Research Institute at Pusa, in India, where, in 1905, he was appointed as Director. For the next 19 years he experimented with a wide range of crops and also with livestock, drawing heavily on the experiences of local Indian farmers. As a result of this work he became aware of the importance of the soil and came to the conclusion that heavily composted, humus-rich soil conferred health on the plants that grew in it, and on the animals that ate them, even if pests or diseases were present in the vicinity. This even applied to highly contagious conditions such as foot and mouth disease. Astonishingly, Howard claimed that his cattle were able to rub noses with beasts from neighbouring farms that had the disease without succumbing to infection.

From Pusa, Howard moved to Indore, in central India, to set up his own institute to investigate this integrated approach to agriculture. It was here that he perfected the art of making compost by carefully mixing animal and plant waste together in specially dug pits, or in heaps. Howard had read reports about agriculture in China and Japan, where the inhabitants returned all waste organic matter to the earth. The Chinese peasants even erected earth-closet toilets by the side of the road for passing travellers to use, as a way of topping up their supplies of 'night soil' (produced from human faeces). They would then compost this with urine, vegetable waste and crop residues and spread it onto the land. The Chinese, alone among civilizations, had maintained the fertility of their agricultural soils for more than 4,000 years because they realized that organic matter is a vitally important component of soil.

Howard later summed up his conclusions in *Farming and Gardening for Health or Disease*, published in 1945. It contains some powerful statements of astonishing simplicity:

> The birthright of all living things is health.
>
> This law is true for soil, plant, animal and man: the health of these four is one connected chain.
>
> Any weakness or defect in the health of any earlier link in the chain is carried on to the next and succeeding links, until it reaches the last, namely man. [...]
>
> The under-nourishment of the soil is at the root of all.

Howard returned to England in 1931 and immediately set about spreading his message to farmers. He was aware that the agricultural establishment would not accept his work because the tide was running too strongly in the opposite direction. During his time in India he had come to recognize that agricultural research was hampered by rigid compartmentalization into specialist subjects such as plant breeding, animal genetics, agricultural economics, and so on. He knew full well that they were linked, but believed that the bigger picture was lost when the research was so fragmented. Perhaps his solutions were so simple that they threatened the careers of those very specialists. As the old saying goes, 'There's none so blind as those who will not see.' Unsurprisingly, the reaction of fertilizer manufacturers was one of total hostility – they were only too aware of what would happen to their profits if Howard's ideas took hold.

Nevertheless, in spite of official reluctance to endorse his views, some enterprising farmers welcomed his fresh approach and adopted his 'Indore Process' of composting. For much of the 1930s Howard criss-crossed the British Empire, visiting farms where his system was being put into practice successfully – places as far apart as Australia, South Africa and Sri Lanka. In England his most notable converts were Friend Sykes, a racehorse breeder whose 750-acre Chantry Farm at Chute in Wiltshire became justly famous, and Frank Newman Turner, a dairy farmer from Bridgwater in Somerset.

But the person responsible for the real breakthrough in public aware-ness about the important relationship that exists between soil, plants, livestock and humans was Lady Eve Balfour, niece of the former British Prime Minister, Arthur Balfour. She had been farming 200 acres at Haughley, near Stowmarket in Suffolk, since the early-1920s and was drawn to Howard's no-nonsense approach to soil husbandry. It troubled her that orthodox scientists didn't accept his research and so she decided to set up a long-term experiment on her farm to prove them wrong. This involved running one section of the farm (which was divided into three separate sections) completely organically, with crops and livestock and relying chiefly on animal manure to maintain the fertility of the soil; running another section also with crops and livestock, but with the soil receiving chemical fertilizers as well as manure; and running the final, smaller, section with no animals and with the crops relying entirely on chemical fertilizers. Everything would be carefully recorded – all farm inputs, yields of crop and livestock products, and the like – and the soil would be sampled for nutrients and other indicators of health and fertility throughout the year.

Surprisingly, Howard was against the idea, believing that the sceptics would never be satisfied, whatever evidence was produced. He also warned her about the heavy financial cost of the enterprise. Government funding was highly unlikely, and no support could be expected from the agricultural industry. In spite of Howard's reservations, Lady Balfour forged ahead and in 1939 the 'Haughley

Experiment' began. It ran for 30 years and while it yielded many valuable insights, it turned out to be ruinously expensive, just as Howard had predicted, and never did produce the clear outcome that Lady Balfour had hoped for. Even so, her belief in the value of naturally derived fertility and organic farming never faltered.

It was left to her book, *The Living Soil*, published in 1943, to mark what is generally regarded as the birth of what we call the 'organic movement'. Her genius lay in bringing together the work of Sir Albert Howard with that of Sir Robert McCarrison, another exceptional scientist, who had concluded that eating food that was fresh, whole and had undergone minimal processing was the best guarantee of human health. To Lady Balfour, Howard's emphasis on a naturally fertilized soil as the foundation of good health dovetailed perfectly with McCarrison's belief in the value of freshly prepared wholefoods.

Sir Albert Howard, Lady Balfour and the other British organic pioneers believed so wholeheartedly in the health-giving benefits of organic growing that they considered the use of pesticides to be unnecessary. DDT (dichloro-diphenyl-trichloroethane), and other organochlorine and organophosphate pesticides – the chemicals that were to cause so much harm to wildlife in the future – weren't introduced into agriculture until after the Second World War. In Howard's time, most of the insecticides were derived from plants and broke down quickly in the soil, so they didn't end up in food or cause any lasting damage to the environment. That would be a problem for future generations to grapple with.

But the health of the nation was an important preoccupation in the 1930s, as indeed it is today, though for entirely different reasons. Britain was deeply divided by poverty at the time: a nationwide nutritional survey had concluded that more than a third of the population was so poor that it couldn't afford an adequate diet, and a fifth of all children was chronically undernourished. Large numbers of people subsisted on a diet of white bread, margarine, tinned meat, tinned vegetables and sweet tea – the opposite of McCarrison's recommendations. Little wonder that ill-health and disease abounded. Cases of the bone-softening condition, rickets, for example, which occurs when the body doesn't receive enough vitamin D for calcium to be properly absorbed, were commonplace.

A problem less well recognized by the world at large, but equally worrying for the organic movement, was the issue of food security, arising from widespread soil erosion in the major food-producing regions of the world, due largely to a failure to return organic matter to the land – the very thing that Sir Albert Howard warned about. As he and the organic movement knew, without this living fraction of the soil to bind the other mineral elements, it simply blows away, as it did in the Great Dust Bowl of the American prairies, where day turned into night for weeks on end as the sky was blacked out by vast storm-clouds of airborne soil particles. Less dramatic but equally catastrophic losses were taking place on the Russian steppes, on the dry lands of Australia and the hills of New Zealand. According to Lady Balfour, more soil had been lost in the 20 years since 1914 than in the entire previous history of the world. And to bring that up to date, almost two billion hectares of farmland were destroyed during the 20th century by soil erosion, desertification and salinization, an area greater than the global total of land being farmed today, according to the United Nation's Environment Programme. And the rate of loss is accelerating.

Jackie and I live in the grain-growing county of Norfolk and here, on a windy day even now, you can see soil billowing around on farmland that has been deprived of the vital organic matter that 'glues' it together. These tiny suspended particles of dust eventually end up in the sea. In other, hillier parts of the country, on fields that have also been depleted of organic matter, rainwater sluices soil particles rapidly downhill along tractor wheel runnels, to end up in great, delta-like deposits of sediment at the bottom. It makes you wonder how much longer this level of destruction can be sustained before the world experiences global hunger on an unprecedented scale.

Lady Balfour's book, *The Living Soil*, was an immediate success and sold out quickly. It ran to more than eight editions and is still in print today. Some who read her book wanted to set up an organization to research into, and promote the link between, a healthy soil and health in plants, animals and people. Three years later, in 1946, the Soil

Association was born, with Lady Balfour at its head. It has grown to become Britain's largest certifier of organic food and is a passionate and vigorous advocate of organic farming worldwide.

A look at these early years of the organic movement would not be complete without mentioning biodynamic growing. This somewhat esoteric approach to farming, with its emphasis on celestial influences, began in 1924, when Rudolf Steiner, an Austrian philosopher, gave a short series of lectures on agriculture. Biodynamic farming is not easy to explain, but it is often described as organic 'plus'. While bio-dynamic farmers conform to the majority of the practices that are used by organic farmers and growers, and avoid artificial fertilizers and pesticides, they also plant, tend and harvest their crops at times determined by the phases of the moon and the position of the con-stellations. They also spray highly diluted concentrations of rather unusual preparations made from medicinal herbs and animal by-products onto their fields, plants and compost heaps – these are care-fully produced according to strict instructions laid down by Steiner.

Unfortunately, Steiner died only a year after giving his lectures and was therefore unable to justify or develop his agricultural theories, but his work was carried on by a student of his, Dr Ehrenfried Pfeiffer, who created an impressive biodynamic farm at Walcheren in The Netherlands.

The Biodynamic Agricultural Association was established in Britain in 1929, and although it has always had a small band of enthusiasts ever since, it has never been as popular here as it has on the Continent. Some of the best organic farms in Europe I have ever seen are biodynamic – although I couldn't say the extent to which this is due to the use of preparations that are claimed to improve soil and plant health.

A certain amount of independent evidence does exist to show that lunar cycles influence the germination and subsequent growth of plants, but most of what Steiner propounded has not been satisfacto-rily corroborated scientifically. But, of course, this does not necessarily make it untrue. Sir Albert Howard had little time for biodynamic farming and considered the emphasis on cosmic forces an unnecessary distraction. And there can be little doubt that it gave ammunition to critics of the organic approach, who, with some justification, labelled it 'muck and mystery'.

In the United States, Howard's ideas found a voice in Jerome Rodale, who ran a publishing business from his farm at Emmaus, Pennsylvania. He had heard McCarrison lecture in the 1920s and came across Howard's book *An Agricultural Testament* in 1941, which he brought out as an American edition. Like Lady Balfour, he recognized the synergy between the ideas of McCarrison and Howard, and in 1942 launched the magazine *Organic Farming and Gardening*. Rodale was the first person to popularize the use of the word 'organic' for what had previously been described as compost growing, fertility farming or a number of similar-sounding terms. He was using it according to one of its dictionary definitions as 'fitting together harmoniously as necessary parts of a whole, the whole being more than the sum of the parts' – which, to Rodale, seemed to best sum up an agricultural philosophy that was in harmony with nature. The name stuck, but it upset chemists of a pedantic turn of mind, who took exception to what they considered to be the highjacking of 'their' word, which is also defined in the diction-ary in the context of 'organic chemistry', or compounds that contain carbon. Three years later, in 1945, Rodale renamed his magazine *Organic Gardening* – it was the first publication of its kind and quickly attracted a big following. Amazingly, it is still the most widely read gardening magazine in the world today, with a circulation of more than a million copies. Rodale felt that organic gardening was a natural extension of organic agriculture, as indeed it is, sharing the same philosophical underpinning and having its roots in the research, insights and practical examples of those early organic farming visionaries of the 20th century. The revolutionary idea of feeding the soil with compost, which began to be popularized by Howard and others from the 1930s onwards, was the basis of organic gardening as we know it today.

The first gardener to be attracted to this new philosophy was F.C. King, who managed the grounds at the historic property of Levens Hall in Cumbria. He had been making compost enthusiastically since 1931 when he read Howard's first book, *The Waste Products of Agriculture*. That same year he put his theories about the disease-resisting properties of compost-fed land to the test, and planted heavily virus-infected raspberry plants into a patch of fertile soil. The usual advice given for the treatment of plants affected by viruses, even today, is to dig them up and burn them – there are no chemical remedies. King's raspberries, however, recovered completely and twelve years later, when Howard paid him a visit, he was able to show him a flourishing bed of soft fruit.

King described his experiences in his *Gardening with Compost*, which came out in 1940, making it the first book in the world on organic gardening. He followed it up with *The Compost Gardener*, which contained a full description of his methods, along with his views on diverse subjects, including how children should cook the vegetables they grow in their school gardens.

Other organic gardeners from those early years included Ben Easey, author of *Practical Organic Gardening*, in 1955, and Maye Bruce who wrote *Commonsense Compost Making*, published in 1945. In her book she describes how to make and use a compost activator called the Quick Return (QR) herbal preparation, which contains a mixture of extracts of wild flowers, oak bark and honey. You can still buy QR compost activator today.

Dr W.E. Shewell-Cooper, who was also a prolific gardening author at that time, had organic leanings too. He was Director of the Thaxted Horticultural College in Essex for ten years and wrote *The Complete Vegetable Grower* in 1955, setting up the Good Gardeners' Association in the same year. In an earlier book about the gardens of the royal palaces he mentions that composting was the norm at all the royal residences, including Buckingham Palace. His own garden looked as neat and tidy as any royal grounds. Being an absolute martinet, he wouldn't suffer a single weed in the garden, his lawns were immaculate and the tools in the tool-shed sparkled; and he certainly knew his compost, as Jackie and I realized when we visited him.

And so we come to the most famous organic gardener of his generation in Britain, Lawrence D. Hills, who will play a major part in our story from now on. He was the founder of the Henry Doubleday Research Association (HDRA), which was to become the driving force in establishing organic gardening in Britain.

Chapter Two

PHILOSOPHY INTO PRACTICE

Lawrence D. Hills was to become the grand old man of the organic movement, but his background was unexceptional. Born in Dartmouth, Devon, in 1911, the middle child of a family of three, he was a sickly infant who suffered from chronic digestive problems. His mother was warned by the medical authorities that he was unlikely to live for more than a few years, even though they didn't fully understand what was wrong with him. Confined to a wheelchair for his entire childhood and unable to attend school, Lawrence was educated at home by his mother. During his teens his health improved and his doctor suggested tentatively that he should make the most of this period of remission by getting a job in the fresh air. To its credit, the local council's parks department agreed to take on the 16-year-old as an unpaid pupil for a period of twelve months and, much to everyone's surprise, he survived the physical ordeal in relatively good shape, even though he recognized that the life of a park keeper was not for him. He wanted to do real, 'hands-on' gardening – which, in those days, meant following the traditional training route of a horticulturalist by becoming an apprentice for three years, an 'improver' for another couple of years, a 'journeyman' to gain even wider experience and, finally, a 'master gardener'.

Although opportunities in horticulture were not as abundant as they had been during the heyday of the profession between the mid-19th and early-20th centuries, there were still plenty of jobs around, and at Bexleyheath, a few miles from Dartford, Lawrence found the post he wanted. Messrs A. Parris & Sons, a small nursery specializing in ornamentals and glasshouse vegetables, recruited apprentices on a regular basis and, despite Lawrence's poor health record, his infectious enthusiasm won him a place. He was appointed on a wage of six shillings a week, with the promise of progressive increases as he became more skilled. His horticultural career had begun in earnest and, although he didn't realize it at the time, it would blossom and bear magnificent fruit over the next 60 years.

Lawrence describes his progress up the career ladder in detail, with flair and humour, in his autobiography *Fighting Like the Flowers* (1989), but suffice it to say that in the run-up to the Second World War he worked at a number of different nurseries, punctuated by lengthy spells in hospital when his health broke down. It was while recuperating from one of these unfortunate episodes that he began to write, mainly as an insurance against the time when he might not be able to do any physical work at all. He obviously had talent as a writer: he became a successful journalist, contributing articles to *Popular Gardening* and other magazines and by 1950 had two books to his name, one of which, *The Propagation of Alpines*, is still considered by many to be the definitive work on the subject.

Lawrence had spent the war years as one of the ground crew in the Royal Air Force and during his time at a base in Cambridgeshire he came, indirectly, into contact with Sir Albert Howard. He had bought a second-hand copy of *The Waste Products of Agriculture* in a local bookshop and read about Howard's experiments on the composting of human waste. There were no flush toilets at the base – waste products were merely buried – so Lawrence wrote to Howard asking if there was a more productive way of dealing with this potentially valuable resource. True to form, Howard responded with a nine-page letter of advice, but the authorities took a dim view of the idea and were unwilling to allow a disappointed Lawrence to experiment!

When the war was over Lawrence worked for his uncle at a small research farm at Southery in Norfolk, testing new and improved feedstuffs for cattle and other livestock. For two years he trialled a wide range of grasses, peas, beans and other crops, but what surprised and impressed him most was a herb called comfrey (*Symphytum* x *uplandicum*), which he had bought from an obscure nursery in Essex. The plant grew spectacularly well, far out-performing his other trial crops and, best of all, the cattle and pigs loved it.

In his spare time, as usual, Lawrence took to writing – on this occasion for a magazine called *The Farmer*, published by Frank Newman Turner. Much to his delight, his articles on comfrey and its virtues brought a steady stream of orders to his uncle's farm, and it even looked as though the extra comfrey sales would expand into a successful business. But then disaster struck.

In the run-up to Christmas 1950 he was taken ill suddenly and rushed into Addenbrookes Hospital in Cambridge with severe digestive problems and afterwards spent many months convalescing. As he had predicted, the time had come for him to stop all physical work for the sake of his health. This latest attack had almost killed him, so he thought that from then on he would have to rely solely on writing to earn a living. One of his former customers suggested he should write a book about comfrey, but Faber and Faber, his publishers, were doubtful that such a specialized title would sell. However, Lawrence had forged a rapport with Richard de la Mare, the company's Chairman, who pushed the book through.

Writing the book took up much of his time over the next couple of years, and it was while undertaking research on the origins of the plant that he learned about an earlier comfrey enthusiast, Henry Doubleday. A 19th-century businessman from Coggeshall in Essex, Doubleday had spent much of his life investigating and promoting the crop, and this struck a chord with Lawrence. In 1953 Lawrence's book, *Russian Comfrey*, was finally published and, much to his and everyone else's surprise, was a huge success. Fan mail poured in, with people not only wanting to know where they could buy plants but also asking lots of other questions that weren't covered in the book. Lawrence was overwhelmed: should he drop the entire project or take it further, he wondered? Eventually he decided on the latter and came up with the idea of renting a patch of land where he could grow comfrey experimentally, sharing his experiences with other keen comfrey growers around the world. Somewhere in Essex perhaps, he thought, where land was reasonably cheap, and close to where Henry Doubleday had lived and worked. At first his searches drew a blank, but then a property in Bocking, on the outskirts of the market town of Braintree, caught his eye. Although it was just an ordinary three-bedroom semi, it came with a decent-sized garden and, more importantly, a little further along the lane there was a patch of derelict land available for rent. That clinched it. He bought the house in December 1954 and he and his elderly mother and father moved into 20 Convent Lane. Shortly afterwards he signed an agreement with the sand and gravel company that owned the land down the road, which entitled him to rent the two-acre plot that he wanted to become his 'trial ground'.

Lawrence was still not sure where all this would take him. Comfrey was obviously the chief focus of his interest, but through his friendship with Frank Newman Turner he was also aware of the work of Lady Balfour and her circle of organic farming pioneers. Lawrence had been one of the earliest members of the Soil Association and was already a regular contributor of organic gardening know-how to the organization's quarterly journal, *Mother Earth*. At Bocking, therefore, having first cleared the weeds from his experimental trial ground, he began to set up not only comfrey beds but plots that would allow him to investigate organic gardening methods.

Time passed uneventfully, but then, in 1957, gardeners and naturalists became aware of a disturbing new phenomenon. Foxgloves, lupins and some other plants were assuming weird, unnatural shapes: stems that were far wider and flatter than normal and flowers that were grotesquely misshapen. Such abnormalities are not unknown in the plant world – flattened, 'fasciated' stems show up periodically when new varieties are bred – but what was so striking was the huge number of these freaks. At first, weedkillers were thought to be the cause as they are capable of producing effects like this, but the problem was so widespread, and occurred in such out-of-the-way places, that it was thought highly unlikely that they were responsible. Lawrence, like many gardeners throughout Britain and mainland Europe, was intrigued and keen to discover the cause of the problem.

'If not pesticides, what could be causing these abnormalities?' he wondered. He wrote letters to the national newspapers asking readers to send him details of their own experiences – anything that might help to explain this strange phenomenon. Botanists and other plant experts picked up his reports, and at last the mystery was explained. The culprit, he was told, was atmospheric radioactive fallout from the atom-bomb tests of the mid-50s. Minute particles of dust had apparently been absorbed through the leaves causing genetic mutations, which were passed on to subsequent generations. At first the authorities denied that the A-bomb was responsible, but the evidence was inescapable and within a few years intense public pressure from people like Lawrence brought above-ground nuclear testing to a stop.

By 1958 he was in regular correspondence with scores of like-minded people, including comfrey growers, organic enthusiasts and those who were worried about nuclear proliferation. He knew then that he had to choose a specific area of work on which to concentrate, but that same year he was appointed gardening correspondent to *The Observer* newspaper. This brought things to a head. Should he formalize his practical, experimental work on the Bocking trial ground by setting up a proper research organization or should he stick to writing full-time? The research could provide an income if he could attract paying members but, in the short term, he would have to carry on writing in order to subsidize it.

In truth there was no real contest – he was determined to start his own research station. To get things going he contacted Robert Pollard, a London solicitor who specialized in charity law. Robert had sent Lawrence a donation during the 'freak plants' campaign, offering legal assistance, so he was a natural point of call for advice. At their meeting, in Robert's upstairs office, he told him that one thing was going to make his organization different from the rest: his researchers wouldn't be experts in white coats, bent over laboratory benches, they'd be ordinary people. With Lawrence's help and encouragement the talents of the gardeners of Britain would be harnessed to become a mighty army of experimenters and their combined results would form the bedrock of organic gardening practice. Faced with such an interesting and irresistible concept, Robert readily agreed to devise a charitable constitution and, knowing that Lawrence had next-to-nothing to live on, asked him for a dozen comfrey plants instead of his usual fee of 50 guineas.

And so Britain's first organic research organization was born, named after Henry Doubleday, in honour of his pioneering work with comfrey. The formal memorandum and articles that were drawn up by Robert Pollard gave the fledgling HDRA considerable scope. The remit, as one might expect, included research on comfrey, but also into discovering improved methods of organic farming and gardening, and whenever Lawrence was asked about the guiding principles of the organization he always referred to two sayings attributable to devout Quaker, Henry Doubleday: 'Observe the works of God in humbleness' and 'Search always for the truth that harms no man.' Lawrence was known to add personally, 'I don't want to die rich; I just want to change the world.' And, in his own way, that's precisely what he went on to do.

In 1961 he was given the opportunity to buy the freehold to the trial ground, but it cost £2,500, an enormous sum in those days. If not for the generosity of the members, who rallied round and stumped up the cash at this point, the purchase wouldn't have been possible. It was a remarkable achievement, given that HDRA had just 600 members at the time. Although Lawrence was making occasional waves in the media, the growth in members was still frustratingly small – but he battled on regardless. There was important work to be done.

Throughout the 1960s persistent chemicals such as DDT were being used in a cavalier fashion on farms and gardens alike, with little thought or knowledge of the consequences. Then, in 1962, an eminent biologist from the United States, Rachel Carson, warned about the dangers of pesticides in her book *Silent Spring*. Although this caused a major stir at the time, things generally continued much as before, with any voices of protest being drowned out by the combined forces of the chemical industry and the agricultural establishment. The organic opposition, such as it was, was largely ignored.

The 60s also brought personal sadness to Lawrence when his father died in 1961, aged 80. That same year he met Hilda 'Cherry' Brooke – the woman who was destined to become his wife and the joy of his life. She lived in South Africa, where she grew comfrey and was actively involved with the local branch of the Soil Association. Cherry had come across Lawrence's writings years before and had been in correspondence with him ever since. So in the summer of 1961, on one of her periodic visits to England, she decided to stop off at Braintree. Despite their age difference – she was 65 and he was 50 – it was love at first sight and three years later they were married.

Much to her credit, Cherry, a self-taught health expert, diagnosed that Lawrence was suffering from coeliac disease – a hyper-sensitivity in the gut to gluten, the protein in wheat that is responsible for the elasticity in dough that also occurs in other cereals. She immediately took him in hand and banished all traces of wheat from his diet, building him up instead on a gluten-free and wholefood regime, which put paid at last to the crippling illness that had wrought such havoc. She also stopped his 40-a-day cigarette habit. His health improved dramatically and within weeks he was looking 20 years younger.

The trial ground at Bocking, with its research plots cut roughly out of the turf, was strictly utilitarian – a place where he could discover organic answers to the many everyday problems that beset amateur gardeners. The land ran to a little under two acres, most of which could be seen in a single glance. Shaped somewhat like a wedge of cheese, with the broad end adjacent to the road, it was mostly flat, except for the farthest, narrowest section, which sloped down gently southwards to a point. Beyond this was a flooded gravel pit, owned by the local angling society. The lake was a delightfully peaceful spot, where Lawrence and Cherry had obtained permission to walk – an opportunity they took on most evenings. The land beyond the wire-netting fence that marked the eastern boundary was rough and uncultivated, and a haven for wildlife, especially rabbits, which proved to be a problem when they burrowed into the trial ground and ruined Lawrence's plots.

Over the next few years Lawrence established open days at Bocking for the members (there were usually two such days each summer), when 50 people or more would turn up, all as keen as mustard. One hot and sunny afternoon in July 1969, for example, a group of around 30 enthusiasts clustered around Lawrence. He was a stout, middle-aged man, wearing a navy blue short-sleeved shirt under a cream safari suit jacket with short trousers, brown brogues and olive-green long socks. A straw trilby that had seen better days was perched jauntily on his head, from which a few wisps of steel-grey hair struggled to escape. For those making their first visit, Lawrence explained the history of the HDRA, which, he said proudly, had just celebrated its tenth birthday.

Lawrence began his tour with his magnificent collection of comfrey cultivars, most of them strains of Russian comfrey (*Symphytum x uplandicum*), descendants of the original plants that Henry Doubleday had introduced from St Petersburg in the mid-1870s. Lawrence had been collecting comfrey plants for most of the 1950s and had classified them according to their growth characteristics, identifying them by what he termed 'Bocking numbers'. He explained that livestock preferred the taste of Bocking 4, whereas Bocking 14 was the best strain for gardeners because it usually out-yielded all the rest and the leaves could be harvested three or four times each season, for use as a mulch, a liquid feed, or in compost. His current trials, he went on, involved lining potato trenches with freshly cut comfrey leaves to supply the growing tubers with an extra source of nitrogen and potash.

Lawrence led the crocodile of visitors along the narrow path, talking at high speed as he went, making it difficult for the stragglers at the rear to keep up with his mercurial train of thought. Those who knew him well were accustomed to his quick-fire delivery, like a burst of machine-gun bullets, but it could be a daunting experience for anyone meeting him for the first time. Arriving at a broader patch of grass in front of a small, green tool shed he stopped to wait for the rest of the group to catch up before starting to speak.

'These eight plots are the most exciting part of the trial ground this season,' he said, pointing to four beds on either side of the main path, each with sides of about eight feet, laid out in the shape of one big square.

'Unfortunately,' he went on, 'this potato trial is not very exciting to look at now. The real climax will be when we have the figures later in the year.'

The visitors could see what he meant. Two of the plots on each side were planted up with potatoes, while on the remainder were tall plants, around three to four feet high, which had deeply divided, dark-green foliage.

'These are Mexican marigolds, the "Sacred Weed" of the Chavins, the prehistoric people of Peru,' Lawrence announced boldly, explaining that the Chavins were growing potatoes in the Andes over 1,000 years before the Incas.

'And I very much hope that they're going to be the answer to the potato eelworm pest, which these plots are riddled with,' he continued, adding that if potatoes are grown in the same patch of ground year after year, the land will eventually succumb to a pest called potato eelworm, otherwise known as potato sickness. He explained that this microscopic, thread-like organism tunnels into the roots, stunting the plant and rendering it incapable of producing more than a handful of tiny tubers. 'Gardeners who practise crop rotation can usually avoid the problem, but it's often found on allotments and it can be a major disaster for farmers.'

In order to study the pest, Lawrence had grown potatoes continuously on that plot for the past seven years, until he had built up a severe infestation of eelworm cysts – the spherical pin-head-sized structures that protect up to 600 eggs in a state of 'suspended animation'. They can remain like this for up to seven years until triggered into life by the chemical 'scent' the potato root exudes. Apparently, the Chavins, for whom the potato was an important staple crop, discovered that when the marigolds (*Tagetes minuta*, so-called by the 18th-century Swedish botanist Carolus Linnaeus after the insignificant pale yellow, groundsel-like flowers, rather than the size of the plant) were grown on land infested with eelworm, the pest miraculously disappeared.

Warming to his subject evermore, Lawrence said that recent research at Swansea University by a Dr Curtis had shown that the roots of *Tagetes minuta* (and not any other types of marigold, apparently) secrete chemicals known as thiophenes, which are somehow able to destroy or deaden the sensitivity of the eelworm's detector mechanisms. Thiophenes are present as an impurity in crude oil and Dr Curtis had been supported by a grant from British Petroleum (BP) in the hope of being able to develop a synthetic anti-eelworm pesticide. However, when Lawrence had last contacted him he had been told that the compounds only work when they are secreted from the roots, not when sprayed onto the soil, so the oil giant had withdrawn its funding. 'Like so many things, it'll only work by nature's methods,' Lawrence stated wisely.

You may be wondering why the trial Lawrence described was being conducted on a collection of small plots, rather than on one single bed that would have been a lot easier to cultivate. As if anticipating this question from his visitors, Lawrence pointed to the poorer growth of the plants in the plots next to the boundary of the property, which were partially shaded by the branches of an overhanging hawthorn tree in the garden next door. This explained, he said, why plots have to be 'replicated' in different places on the same trial in order to cancel out the inevitable differences in soil quality or situation that could otherwise skew the results.

The four-block layout, which was duplicated all over the trial ground, is known as a Latin square. It was the de-facto logo of the organization and was displayed proudly on the front cover of the HDRA newsletter, which was sent to members four times a year. The newsletter was a highly idiosyncratic publication in those early days. It was printed, for reasons of economy, on poor quality paper and stapled together with a coloured paper cover – one edition might be pink, the next blue, and so on. There was no concession to design or aesthetics – it was the information inside that concerned Lawrence. Resembling a small paperback in format, it had anything from 36 to over 70 pages, depending on how much there was to report. As well as general news, it contained information about the trial-ground experiments, facts about comfrey, nutritional advice from Cherry and anything else that took Lawrence's fancy. Basically, he just kept on writing until he ran out of things to say!

The members' experiments were HDRA's raison d'être, and the spring newsletter, which came out in February, was always the thickest because it contained the details of the current year's trials, together with reports sent in by members on what had happened the previous year – often printed verbatim. Many of the trial-ground experiments were also being repeated by members in their own gardens, and their combined conclusions, drawn from the length and breadth of Britain, on soils that vary from almost pure sand to the heaviest of clays, gave a potent extra credibility to the results. This was replication par excellence and, because it works so well statistically, it is still carried on by members today. In 1969, needless to say, the potato eelworm cure was also being tried out by the members, and Lawrence had to ask Australian and South African members who collected seed from *Tagetes* plants growing in the wild to send extras supplies to give away to the hundreds of members who wanted to give it a go.

Most of the experiments were designed to run for at least three years because one season's observations rarely yield meaningful results. What works in a year of normal rainfall, for example, may fail in a drought, and vice-versa. Over a number of years things tend to average out, and it therefore gives you a more accurate picture of the changes taking place, if any.

The *Tagetes* against potato eelworm experiment had been running for at least five years, during which time Lawrence had also been urging members who didn't suffer from eelworm in their gardens to observe whether the root action was effective against any other serious soil-dwelling pests. Their home trials seemed to indicate that it wasn't. But quite by chance a few of them noticed that when *Tagetes* was grown in land that was overrun with weeds, the weeds curled up and died. And not just any old weeds, but the three perennial species that are the most difficult of all to eradicate – the terrible trinity of bindweed, couch grass and ground elder. This had spurred Lawrence on to design a formal trial ground experiment at Bocking, to see if it really worked. He told members that the experiment was near the far gate, if they wanted to look at it, but he wasn't able to discern a clear picture from the trial so far. He said that it seemed that *Tagetes* worked best when it grew to over six feet, and that it was at its most successful when it was pitted against ground elder. It was a lot safer to the environment than toxic weedkillers, he exhorted, so it was worth trying.

Lawrence got carried away easily and spent rather longer than anticipated talking about these miraculous marigolds, so he moved speedily past the composting area, with its row of six compost boxes, to a large nine-block Latin square at the bottom of the trial ground. Three of the plots had been dressed with dried sewage sludge, supplied by the Upper Tame Main Drainage Authority in the West Midlands; another three had been treated with municipal compost made from dustbin rubbish; and the final three had been given compost that had been made on the trial ground. As we already know from his war service, Lawrence was keen to make use of material that would otherwise be wasted. The thought of all that goodness being flushed away upset him – the nitrogen and phosphate in human sewage, and the potash in urine. If it could be returned to the soil as a natural fertilizer, so much the better. Not that the products that he had brought in were without problems. The municipal compost that came from a plant at Leatherhead in Surrey had been made by removing the tin cans from dustbin waste and pulverizing and composting what remained. Unfortunately, it still contained tiny shards of glass and fragments of plastic. Over subsequent decades the soaring quantities of plastic packaging in the rubbish put paid to these early attempts at recycling, but lessons were learned; which is why we are asked to pre-sort our rubbish nowadays. And sewage sludge sometimes contained worrying amounts of lead and other heavy metals, although not in this case. The crops on all three of the beds were looking good, but if the previous year's experiences were anything to go by, those grown on the sludge-treated beds would eventually do best.

As Lawrence turned and began to re-trace his steps, it must have occurred to the visitors that he couldn't possibly have managed to do all this work on his own. In truth, he could only afford to pay for part-time help in the gardens, along with his next-door neighbours,

Ron Suckling and his teenage son Michael, who used to cut the grass paths most Saturdays. But that still left a lot of outdoor labour, which he had to do himself. This was in addition to his column in *The Observer*, the HDRA newsletter and answering anything between 50 and 100 letters from members each week. Then there were all the booklets and leaflets he wrote that summarized the experimental results. Lawrence's most successful publication at the time was *Pest Control Without Poisons*, which was originally published in 1964 and was already in its third edition, but *Weedkillers Without Worry* would follow shortly. He certainly had the sub-editor's gift for alliteration and catchy titles! A leaflet urging gardeners to make compost rather than to light bonfires was also successful. Entitled *Give up Smoking Bonfires*, it was written early in the spring of 1969, and he had already given away a quarter of a million copies to local authorities. On top of this, he was well on the way to completing the manuscript for a book called *Grow Your Own Fruit and Vegetables*, which Faber and Faber subsequently published in 1971. This was to become a bible for generations of aspiring organic gardeners.

Back at the tour Lawrence pointed out some work he was doing with hoverflies. These striking looking insects, which resemble slim wasps (but are harmless), feed on nectar, but their larvae are voracious predators of greenfly and other sap-sucking creatures, so it makes sense to lure them into the garden. The question was, which plants were the most attractive to these useful pest controllers? He had planted buckwheat, mustard and French parsley, he said, to see which they preferred. And then, with a twinkle in his eye, he urged everyone present to set up 'hoverfly corners' in their gardens and insisted that 'insect watching' was a far more useful and interesting hobby than ornithology!

Lawrence had at least another half-hour to go before the tour ended, during which time he described strawberry variety trials, Japanese pumpkin breeding experiments ('Fertile Freda' and 'Yellow Yvonne' were the hot favourites this year), 'no-digging' beds and various methods of supporting runner beans. Before the exhausted visitors finally got away, they had time for a reviving cup of tea and a scone baked by Cherry, taken in a small wooden cedar garage, which doubled as a café, shop and meeting room. Apart from the tool store, and a small packing shed where comfrey plants were despatched to addresses around the world, this was the only other building on site, with Lawrence conducting all the administration of the organization from the spare bedroom at his home. What struck members was the sheer energy of the man, his infectious enthusiasm and his seemingly endless knowledge. He had achieved so much, despite having worked almost single-handedly.

Issues such as recycling and wildlife gardening, which the present generation is only now coming to terms with, were common currency at HDRA 40 years ago, and as an organization, it would forever be ahead of its time. The Association entered the 1970s with a committed band of around 2,000 members, each paying an annual subscription of two pounds. Considering the shoestring nature of the project, the organization had made solid, if unspectacular, progress. But in the wider world Lawrence could see that things were starting to change. The stirrings of a latent environmental movement were just beginning, as groups like Friends of the Earth and Greenpeace began to draw attention to recycling and other issues, and some people were even moving to the countryside to set up communal, 'self-sufficient' smallholdings. He realized that the time was right to expand his operations, but to do that he would need to employ more staff. Who would pay for it? HDRA was generating a small annual surplus on the back of membership income and sales of comfrey, but this was hardly enough to cover additional salaries. Could he capitalize on youthful idealism instead, he wondered? A couple of weeks later, he put an advert in *The Times* appealing for a young couple willing to work for board and lodgings only. 'It's worth a try,' he thought, 'but will anyone be interested?'

Chapter Three

NEW ROOTS

WHEN LAWRENCE HILLS'S advertisement appeared in *The Times* in 1972, Jackie and I were scientists, just out of university. I was working as a civil engineer and she was a biologist. Our jobs were interesting enough but, as passionate conservationists, we started to wonder whether we should look for work that was more closely connected to environmental issues. We'd been keen on supporting organic food production for some time and were therefore intrigued by the advert.

We knew that the environment was being damaged, but it wasn't until 1972 that the seriously deteriorating state of the Earth was really brought home to us. This was when the United Nations Conference on the Human Environment in Stockholm made it clear that humans were responsible for a list of ecological disasters on a massive scale, including the destruction of the rainforests, over-fishing, atmospheric pollution and the extinction of thousands of animals and plants.

Around the same time, a team of experts at the Massachusetts Institute of Technology published a book called *The Limits to Growth*. They had fed information on topics such as population growth, global fuel consumption and worldwide pollution into a vast computer in an attempt to predict what life would be like in the 21st century. The results were depressing. The authors warned that unless we made drastic changes to the way we lived, the future looked bleak. Catastrophic global degradation of the environment, the depletion of oil supplies and deaths on an unprecedented scale due to insufficient food and inadequate fresh water for an expanding population, were inevitable, they insisted, possibly as soon as 2030. It was a frightening thought.

The book received a massively hostile reception. Its critics refused to accept that oil might be in danger of running out, asserting that a technological fix would be found for any future environmental problems. But what if they were wrong and the Earth really was in a dangerously vulnerable state? Surely we should be doing our bit to save it?

This was why the job at HDRA interested us. But we had just taken out a mortgage on our first house and were settling down to married life, with reasonably well-paid jobs and good career prospects, so the idea of taking up unsalaried positions was absurd. By rights we shouldn't have given it a second thought and yet we knew that organic food production should be encouraged because the chemicals that were being widely used in conventional agriculture and horticulture at the time were responsible for a considerable amount of the worldwide environmental damage. We read the job advert again and decided that it was worth finding out more, so Jackie sent off an enthusiastic letter asking for details.

The reply came a few days later, on Christmas Eve. 'Dear Mrs Gear, you sound exactly what we want, but the question is whether you have read our advertisement carefully. It says clearly "no salary" and you can see from the accounts how little money we have. So far this year we have had five post-graduates after jobs and we cannot afford to pay any salaries.' The letter went on to describe what the job would entail – which was, essentially, responsibility for all the scientific work of the organization. It ended with a breathless 'Let us know quickly when you can come and see us,' signed Lawrence D. Hills, Director, Henry Doubleday Research Association (HDRA). We had landed ourselves with an interview, but were we what he wanted?

As we prepared more detailed CVs, we wondered what to include about ourselves. Jackie was from Swansea, in Wales, and she and her younger brother, Graham, would often go on long walks with their mum and dad along the miles of beach and into the fields and woodlands of the nearby Gower peninsula. It was here that she had forged a deep passion for the natural world, and it's easy to see, looking back, why she grew up wanting to protect the environment.

As for me, I come from what used to be known as the industrial Midlands, growing up in Beeston, a suburb of Nottingham. Mum stayed at home to bring up my younger sister, Betty, and me, and dad was a travelling salesman. But his real pleasure was his allotment, where he often took me as a young lad, perched jauntily on the front of his bike. You could say gardening was in my blood!

Jackie and I had enjoyed school. Having passed our 'A' Levels, we each decided to go to the University of Wales in Swansea. Jackie's dad was ill at the time so she didn't want to go further afield. We met in the autumn of 1968, when I was in the second year of a civil engineering course and she had just begun a degree in zoology. Back in the late 60s the student population was less than a quarter of what it is today, so the place had an exciting and intimate feel. The real difference between then and now, though, can be summed up in one word – politics. Students in the late 1960s were radicalized to an extent not seen before or since. Opposition to the Vietnam War galvanized students in American universities into action that spilled over to Britain, and there were other international issues that we personally felt strongly about, such as abolition of the appalling apartheid system in South Africa.

At Swansea it was not unusual for college meetings to attract as many as 2,000 students. We always went along, and our natural sympathy was usually with the anarchists, whose views on the importance of individual responsibility struck a chord. We were full of idealism – a combination, I suppose, of the self-realization that developed as we learned more about what was going on in the world and the Christian values we had been brought up with.

But our life at college wasn't all doom and gloom. We loved tramping over Jackie's stunningly beautiful Gower coast – the first officially designated area of 'outstanding natural beauty' in Britain. According to visitors in the 17th century, Swansea itself had once been an earthly paradise. But that was before the dark and deathly hand of industrialization destroyed it. Jackie gained first-hand experience of this devastation, and the legacy of pollution, in her final degree year, when she had to undertake a research project for her dissertation. She decided to carry out an investigation into the deaths of a number of horses that had lived near a lead-smelting works in the countryside to the northeast of Swansea. There was a suspicion that they'd been poisoned by eating grass contaminated with lead or cadmium emitted from the factory – the only one still remaining from the hundreds that once existed. We collected samples of the grass and soil for analysis from the moorland and meadows where the horses had been grazing; my role, as boy-friend, was a humble bag carrier. Back in the lab Jackie analysed their livers and other organs to see if they contained heavy metals.

The smelter was situated close to the village of Llansamlet in an area known as the Lower Swansea Valley, which was famous, or perhaps that should be infamous, in the late-18th and early-19th centuries for the copper, zinc and lead that was processed on an epic scale along the River Tawe, which ran through it. At their height, the Swansea furnaces accounted for 90 per cent of all the copper smelted in Britain. Although this had brought work to many, and great wealth to a few, the downside was appalling. The life expectancy of Swansea metal workers in the 1880s was just 24 years, so they were issued with a coffin when they started work. Toxic fumes from arsenic and sulphur had filled the air, killing trees and crops and contaminating the pasture. The industry eventually died away in the early part of the 20th century, but its poisoned earth remained for another 50 years.

Jackie's research indicated that lead pollution had indeed been responsible for killing the horses, because some of their organs were heavily contaminated. The smelter appeared to be the obvious culprit – sample results showed steadily declining lead levels the further downwind you travelled away from the smokestack. Thankfully, the smelting works went bust not long after she had submitted her dissertation, but the experience left both of us with a lasting impres-sion of the dangers from unrestricted pollution.

In the summer of 1971 Jackie was awarded an honours degree in zoology, I received my MSc and we were married a month later. A few days after the ceremony she began work, running a water pollution control laboratory for Gower Rural District Council. Although we hadn't had the time for a honeymoon, at least she loved her job! It consisted, basically, of collecting samples of the treated effluent from the Gower's various sewerage works, and also samples from the local rivers and sea water, and then analysing them to make sure that levels of various pollutants weren't exceeding government limits. At the time she used to be fond of quipping, 'Sewage is my bread and butter!' or 'You don't go swimming in Swansea Bay, you just go through the motions!'

After working there for a year or so Jackie received a letter from Lawrence Hills asking if Gower Council sold dried sewage sludge to gardeners. He was, he explained, writing *The Good Sludge Guide* – along the same lines as *The Good Food Guide*, but much more useful! He also asked about the lead content of the Gower sewage sludge. In her reply she told him that her council sold a liquid effluent to farmers for spraying onto their fields but that there was, unfortunately, nothing in a dried form available to gardeners. As to the lead content, she commented, hers was a predominately rural authority, with few cars and factories, so it was unlikely to be present. She knew that lead in sewage was mainly a problem in the cities, where factory wastes and leaded petrol emissions from cars washed into the drains, but as she thought more about his question, she worried about whether the people who were eating vegetables fertilized with lead-contaminated sewage sludge would eventually suffer the same fate as the poor old horses at Llansamlet.

Jackie's reply to HDRA was rewarded with a polite thank-you note from Lawrence and also a flyer advertising copies of his forthcoming *The Good Sludge Guide* at a special pre-publication discount. It's a funny old world though, because long before the book had rolled off the presses, he had placed that personal advert in *The Times*, and she and I were now committed to going to find out whether we would be working with him.

We were summoned to the small village of Bocking, near Braintree, in Essex. The proud owners of a Morris 1,000 Traveller, we could have driven there but it was an old banger of a car, so we decided not to risk the long drive from Swansea and took the train instead. After a mammoth journey we jumped into a taxi, which eventually dropped us at 20 Convent Lane, HDRA's headquarters.

What we saw was an unprepossessing 1930s red-brick semi-detached house, with metal-framed windows and a solid-looking green door. The small front garden was laid down to lawn, with flower borders, a nice little cherry tree and a somewhat unkempt rosemary hedge. We'd phoned from the station to say we'd arrived, so Lawrence and Cherry were waiting on the step to greet us.

'Do come in,' said Cherry in a richly modulated voice. We followed her into the hall, Lawrence immediately chipping in with news of his latest project – something to do with providing over-wintering accommodation for hibernating ladybirds.

We were ushered into the living room and sat down, side by side, on a somewhat battered sofa. They were obviously 'posh', although everything looked a bit scruffy.

'Tea,' declared Cherry, 'comfrey or Darjeeling?' We hadn't a clue, having only ever drunk Typhoo. I glanced at Jackie. Was this some sort of test?

'Comfrey,' we said in unison. Cherry beamed: right answer.

'Lawrence always has his with honey,' she said, looking directly at us. We nodded agreement.

While the tea was being prepared we looked around at the deep-winged armchair in one corner, used by Lawrence, and the smaller version opposite for Cherry, and the large, square, oak table with four wheel-back chairs. Decorations included two gloomy pictures of naval scenes, which we were told had been painted by Lawrence's father. Curiously, we couldn't see any books, but these, we learned later, were in the upstairs back bedroom that served as Lawrence's office.

We were handed the tea in two china cups that still bore traces of grease (we later discovered that washing-up liquid, along with all modern cleaning aids, was expressly forbidden due to its polluting action). The muddy green liquid smelt strongly of honey, which, regrettably, didn't entirely mask the unusual taste of the comfrey!

A well-padded Lawrence flopped back into his armchair. He had a pleasant rounded face, virtually no hair, and a heavy pair of black prescription spectacles, which framed sparkling eyes. Although it was a warmish day, he was dressed in a heavy tweed jacket with leather elbow patches, a checked shirt with a plain green tie, loosened at the neck (and flecked with whatever he had eaten for lunch), olive green cord gaiters with matching socks and sturdy brown brogues. He had a knitted brow – as though time was running out and he simply had to get on as quickly as possible. This, we were to learn, was the normal repose of his face, but at the time it was disconcerting. Cherry, dressed in a loose cotton summer frock and sandals, sat bolt upright at the table. We were told that she had been a physiotherapist. It showed.

Lawrence began talking, with machine-gun rapidity. Words tumbled over themselves. He barely paused for breath, all the time his eyes alive with passion. I suppose we must have said something about ourselves too and what we were doing, but if so it's long forgotten. Our abiding memory is of being carried along on a wave of ideas by this amazing, charismatic man.

'Let me show you the trial ground,' he said finally. Dazed, we stepped out of the back door, paused to look down the long, narrow garden bursting with fruit and vegetables, then we all walked down the lane to a small, green, wrought-iron garden gate that had a cast aluminium sign in battleship grey, announcing that this was the premises of 'The Henry Doubleday Research Association, registered charity no. 298104, all enquiries to the Director/Secretary, 20 Convent Lane.'

'It's just under two acres,' explained Lawrence, scurrying along a grass path between lots of small, square plots, giving hurried explanations about this and that trial as we went. At the very bottom, nestling in a small copse of willow trees, was an elderly green touring caravan.

'That would be your home,' he pointed, beaming.

'Hold on,' we thought. 'Does that mean we've got the job?' Apparently it did, and back at the house there remained one more thing to be discussed. How were we going to live with no salary?

'About the money,' I said. Lawrence looked anxiously at Cherry.

'We can't really manage on no wages at all,' I continued. 'We were wondering if you could pay us five pounds a week.' Lawrence's face fell; Cherry's was impassive.

'We know there's full board, but we'll need money for phone calls home, travelling to see our families, that sort of thing,' explained Jackie. After what seemed an age, Lawrence finally agreed that he could probably just about afford a fiver a week for the two of us.

'Five pounds each,' we insisted.

We could see that this was a real shock. We imagined what must be going through his mind ... ten pounds a week – that worked out at £500 a year. HDRA would be bankrupted! But after agonizing for a few minutes, he agreed to offer us a fiver apiece. Now we knew exactly what we would be letting ourselves in for.

On the train going back we talked about what we should do. We'd be working together, doing something of real environmental importance, with one of the foremost elder statesmen of the organic movement. Set against that, it would mean the end of our careers. Then there was the money. We were currently earning the princely sum of £5,000 a year. And our families weren't well off. They couldn't bail us out if we got into trouble, and we wouldn't be able to help them in the future either. We would be trading our own house for a caravan, and we couldn't possibly afford to run a car. On top of this, Jackie would have to say goodbye to her beloved family in Swansea. It would be a massive wrench for her to leave the three of them. She felt torn apart. Common sense told us that we would be mad to give everything up. But we were young and idealistic and it seemed like the right thing to do – almost like a calling. Back in Swansea, we talked it over with our respective families and with their blessing we finally decided to commit. I rang Lawrence to tell him. He was delighted.

'Wonderful news,' he enthused. 'When can you come?'

'We're putting the house on the market right away,' I said, 'and we expect to be with you before the end of the summer.'

As it turned out, the economy took an unexpected turn for the worse, not helped by war in the Middle East, which sent fuel prices soaring. People were understandably reluctant to buy houses, and so ours remained unsold until December 1973. We gave away most of our furniture and passed on the beloved Morris to a friend. Christmas was spent quietly with Jackie's family and then, early in the New Year, we packed our few remaining possessions and left Swansea. Jackie cried most of the way to Braintree.

It took us a while to settle into our new home. Jackie immediately declared the caravan unfit to live in and embarked on a major overhaul, which included a thorough scrub down and then the purchase of some rich red Sanderson, William Morris patterned material, reduced in the sale, which she made into curtains. She did her best to create a cosy little nest but, looking back, going to live in a touring caravan in the middle of winter was not the cleverest of moves. There were no toilet facilities for a start – the nearest loo was about 50 yards away in a green wooden shed the size and shape of a telephone box. Inside there was a large bucket containing a blue, scented liquid. At night, in the pitch black, you couldn't spot the spiders, which had always been a phobia of mine. Even with the door open, looking up at the stars, I found the thought of them crawling all around me unsettling. Jackie would even have preferred to use an open field – but this was not an option!

The only really comfortable place to relax was in what was known as 'the Pye House'. Almost all the buildings on site had been paid for by HDRA's members and when someone handed over a significant amount of money, they would be honoured by having the structure named after them. In 1970, Jack and Mary Pye had paid for the construction of an asbestos and timber building – a large shed really – which housed the HDRA office at one end and a spare room at the other end that we could use as a sitting room. The main entrance to the office was a 10ft x 4ft foyer, which doubled as our kitchen and had been kitted out with an ancient electric cooker and an old Belfast sink. Even more bizarrely, this old sink was all that we had for our personal ablutions (apart from a once-a-week bath at Number 20), which meant that on a couple of occasions, office girls arriving early to work were startled to discover Jackie standing stark naked at the sink having her morning wash. Well, it was the 70s!

Next to the foyer was a small, makeshift living room, which had a couple of tatty armchairs, a sofa and post-war dining table. This room also received the William Morris treatment from Jackie – but this time she could only find material in the bargain bin for cushions and curtains in a jolly shade of lime green. It would have to do. We didn't have a television, but our pride and joy was a much-loved Dansette Junior record player, from which music, ranging from rock to classical, could be heard playing on most evenings.

During the day we concentrated on our work on the trial ground with Lawrence, who kept us so busy that we didn't have time to think. We were truly privileged to be working alongside the great man himself. When the weather was wet he showed us how to do routine jobs inside, such as cutting up comfrey roots for re-planting, stringing onions or storing carrots over the winter in a tea-chest filled with sand. Outside, we helped him to prepare the plots for the new season's trials. He declared that what really made a good gardener was knowing what to do and when to do it – recognizing priorities according to the season, the weather, or whatever circumstance dictated. For example, if the evening forecast predicted frost that night, you must leave your comfortable armchair in order to put some protection over your vulnerable young potatoes peeping out of the soil. You had to be ever-watchful in the garden, he explained, and notice all the little messages that the plants, the soil or even the birds were sending you. Knowing the life-cycles of all the plant pests, recognizing which plants would grow best in the shade, or which would thrive in the full sun, were among the multitude of facts we were expected to learn if we wanted to become good gardeners.

Before arriving at Bocking, Jackie and I had assumed that organic gardening meant not using chemical fertilizers and pesticides. But the more we listened to Lawrence, the more we realized that this was a highly simplistic explanation. Organic gardening is, among other things, a positive way of growing that extols natural methods, such as composting to improve the soil, and encourages ladybirds and garden-friendly wildlife to keep pests in check. Although an expert, Lawrence was always trying to improve his own organic gardening methods – hence the various trials that lay spread out all around us. Before we were let loose on the experimental beds, he taught us all about composting, the foundation of the organic philosophy. This involved loading up the battery of compost bins with discarded tomato-plant haulm (stems, shoots and leaves) from the commercial glasshouse grower next door – the nearest bulk plant waste to hand. Lawrence was convinced that these three-foot square wooden containers, known as New Zealand Boxes (after the New Zealand Compost Club, now called the Soil and Health Association of New Zealand, whose members invented the design), were the best. I have to agree, having tried numerous other bins over the years. In just six weeks, by turning the contents once, the bins produced the most wonderful dark, sweet-smelling compost – a perfect soil conditioner.

The trial that interested us most in our first year wasn't anything to do with the merits of compost or with pest control techniques. It was called 'Survival Gardening' and it was being tried as a members' experiment. We learned that the fact that gardeners up and down the country were replicating it made the results even more viable statistically. Its raison d'être was to ascertain the weight of the total vegetable crop that it was reasonable to expect from an average-size garden, and whether one could grow enough to supply a family all year round. The trial went on for a decade and although results were not as clear-cut as Lawrence would have liked, it looked as though a plot of land of about 300 square yards was enough to feed an average family. Coincidentally, this is the size of a standard ten-rod allotment. They knew what they were doing in the old days!

At the start of this trial Lawrence had thought that first-time gardeners anywhere and everywhere might welcome a simplified vegetable growing guide. Taking his cue from the wartime 'Dig for Victory' campaign, he came up with a six-page leaflet called *Dig for Survival*, which was given away free to anyone who wrote in to us with a stamped and addressed envelope. Rather than spending money on advertising, he decided to do a mail shot to promote it. At Bocking this was known as a 'jump-in', which involved sending a standard letter to all of Britain's national and regional newspapers, selecting a particular topical issue that suited Lawrence's case. This time he chose the rising cost of food, which enabled him to suggest that people could save money by growing their own vegetables. He ended his letter with an offer of a free copy of *Dig for Survival*, a real incentive for the reader, but he would also send out an HDRA enrolment form to persuade them to become members – the organization's life-blood. This took place long before computerized databases were available, so it involved typing hundreds of letters – but it was worth all the hard work because invariably they were published.

Requests for the leaflet flooded in, running at one stage to over 900 a day. It was still going strong two months later and, during this period, opening and responding to the huge amount of mail was more than Cherry and Lawrence could cope with alone. In less hectic times they would normally open letters shortly after seven o'clock in the morning, when the mail was delivered. The two of them would sit up in bed contentedly, with the post strewn over the bedcovers, picking out choice letters to read out to one another. Now Jackie and I were drafted in to help, but even so, on some days, it took us well into mid-morning before we finished opening the letters and sending out the leaflets. These were jolly occasions, which we wouldn't have missed for the world, with both Lawrence and Cherry happily holding forth to their captive but appreciative audience.

Aside from us, from the point of view of hired help, Lawrence ran an extremely tight ship. Mrs Adams, the office secretary, and her young assistant, Karen, were responsible for the clerical side of things, while lanky Rose, with a sharp tongue but a heart of gold, was in charge of the mail-order department, ably assisted by motherly 'Auntie Vi'. Two other ladies, Anne Long and Mrs Johnson, both pleasant and quietly efficient, took dictation from Lawrence during the evenings and typed up the letters at home. At the height of the 'Dig for Survival' campaign, however, absolutely everyone was enlisted to help stuff the various items of literature into the waiting envelopes. Lawrence then bundled them into two large shopping bags and cycled down to the village post office, the heavily laden carriers dangling precariously from his handlebars.

All this time Lawrence had been working flat out. As well as responding to requests for *Dig for Survival* and related interviews with the press and radio, he was dealing with countless queries from would-be members; he was often at his desk for 14 hours a day. It was therefore little surprise when he was taken ill, with what the doctor described as nervous exhaustion. Unfortunately, the all-important HDRA Annual General Meeting (AGM) was due to take place in just ten days' time and he obviously wasn't well enough to run the entire proceedings, so Jackie and I were summoned to his bedside for crisis talks. He thought that he might recover sufficiently to manage the AGM committee meeting in the morning, but an hour-long lecture to HDRA's members would be beyond him, so he informed us that we would have to do it. Apart from presenting our college dissertations to fellow students and a panel of lecturers, neither of us had ever spoken in public before. And yet we had just over a week to become experts on 'Methane from waste'!

The current energy crisis was the reason behind this choice of topic. The world had received a nasty shock the previous year when, in response to the Yom Kippur war with Israel in October 1973, the Arab oil exporting nations had threatened to withhold oil supplies and had quadrupled their prices. In Britain, ration books for petrol were issued to all drivers and there was a lot of talk about what would happen in a future that was short of fuel. All manner of alternative energy sources were under consideration, one of which was methane gas, produced from sewage effluent. Even though the subject of methane production was familiar to Jackie, thanks to her days at the sewage works, I really fancied doing the talk, so she agreed to help me to get 30 or so slides together and assemble a set of rough notes.

On the big day, the four of us – Jackie, Cherry, a peaky-looking Lawrence and I – piled into an empty carriage compartment for the hour-long train journey to London and the AGM. Our destination was St Georges in the East, an elegant 18th-century church, designed by Nicholas Hawksmoor, in the heart of the East End, which had miraculously survived the Blitz. HDRA had first come here in 1973, the previous year, and it would remain its chosen venue for AGMs until 1978.

There were around 3,000 HDRA members at this time, all of whom had the right to attend the AGM, if they wished. Each member paid an annual subscription of three pounds, for which they were entitled to: a quarterly newsletter, free organic gardening advice from Lawrence, buy books and other sundries at a discount by mail order, take part in the members' experiments, and attend the open day and the AGM. HDRA's Committee at the time, which was represented there by as many trustees as possible, was made up of 16 enthusiasts, a mixed and lively bunch – in those days, it has to be said, it was a little weighted by Lawrence's and Cherry's useful personal friends and contacts, but none the worse for that. The committee also included several scientists, a lawyer, a doctor, two nutritionists and an accountant. Presiding over things, as Chairman and President, was Lord Kitchener, HDRA's most notable member. He is the great nephew of Lord Kitchener of Khartoum (the fearsome First World War leader whose stern countenance appeared on the famous recruitment poster 'Your Country Needs You!') – but despite the ancestral links, you'd be hard put to find a more pleasant, self-effacing individual. This doesn't mean, however, that he wasn't a strong contributor – far from it. An extremely astute and intelligent man, he remained a real asset to the organization for some 30 years.

Attending the meeting for the first time was Dr Bill Blyth, an eminent research scientist employed by the Medical Research Council, who was also one of HDRA's most assiduous experimenting members. In future years Bill was to become a major force in the Association as its Chairman.

We were immediately struck by how excited the members were as they filed into the hall, several telling us how relieved they felt that Lawrence was at last sharing the burden of running the organization with two younger assistants. In such a welcoming environment my nerves melted away and I think I made a reasonable fist of my first public address. Everybody clapped at any rate! The day went better than we had hoped and Lawrence was happy. We went home tired but contented.

The other big event in the HDRA calendar was the twice-annual trial-ground open day, one of which I've already mentioned. Now, however, among her many other duties on the day, it was Jackie's responsibility to provide refreshments for the hundred or so members. Tea was taken in the Bigg Building, a large, second-hand wooden shed that was erected in 1972, thanks to a £100 donation from – yes, you've guessed – a Mrs Bigg, of Jersey. Jackie set up the rickety old trestle tables and folding benches, assembled the motley assortment of crockery and plastic washing-up bowls full of freshly picked lettuces and, last but not least, laid out the scores of scones, malt loaves and wholemeal bread she'd been baking since the crack of dawn. Her biggest worry was that she and I would have to wash up all the used crockery in between sittings with no running water. But as it happened, there was such a buzz about the place as visitors came in from Lawrence's tour, that we both loved every minute.

Our first year at HDRA had proved to be a good one for the organization in general. The 'Dig for Survival' campaign had produced over 1,000 new members and income had increased by more than 50 per cent, so that even after paying our wages, and other costs, the Association had recorded a £5,000 surplus, the largest in its history. As Christmas drew near Lawrence called us into his office. He said he was so pleased with the way we were working that he wanted to make me Deputy Director of HDRA and Jackie Director of Analytical Research. The best was yet to come, when he added, 'I propose to double both your salaries to £10 a week.' Now, we thought, we can really live it up!

He also said that Jackie and I couldn't go on living in the caravan in the long term, and that he was confident that HDRA's members would be willing to donate enough funds to build a new bungalow for Cherry and him on the trial ground, leaving Number 20 free for Jackie and me.

The next few months sped by and before we knew it, planning permission was granted for the bungalow. With Lord Kitchener heading an appeal, the money was raised quickly and the foundations were dug early in the New Year. By late May we were able to move into the positively commodious accommodation of Number 20.

Our time at Bocking had been a helter-skelter learning experience: gardening for the first time, managing building construction, meeting members and reorganizing the office, let alone all the baking, preserving and catering. We knew we'd made the right decision to come to HDRA. As far as we were aware, this was the only organic horticultural organization of its kind in the world and we felt instinctively that an interesting future lay ahead for us, and for the Association.

Chapter Four

THE GOOD LIFE

W**E EMBRACED A WHOLE** new lifestyle at Bocking, and it suited us. It was what we wanted. It was why we'd left our conventional careers behind. We were the 'love and peace' generation who believed naively that we could make a better world. Many of us 'opted out', some literally taking to the hills to set up self-sufficient smallholdings. Jackie and I just wanted to bring all the strands of our life together into one cohesive existence. At Bocking we were able to study organic gardening and to learn how to grow fruit and vegetables from an acknowledged master so that in the future we could persuade others to do it too. This life also encompassed our need for mental stimulation, physical activity, a spiritual dimension and time for family and friends. Jackie started going to yoga classes and we both learned how to manage without modern household gadgets, like a washing machine.

We also discovered how to avoid chemical household cleaners and use more natural substances instead, such as bicarbonate of soda and white vinegar. When we shopped we avoided unnecessary packaging and even took to buying our apple juice in a re-useable glass bottle, which was re-filled from a large container in a local wholefood shop. It was a much simpler lifestyle than our old nine-to-five existence, and we were happy, even though we were broke most of the time. We rejected all processed food in favour of naturally produced wholefoods. Somehow, homely activities, such as grinding organic wheat and making our own bread to share with others over a simple meal of home-grown fresh produce, were joyful occasions and reinforced our belief that there really was a better way to live. It was all the more special because we were following in the path of other like-minded individuals – the Hills and, before them, Lady Balfour, Sir Albert Howard and Sir Robert McCarrison.

A highly qualified medic, McCarrison (1876–1960) had spent most of his career working for the British administration in India, where he was employed as the Director of Nutrition, charged with improving the well-being of the citizens of the Raj. He believed that good nutrition was the basis of good health. It all began in his travels across the sub-continent, where he noticed that the physique and health of some Indian races were better than others. People living in the north – Sikhs, Punjabis and Pathans – were far taller and generally in better shape than the Madrassis from the south. After investigating all the various factors involved, McCarrison came to the conclusion that it was their food that was making the difference. The northern diet was based on whole wheat, milk, dairy products, pulses, fresh fruit and vegetables and modest amounts of meat; while the diet of the south comprised, in the main, white rice, lentils and coconuts.

McCarrison set up scientific experiments involving two sets of rats to see how different diets affected them. The northern Indian diet was given to one set of rats; the southern Indian diet to the other – with astonishing consequences. Rats fed on the northern, wholefood diet grew up to be sleek, fit and fertile, free from disease, and they lived together harmoniously. Rats eating the southern diet were smaller, had significantly less energy and tended to suffer from degenerative diseases. McCarrison concluded that what happened to the two groups of rats faithfully reproduced what was happening to the two groups of Indians, establishing that there was a clear link between diet and health.

To see if he would get the same results in a different setting, he then turned his focus on the diet of the British working classes. Being short of money, their diet was based on white bread, margarine, tinned vegetables, canned meat, tinned jam, tea, sugar and milk. He gave his laboratory rats the same food to see how they would be affected by it. As he had expected the creatures grew poorly and lived unhappily together. Some developed a craving for tea and sugar, and 60 days into the experiment the bigger rats started to kill the weaker ones. McCarrison was forced to separate the remainder after three had died. At the end of the experiment all the rats were examined and their post-mortems revealed widespread gastro-intestinal and pulmonary disorders. No coincidence, he mooted, that these were two of the most frequently encountered diseases among the poorer classes at the time. McCarrison's experiments ran for more than 20 years, involving many generations of rats. When summing up his life's work, he concluded that sound nutrition, based on food that was fresh, whole, and little altered by preparation, was the foundation of good health. He was convinced that there was a 'factor', as yet unidentified, in wholesome food that was not accounted for if it was only analysed for its proteins, fats, carbohydrates, vitamins and minerals. This elusive 'something', he believed, was responsible for the natural immunity to disease he had observed in the healthiest Indian tribes and in his healthiest laboratory animals.

When we lived at Bocking, many people, including Lawrence and Cherry, called this mysterious factor the 'life force'. They believed that freshly picked, raw vegetables and fruit, grown organically, as nature intended, still contained some 'energy' from the living plants, and this is what they thought of as the life force. Jackie and I believed that whatever you called it, it seemed to make sense. So we ate organic home-grown fresh produce, unpeeled and uncooked, by preference. We also opted for wholegrain bread, pasta and rice, cold-pressed, virgin vegetable oils, and unpasteurised local milk, buying a small amount of fresh meat and fish, plus lots of dried beans and lentils. The nearest we came to buying processed food was butter, cheese and tins of tomato purée. In the winter this satisfying nourishment was supplemented by our own bottled fruit – usually raspberries, cherries or blackcurrants. It didn't contain any sugar but was still sweet enough to enjoy, and we ate it with homemade yogurt, cultured in the airing cupboard! We loved our new diet.

Twice a week Jackie would make bread, which smelt intoxicating. The hard thing was to stop yourself from eating a whole loaf at one sitting! What made it extra special was that we used freshly milled organic flour, made from wheat bought direct from Pimhill Farm in Shropshire, run by Sam Mayall, one of the leading lights of the Soil Association. We would order a hundredweight sack of whole grains at a time, storing it in a mouse-proof metal dustbin in the shed at Number 20, where we also kept our Atlas mill – a glorious piece of red and blue ironmongery, looking for all the world as though it had come from the 1851 Great Exhibition. It was simplicity itself to operate and I could produce exceptionally fine flour in just under ten minutes, although it was easier to settle for a slightly coarser mix! Jackie and I shared grinding duties but she went at it more sedately, gently glowing during her 20-minute stint. Needless to say, the flour was 100 per cent wholemeal.

Cherry had taught Jackie how to make a 'Doris Grant' loaf. Ordinary bread involves a fair amount of time spent kneading, but with the Grant recipe the dough is much wetter – more like a cake mix – and it only has to rise once before baking, the yeast rising easily in the warm water and molasses treacle (the only sweetener, along with honey, that we used). The resulting loaf – dense, moist and in the shape of a brick – retained its freshness for days, not that it ever lasted that long. Doris Grant got our vote for her loaf recipe alone, but we discovered that she had other amazing talents. She was a keen advocate of wholefood cooking and the author of a bestselling book called *Your Daily Bread*. One of Lawrence's oldest friends, she had been on HDRA's founding committee back in 1958, but in the 1990s she became known to a whole new generation for her 'food combining' dietary and cook books. Jackie and I became good friends and admirers after we met her for the first time about 15 years ago. She and her husband were then in their 90s and lived in a first-floor retirement apartment in Poole, Dorset. When we were invited to their home to meet them we'd expected Doris to be a homely figure in a sloppy jumper and a long tweed skirt

– a sort of geriatric hippy-earth-mother. Imagine our astonishment when we were greeted by a petite, immaculately coiffured figure, smartly dressed in a Barbara Cartland-style, pale yellow twin-set. Doris was the only person we had ever known to have a white shag-pile carpet in the kitchen – not at all like most other organic households we'd encountered. Over tea with her own-recipe bread, cut into gossamer thin wafers by her husband Gordon, she entertained us with stories of the early days. The secret of their long lives, she informed us, was her homemade bread, plus a tot of whisky at bedtime! Sadly they are both dead now, but we'll never forget Doris – Jackie still uses her bread recipe and has all her books. Although a wholefood diet may seem a bit restrictive if you haven't tried it, I can honestly say that we both felt better than we could ever remember.

Mind you, we had been force-fed with brewer's yeast by Cherry for weeks when we first started. This was the only food supplement allowed by her (apart from Acerola Cherry vitamin C tablets) because it contains lots of B vitamins. When we'd first arrived she decided we both looked a bit 'peaky', especially Jackie, who apparently had a classic butterfly-shaped area of faint redness over her nose and cheeks. I can't say that I'd ever noticed, but Cherry assured me it was a sure sign of vitamin B deficiency. Being cruel to be kind, she elected to give us brewer's yeast powder mixed with water every morning. The problem was, the yeast didn't dissolve properly in the liquid. Ugh! I still shudder to think about it. It was a bitter experience, literally. Still, it did the trick – we felt a lot healthier after a couple of months and Jackie's 'red butterfly' disappeared. In time, when Cherry thought we were benefiting from eating our new, wholefood, vitamin-rich diet, the treatment ceased, and I can't say we were unhappy about this!

Jackie respected Cherry greatly for her vast knowledge of nutrition and health, and she hungrily absorbed her every word. She realized, excitedly, that far from being at odds with the biochemistry and physiology she'd studied at university, it all made perfect sense – she picked Cherry's brains incessantly from then on. Lawrence's wife was an exceptional woman. She didn't accept any facts about nutrition without going back to the original scientific papers to verify the information, and she and Jackie made regular trips to the medical library at Chelmsford in Essex, where they would delve into the mysteries of, say, a particular trace element and the part it played in our diets, or the role of nicotinic acid.

When Cherry died, many years later, Jackie took up the wholefood banner in the organization and became the driving force for promoting an organic wholefood diet as the healthiest way to eat. Jackie was convinced that if everyone stopped eating so-called 'convenience' food – the forerunner to our 'junk' food – and started eating plenty of fresh, organic fruit and vegetables, there would be far fewer cases of cancer, heart disease, intestinal disorders and other chronic illnesses. It was little short of a tragedy that the medical profession refused to accept what was, to her, blindingly obvious – that it was better to eat a healthy diet, which would help to prevent disease, rather than to eat a bad diet, which could result in untreatable medical consequences later in life.

Jackie had always enjoyed cooking. Her mother's generation had, in general, made sure that they passed their culinary skills on to their daughters, and Phyllis, her mum, was no exception. One of my most endearing memories of her was the steaming dish of tasty lamb and vegetable stew that invariably greeted us when we arrived in Swansea, tired out after having hitch-hiked the 250-mile journey from Braintree. Jackie's Welsh grandmother made a mean Bara Brith, or fruit loaf, and the most mouthwatering Welsh cakes I've ever tasted, so Jackie already had a wealth of recipes in her head that she could turn her hand to when we settled down together. How she knows instinctively what will happen when you combine different ingredients is a mystery to me. Politically incorrect, I know, but I'm not embarrassed by my lack of culinary skills. Quite the opposite, in fact, because we both believe that in any relationship each person should try to fulfil their potential by playing to their individual strengths. Well, that's the theory anyway!

By the summer of 1975 Jackie was also cooking for up to four student gardeners, whom we had persuaded Lawrence to take on to help us. At first we could only accommodate two students at a time because they stayed in a newly bought two-berth, second-hand caravan situated next to ours, but once we had moved into the house it freed up our caravan for two more. Our first student was Charlie Wacher, who stayed with us for three months. He was a quiet, soft-spoken, thoughtful man in his early 30s, with a clear, penetrating gaze. He was hoping to grow organic vegetables for a living, something that few others were doing at the time, but the scale of production at Bocking was too small, so he left after a while to seek more relevant experience elsewhere. Although he succeeded in his aim and eventually farmed organically in mid-Wales, becoming a founder member of the Organic Growers Association, his life was tragically cut short a few years later. He had been a truly wise and lovely man.

At Braintree, he was followed by Liz Moore and Jim Buckland, neither of whom knew anything about growing when they arrived. Liz had been a teacher and became a lifelong friend of ours. Jim, a chirpy Londoner, was far more single-minded about pursuing a career in horticulture than Liz and most of the other students who came after him. After twelve months with HDRA he left to do the prestigious diploma course at Kew Gardens. Some years later, he and his wife Sarah (also good mates of ours) took over and restored the near-derelict walled kitchen garden and run-down grounds at West Dean College, near Chichester in Sussex, turning them into one of the finest gardens in England.

After a year or so we found that we were attracting students from abroad as well as from Britain. Chris Dawson, for example, came from New Zealand and seemed to be drawn more to the dietary side of HDRA's work than to the gardening. He was a great food experimenter, devising his own gluten-free bread recipe, which earned him the nickname 'the Dawson loafer' from a fellow Aussie student. He moved to Japan when his studentship ended and we lost touch. But years later we came across him again at an organic food show, by which time he had become the Managing Director of a major health food company, importing Japanese health foods into Britain.

Then David Lofts from the USA came to work with us. He was an accomplished violinist but earned his living playing multiple games of chess. He had turned up in England as part of a tour of Europe. I forget how he found us, but he had a striking face with over-sized spectacles in circular black frames, a shock of curly dark hair and an infectious laugh. Dave was great company and we were sorry to see him go after almost a year, but we still keep in touch. He now lives the self-sufficient life in the French Pyrenees.

You can tell that the students were an interesting bunch. Sitting down to eat with them in our sunny, yellow kitchen, around our huge farmhouse table, everyone sunburned and exhausted but bursting with conversation, were always happy times. We were very optimistic. Very 70s!

Jackie did all the cooking and there were never fewer than six people for lunch, so the catering arrangements were sometimes complicated. Both Jackie and I ate meat, as did Lawrence and Cherry, but it was not unusual for students to be vegetarian, vegan, macrobiotic or occasionally even fruitarian. Indeed, when Jackie first started teaching yoga she adopted a macrobiotic diet herself for over two years. Vegetarians who didn't eat meat on principle would sometimes criticize us for our meat-eating ways. But we would retaliate by saying that in order to produce milk a cow must become pregnant and give birth to a calf. If the calf is male, it will either be killed within days of being born and the carcase disposed of, or it will be raised and killed for its meat. Above all, a farm has to pay its way (even non-intensive farming is a commercial enterprise), so an animal is not going to be allowed to live and die naturally because of the cost of the food it would consume throughout its lifetime. Vegetarians may not be prepared to eat meat themselves but someone else will. And it's a similar story as far as eating eggs is concerned, incidentally. To us it's even worse because of the short and extremely unpleasant lives most hens live under 'battery' conditions (the average life of a battery hen is just over one year – after this it's destined for pet food or meat pies). If, as vegetarians, you want to enjoy the pleasures of milk, cheese and other dairy products, you have to accept that animals have to die in the process of providing them for you. And how can you condemn meat-eating communities, born through no fault of their own in harsh, rocky terrain, who, if they didn't eat lamb or goat, say, would perish because nothing else would grow in such a harsh environment?

On the other hand, I can fully understand why anyone should recoil from eating meat produced by factory farming. Jackie and I will have no truck with it, refusing to buy broiler chickens, eggs from batteries, indoor-reared pork or any other intensively raised livestock products. We believe it's important to respect animals, and our duty to make sure that they live stress-free lives and are put to death humanely. We eat organic meat because we know it's produced according to the highest welfare standards, which prohibit close confinement of livestock and, on the whole, allow creatures to live as natural a life as possible. In any case, in our view animals are a vital element of an organic farm, contributing to the long-term fertility of its land. Admittedly there have been attempts to set up livestock-free organic farms, but veganic experiments like these often fail. Farm animals have been an important part of agriculture for thousands of years, and their production, within limits, should continue, but only on the basis of proper respect for the needs of the animal, a humane death and with due consideration for the environment. Regrettably, we are a long way from achieving these basic goals on the majority of the world's farms.

We used to host what were known as WWOOF weekends at Bocking every couple of months, with Jackie cooking for four extra hungry mouths. WWOOF stands for Working Weekends On Organic Farms, or at least it did back in the 70s, when it was devised by Sue Coppard, a London-based administrator, who longed to find a low-cost way of escaping to the countryside at the end of a week's work. The idea was that the host farm provided free board and lodgings, in return for work on the land; so for the farmer it meant useful labour at little cost. The WWOOFer, on the other hand, would receive good food in pleasant surroundings and experience organic farming first hand, in return for a couple of days of work. Both parties enjoyed the convivial atmosphere that WWOOF gatherings invariably engendered. They were timed by us to coincide with major events such as harvesting or large-scale compost making. Because of accommodation difficulties we had to restrict numbers and relied on setting up camp beds in our spare rooms. One WWOOFer, David Albon, later became my brother-in-law by marrying my sister Betty. Even now, many years later, he remembers enjoying Jackie's homemade lunches in the heady days of his WWOOF weekends. Like all great ideas, news about WWOOF spread worldwide and you can now find the organization operating in over 30 countries. The same acronym is still used, but the letters now stand for World Wide Opportunities on Organic Farms.

Our visitors automatically participated in our self-sufficient lifestyle, benefiting from our fruit and vegetables all year round. The garden at Number 20 always had a good selection of fruit, so raspberries, gooseberries, blackcurrants, rhubarb and cherries would all find their way onto the menu, depending on the time of year. Although some were eaten the same day (who can resist fresh raspberries?), the majority were bottled for consumption during the winter. Cherry, cleverly, made specially adapted aprons, with a pouch in front that was large enough to hold two Kilner bottling jars side by side to pick into. Then all you had to do was to take the full jars into the kitchen, add cold water to them, screw the lids down loosely, slowly heat in a water-bath to sterilization temperature, remove them, tighten the lids, and Bob's your uncle. No sugar, no fuss, no problem. Tomatoes came in for the same treatment. We would squirrel away hundreds of bottles of fruit in our loft that would provide us with delicious desserts every day of the year.

Once you start on a quest for self-sufficiency it can become seriously addictive, and before long we had acquired a dozen hens, which lived in a moveable ark on the trial ground, keeping us well supplied with fresh eggs and the occasional roast dinner. I also took up beekeeping, under the watchful eye of the Braintree Beekeepers Association, which was run by an elderly gentleman called Alf Gunn, who got me started with a borrowed hive and my first swarm. Alf had kept bees all his life and had no fear of being stung. Not for him the traditional beekeeper's outfit of white protective suit, gloves and veil – he administered a light puff of smoke into the hive to quieten the occupants and that was it. Funnily enough, the bees seemed to sense his calm gentleness and rarely attacked him. I was less sanguine about the prospect of being stung, so I made sure that I was fully covered each time I inspected the colonies. One day, though, I made the serious error of wearing a 'hard hat' from my old civil engineering days, and a little blighter got in through the ventilation holes and stung me repeatedly – not dying, as bees usually do when they leave their sting in your skin, because my skull was too thick!

For her part, Jackie took to making preserves, drying herbs and culturing her own yogurt. Looking back, I'm amazed she managed to find the time, given that our HDRA duties kept us on the trial ground for long hours at a stretch and that she cooked for all the students and WWOOFers. We even made our own wine, until one night the blackcurrants gently fermenting on the electric storage heaters got too hot, popped their corks and exploded, leaving sticky, purple gunge over our brand new wallpaper, our beautiful pine furniture and, more importantly, us. We've never made wine since!

Our own efforts to live a more self-reliant life mirrored similar attempts taking place elsewhere in Britain. Many 'back-to-the-landers' were inspired by the writings of John Seymour, whose books on self-sufficiency acquired almost cult status in the mid-1970s. Then in his early 60s, Seymour spent his working life as a writer and broadcaster, based on a small farm in Suffolk. Following the unexpected success of *The Fat of the Land*, a book he wrote with his wife Sally, who supplied the illustrations, he moved to Pembrokeshire. His farm there at Fachongle Isaf quickly became a mecca for anyone wanting first-hand experience of the 'good life'. Land was relatively cheap in West Wales and it became the hub of scores of experimental communities, set up to get back to the land. Inevitably, many found-ered, leaving a trail of disintegrating relationships in their wake (including Seymour's own marriage). Add to this the harsh realities of attempting to do every-thing yourself and you had a counter-drift of disillusioned young people heading back to the cities. Not all of them failed, however, and those that remained formed the nucleus of organic vegetable pro-ducers that was to emerge a decade later to kick-start commercial production in Britain.

Further up the coast, at the mouth of the Dovey estuary, sits the delightful town of Machynlleth, and it was here in a disused slate quarry in 1973 that Gerard Morgan-Grenville and a small group of like-minded individuals, including Peter Harper, began experimenting with solar and wind power and other forms of alternative energy. Two years later the place opened to the public as the Centre for Alternative Technology (CAT) and although trialling and demonstrating renewable forms of energy was, and still is, its primary focus, there has always been a strong strand of organic growing in CAT's work. Like HDRA, this community was way ahead of its time.

Some of the most durable groups established in the 60s and 70s had a strong spiritual foundation, the most famous being the Findhorn Community on the shores of the Moray Firth in the far north of Scotland. It was started in 1962 by Peter and Eileen Caddy and their friend Dorothy Maclean in a caravan park. Findhorn initially became famous for its remarkable giant cabbages, weighing up to 40lb, and other monster crops that the Caddys grew in their garden, which Eileen attributed to divine intervention (although Lawrence, when he went up to see them, put their success down to heavy applications of pig muck!). The Findhorn Foundation, as it is now known, has expanded beyond all recognition since those early days, with the emphasis now far more on personal awareness and spiritual growth than on organic horticulture.

The self-sufficiency movement found expression elsewhere in Europe, and it was similarly strong in the USA. Interesting parallels exist between Britain and the USA. Just as we had the Seymours, so they had Scott and Helen Nearing, whose book *Living the Good Life*, published in 1954, became a bible for thousands of homesteaders. Their austere farm near the small town of Jamaica, in Windham County, Vermont, which they moved to in 1932, became a test-bed for an alternative lifestyle that put organic growing at its heart. Each day was apparently divided into three equal blocks of time, almost on monastic lines, and these comprised physical work (what they called 'bread labor'), help in the community and recreational activities. In 1952 they moved to a new farm at Cape Rosier in Maine, where they remained for the rest of their lives. Their later experiences were summed up in *Continuing the Good Life*, which came out in 1979. A succession of *Good Life* titles followed, which reinforced their central message of the need for people to embrace a simpler and more fulfilling existence, in tune with nature. Theirs was a physically demanding life, but it was a long and happy one on the whole; Scott died in 1983, aged 100, and Helen in 1995 at over 90 years old.

We also led a simple, hard-working life at Bocking. We didn't even have a television set, but we did have our record player and we listened to the radio regularly, but most evenings were just spent enjoying conversation. Now and again we would be lucky to have a student like David Lofts, who could play a musical instrument, but we were especially fortunate one year when Louise Williams joined us. She'd been a founder member of the Endellion String Quartet, which was then, as it is now, one of the country's leading ensembles, but she'd felt the need for a break. One day she told us that her ex-husband Colin Carr, a virtuoso cellist, was playing at the Wigmore Hall in London that very lunchtime and the concert was being broadcast by the BBC. Afterwards he would be taking the train to Braintree to see her. To say we were thrilled would not be doing justice to our feelings of joyous anticipation – Jackie and I adore classical music. Sure enough, a few hours after we heard him play on air, we were privileged to hear the two of them, perched on upended wheelbarrows, playing Bach duets. Listening to that sublime music, watching the sun go down over the gardens, is one of our most enduring memories. Looking back on those years in general, we had none of the anxieties that plague so many people in today's materialistic society. Everything was simpler then. We were eating fresh, wholesome, healthy food, most of which we had produced ourselves, and living close to nature. It was a very good life indeed.

Chapter Five

FERTILITY WITHOUT FERTILIZERS

A s INTERESTING AS IT WAS to look after chickens or bottle fruit for the first time, these activities were peripheral to our main responsibility, which was running the experimental trials. Many of the trials concerned soil fertility, and for this we needed an ever-ready supply of compost. As I've mentioned, six New Zealand compost boxes stood in pride of place at the centre of the trial ground. They were the main source of fertility for all the plots and were always in use. One would be empty, waiting for the next batch of garden waste, and another full of finished compost ready to spread onto the land, while the rest contained weeds and other plant material at various stages of decomposition. On summer mornings at daybreak, when stillness hung over the gardens and the air was deliciously cool, at least one bin would nevertheless be gently steaming away. We knew from our thermometer readings that the temperature at the heart of the heaps would regularly reach 150°F (66°C), sometimes getting as high as 160°F (71°C), and only the foolhardy would attempt to delve into the core with bare hands. Lawrence claimed that he knew a man who had cooked an omelette on a newly made compost heap, and although we always wanted to test this extraordinary feat ourselves we never actually got round to it! The heaps only stayed this hot for a day or two and then began to cool down, shrinking in volume all the while, until the contents were forked out and re-positioned in the same box: the well-rotted material from the middle of the heap was moved to the sides and the relatively undecomposed material, which hadn't heated up, was moved from the sides into the middle. This action would provoke another burst of heat, as the new material in the centre began its breakdown. The whole thing would then be left alone for a couple of months by which time the finished compost was ready for use.

Composting is a miraculous business and I still get a thrill from watching a large pile of rough garden waste metamorphose into a neat heap of sweet-smelling, light and friable, earth-like soil conditioner. Lawrence, of course, had compost-making off to a fine art, and we soon got the hang of it. Achieving the right balance of constituents is critical to success. The compost should not include too much woody material or too many sappy substances. Incorporating just the right amount of air and water is also important. The rest is easy. Although it's best to make garden-scale compost in a container, which helps to retain the heat, you can construct a compost heap just as a pile, straight on the ground, if you have large quantities of, say, something like strawy cattle manure or horse manure. Here, the sheer bulk of the material ensures that the high temperatures will be reached easily, but they also have to be turned 'inside out', just liker the smaller heaps, to fully break down the material around the edge. One brilliant side-effect of generating high temperatures in the heap is that it destroys weed seeds and any disease organisms that may be present – a real bonus. For that reason, Lawrence always preferred to use wooden compost bins, which he said retained the heat far better than plastic ones.

We would always attempt to fill a bin in one go, trampling down the contents to create a compact mass, yet not packing it so tightly that air was excluded, and periodically spraying the surface with water if it was a little on the dry side. The effect we were trying to achieve was a moist heap, but not a sodden one. Often we would use freshly-mown grass clippings as an 'activator', because they are rich in nitrogen and heat up rapidly; but Lawrence made a point of trotting down to the composting area in his bedroom slippers each morning to discharge the content of their chamber pot, which is a valuable source of nitrogen and potassium. This use of urine echoed the millennia-old practice of Chinese peasants who, as I've already discussed, also made good use of their bodily waste – hence Lawrence's pet name for it as 'Chairman Mao Special'. Most gardeners, unthinkingly, simply flush away this useful resource.

Many people seem to find compost-making difficult when they first start because they can't get their compost heaps to heat up properly. If this happens to you, don't worry, it's not the end of the world! All heaps rot down eventually, but they may take twelve months or longer to do so – the chief problem being that weed seeds may not be destroyed thoroughly. Heaps usually fail to heat up when they have been made piecemeal fashion rather than all at once, as a 'critical mass' of waste is needed to get the decomposition process going. This is unlikely to happen if material is added in dribs and drabs. If there's insufficient material available to fill at least half a bin, it can be put into black plastic sacks, which are then tied to exclude air and minimize rotting. As soon as sufficient waste has accumulated, the contents of all the sacks can be emptied out and mixed together, at the same time adding fresh green material, such as grass clippings.

At Bocking, even with all six bins producing compost on a near-continuous basis, we never seemed to have enough to satisfy our acre of beds. The sandy loam devoured compost, like light soils everywhere, and whether spread on the soil surface as a mulch, or lightly dug in, it was hard to find any traces of it left by the end of the season. Some was sieved and applied to the seed beds, and some went in the potato trenches and around plants that needed a high level of nutrients, while the rest went on trials that specifically involved compost treatment. We knew from the results of the trials that the overall fertility of the land was rising steadily. It was also noticeable that the composted soil was more resilient to drying out in times of drought (an ever-present risk on the eastern side of the country) because the enhanced level of organic matter ensured better moisture retention. Had the site at Bocking been more clay-like, the effect of adding compost would have been to open the soil up, so that more air and water would be incorporated, thus making it easier to work. All in all, compost is something special!

Microbiologically speaking, our understanding of what actually goes on in a 'hot' compost heap is still far from complete. The process begins when aerobic (air-needing) microbes digest the most easily broken down constituents, causing the heap to start to heat up. Once the temperature gets above 100°F (38°C), thermophilic (heat-loving) micro-organisms, comprising bacteria and fungi, take over. When the thermometer readings climb above 140°F (60°C) the thermophilic fungi die and are followed by other bacteria, along with organisms called actinomycetes, which resemble bacteria but are classified as fungi – actinomycetes are responsible for the earthy smell of compost and damp soil. As the heap begins to cool, the tougher cellulose that remains is digested by more thermophilic fungi and other types of bacteria that only tolerate warm conditions. This is followed by a longer cooling-down phase, during which time fungi have the heap more or less to themselves. It reaches full maturity after larger organisms that are visible to the naked eye, like manure worms, beetles, springtails and mites, pick over whatever undigested material is left.

Under optimum conditions the entire cycle can be accomplished in about six weeks, but it usually takes around three months. I have greatly simplified the whole process, because the number of individual species of bacteria alone runs to many thousands, and even now professional soil scientists are still a long way from comprehending exactly what goes on in a compost heap.

When considering the soil in general, while the function of each of the major classes of soil-dwelling organisms is known, only a handful of the individual interactions that occur there have been accurately decoded. From an organic gardener's point of view, 'nitrogen-fixing' (or *Rhizobia*) bacteria, which live in the pin-head-sized nodules that you can find on the roots of beans, clover and other legumes, are among the most important because they're able to convert gaseous nitrogen into a usable form. It's a beneficial relationship all round. The plants supply carbohydrates that the bacteria feed on, while the bacteria return the favour by supplying the plant with the vital nutrient, nitrate: every plant has, in effect, its own tiny nitrogen fertilizer factory. When the plants die, any nitrate that remains in the nodules is released into the soil, to the benefit of other plants nearby. The nodule-forming bacteria contribute the largest proportion of biologically 'fixed' nitrogen, but there are other free-living forms, such as blue-green algae, inhabiting the spaces between the soil particles, that also contribute a useful amount of nitrogen.

Then there are the mycorrhizal fungi mentioned in the first chapter. There are known to be around 6,000 species of these and they perform a key role in supplying plants with phosphorus. Like *Rhizobia*, they live in symbiosis with plants, invading the root hairs and casting out complex skeins of fungal hyphae (threads) into the soil, like a fisherman laying his nets. They scavenge for nutrients far more effectively than the plant roots could on their own. Certain species of these opportunistic feeders can also defend plants against attack from other harmful fungi by enveloping their roots in an all-embracing protective cloak. Lots of plant species can form these mutually beneficial relationships with mycorrhizae – particularly trees and shrubs. Among vegetables, the onion family appears to be the most adept at exploiting these valuable fungal friends. Cabbages and other brassicas, however, don't appear to generate mycorrhizal associations at all.

There is one organism living in the soil that we do know a lot about – our friend the dear old earthworm. We are much more familiar with these annelids thanks to the patient observations of Charles Darwin in the 19th century. He was captivated by these unassuming little creatures, which collectively perform a heroic task in the soil. On a typical acre of land worms are capable of processing up to 15 tons of earth each year, which they then bring to the surface as castings. Worm casts are much richer in nutrients than the surrounding soil and typically contain five times the nitrogen, seven times the phosphate and as much as eleven times the potash, making them, from a gardening perspective, an ideal ingredient of potting mixtures. As they eat their way through the soil, worms leave behind a tubular network of air- and water-filled tunnels that plant roots readily exploit, while the soil itself, during its passage through the worm's alimentary system, is mixed with chemicals that are secreted during digestion, and is converted into stable crumbs.

All in all, the living soil is an immensely sophisticated biological powerhouse that is responsible for enabling plants to grow successfully in the wild by making the nutrients they need available. Our job, as organic gardeners, is to stimulate the soil so that it performs the same function for us at home. According to Dr R.F. Milton, Director of Research at the Haughley Research Farms for 16 years, the average topsoil in Britain contains sufficient stores of potash, phosphate and trace minerals to allow for 1,000 years of cropping. Even greater mineral reserves exist in the subsoil, but most of them are present in insoluble forms that render them unavailable to plants, unless they are acted upon by micro-organisms in the ways I've just described. It is simply not true, therefore, that chemical fertilizers are essential to replace the minerals that are lost whenever crops and livestock products are removed from the farm. Of course, it pays to return minerals to the soil when plants are harvested, but if this is done by adding compost or other organic 'wastes', the resulting enhanced biological activity 'unlocks' the far greater treasure chest that is already present in the soil.

By contrast, farmers and gardeners who rely on chemicals actually suppress this vital, mineral-producing biological activity, so when an analysis of their soil reveals shortages of key minerals, they respond by adding even more chemicals, which just makes matters worse. Before they know it they are on the cycle of declining soil fertility and ever-increasing chemical use until the soil structure breaks down completely with potentially catastrophic consequences. The truth is – nature just needs a helping hand, not a kick in the teeth!

Artificial nitrogenous fertilizers have a dramatic effect on *Rhizobia*, and other nitrogen-fixing bacteria, killing or severely inhibiting them. Mycorrhizal fungi also suffer when fertilizers are applied, and they can even change, Jekyll-and-Hyde-like, from being beneficial to becoming dangerously parasitic, though all too often they are wiped out before this can happen by chemical fungicides that are being used to treat other fungal diseases. Most chemical fertilizers also tend, over time, to make soils more acid, and hence unattractive to worms, which cannot tolerate a soil pH below 5.0 (pH is a measure of acidity/alkalinity with

7.0 representing neutral). When combined with reduced amounts of organic matter in the soil, as is so often the case, and the use of certain herbicides and fungicides that have wormicidal properties, worms will be killed or driven out completely. An absence of worms from a field, in fact, is one of the most telling indicators of intensive use of chemicals.

The 'locking up' of trace elements can be another unfortunate consequence of using fertilizers, as chemical reactions come into play that make them unavailable to plants. So, the over-zealous application of superphosphate can bring about a deficiency of zinc, for example, just as too much potash results in a shortage of boron, while the over-use of both can lead to the unavailability of magnesium. At the other end of the pH scale, if the soil becomes too alkaline as a result of lime being added as a corrective, the release of boron, manganese, nickel and other trace elements can become impaired. All of this is part of the reason why the mineral and trace element content of much of the food we eat today has dropped dramatically, with potentially alarming consequences for our health.

In a biologically active soil, the level of available nutrients is constantly fluctuating in harmony with the seasons, as Dr Milton discovered. During the winter months, when the coldness of the soil deters microbial activity, soil tests indicate extremely low levels of NPK (nitrogen, phosphorus, potassium). But when spring arrives, days lengthen and soil temperatures increase, the micro-organisms step up a gear and levels of available nutrients increase dramatically, peaking in June and July. And when you come to think about it, this is exactly how it should be, with nature making nutrients available to plants when they are most needed, during the spring and summer months when growth is at its most intense.

Compost is undoubtedly the best source of organic matter that can be added to the soil to stimulate micro-organisms and improve its structure, but there are others – such as leafmould. When a tree sheds its leaves in a riot of autumn colour, the minerals, which have been drawn up from the earth via the roots and incorporated into the foliage all season long, are returned to the soil. The leaves are attacked by fungi and gradually break down, accumulating on the surface as a spongy, dark-brown layer known as leaf litter. This, over time, is incorporated back into the soil by earthworms and surface-living creatures. It is easy to replicate this process in the garden – just heap the leaves into a pile and leave nature to do the rest.

At Bocking we constructed leafmould enclosures similar in size to our compost bins, but made from wire netting instead. Because the trial ground didn't contain many trees and shrubs we used to ask our neighbours for their autumn leaves. They rarely needed much persuading, since the alternative was an afternoon spent choking over a smoky bonfire. The decaying process in a pile of leaves occurs at a much slower rate than in a compost heap, and it can take a couple of years, although you can speed things up by shredding the leaves. A good way of doing this is to sprinkle the leaves over a lawn and then attack them with a rotary mower with a grass box attached. This has the added benefit of incorporating nitrogen-rich grass clippings into the mix. Leafmould is an excellent substitute for peat in seed and potting mixtures, and all soils will benefit from additions of this long-lasting source of humus.

It's commonly assumed that organic gardeners depend on farm-yard manure. This may have been so in the past, but by the 1970s the specialization of British agriculture into either livestock farming or arable cropping meant that certain parts of the country were virtually livestock-free zones, East Anglia being a case in point. If anything, the situation is even more polarized today. Actually, there was a small dairy farm left, not far from us – the last for miles around – and once or twice a year we would ask the farmer to drop off a trailer load of 'muck' in front of a farm gate entrance to the trial ground, at the far end of Convent Lane. What he brought along had been taken from the yard where his animals had lived during the winter, and it consisted of straw, drenched with cattle urine and richly coated with dung. It was heavy and smelly – beautiful stuff! Manure like this should ideally be re-stacked, windrow fashion, with any straw that appears to be on the dry side dampened with a hosepipe, and the whole lot trodden down. This can be hard work, and Jackie and I had the aching muscles to prove it! The heating up of the heap is fierce and rapid, and the stack rots down, transformed and ready for use, within weeks. But if there isn't the time it can be left to rot down as a pile, so long as it's covered with a tarpaulin to keep nutrient loss to a minimum.

Nowadays the most commonly available source of stable manure is from horses that have been bedded on wood shavings or sawdust, rather than straw, so it's essential to ensure that it has decomposed thoroughly before using on the garden. Wood resists breakdown tenaciously, far more so than straw, and even when it's mixed with horse droppings and stable manure, it may take three or more years to decay. It contains a large amount of carbon and requires nitrogen, which is present in the soil, to complete its breakdown, thus potentially depriving any nearby plants of the nitrogen they need. They may then suffer from a deficiency, colourfully known as 'nitrogen robbery'. Patience is essential with horse manure – stack, cover and then wait, and wait! Even so, it may be safest to put it as a mulch onto perennial flower beds, or under trees, rather than risk it on nitrogen-sensitive vegetable plots.

Some manure – especially droppings from birds such as pigeons and poultry – is problematic for the opposite reason, in that it contains concentrated amounts of nitrogen that can 'scorch' plants. The best way to deal with this type of manure is to put it straight onto the compost heap, where it makes an excellent activator; alternatively, if you have a lot, make a separate heap with straw.

However, not everyone is comfortable using animal manures. Vegetarians and vegans, among others, sometimes baulk at using them on principle, especially given the unsatisfactory conditions many farm animals have to endure. For this reason I will never buy chicken manure from battery houses. Fortunately, there is an alternative to using 'factory farmed' waste to provide the soil with additional organic matter – a technique known as 'green manuring' or 'cover cropping'. Certain grasses, legumes and other leafy plants that are appropriate as green manures are sown and then dug into the soil while they are still soft and sappy, breaking down to provide the soil bacteria and fungi with something to feed on. If this happens before the plants become too old and woody there is no fear of nitrogen robbery; and if a leguminous species of green manure, such as clover, is chosen, the soil will also benefit from the release of extra nitrogen as the root nodules decay. Green manures can be sown at any time other than in winter. They can be sown during a short break between crops in the summer months or, more commonly, they can be used in the early autumn as a way of grabbing the plant foods, like nitrate, that might otherwise be flushed from the soil by winter rains. When these plants are dug in the following spring, the nitrogen is released back into the soil by bacterial action and made available for use by the succeeding crop. Good over-wintering green manures include grazing rye (*Secale cereale*) and *Phacelia tanacetifolia*, which aren't 'nitrogen fixers', and winter tares (*Vicia sativa*) and crimson clover (*Trifolium incarnatum*), which are. Green-manure plants will never provide much by way of long-lasting humus but they are an important means of preserving nutrients and form a key part in the cropping plans of most commercial organic vegetable producers, as indeed they did at Bocking, where we used them routinely.

Green manuring is very popular nowadays, as is worm composting. In fact, there's no better way of burnishing one's green credentials than by having a worm bin at home to process unwanted kitchen scraps – but this invaluable way of enhancing soil fertility has been practised for many years. In the mid-1970s, Jack Temple, an organic market gardener living in Surrey, came up with the idea of creating a specially protected environment in which worms could break down vegetable peelings and cooked food waste that could otherwise attract rats if placed in a normal compost bin. He devised a wooden container, similar in size to a regular compost bin, that he half-filled with peat and then seeded with brandling worms (*Eisenia foetida*). These are not the same species found in most garden soils; they are the bright red, stripy worms usually seen in piles of manure, which anglers use as fishing bait. Jack had half a dozen or so of these, which he filled with a mixture of weeds and kitchen waste; he argued that the end product of the worms' digestive efforts was superior to conventionally produced compost. In 1979 he wrote an 18-page booklet describing his system, which was published by the Soil Association under the title *Worm Compost*.

However, it was not Jack's method that became the popular way of utilizing worms. That honour belongs to Mary Appelhof from the

United States, the self-styled 'Worm Woman', whose book *Worms Eat My Garbage* came out in 1982. It has rarely been out of print and is the primer for budding vermiculturalists the world over. Appelhof used a much smaller container – a wooden box that she half-filled with bedding made from shredded paper mixed with leafmould or peat. Her worms were fed an exclusive diet of kitchen waste which, over a period of several months was turned into rich, dark compost that rose gradually up the container. At Bocking we were never completely convinced by Jack's approach to utilizing worms; Mary Appelhof's ideas seemed far more workable, so we began experimenting with worm bins of our own. Nowadays, of course, you can buy specially manufactured worm composting kits, complete with worms, and most designs even have traps to collect the drainage liquor, which can be watered onto the compost heap. One of the great things about these wiggly workers is that the compost they produce doesn't smell if the worm bin is working well. Consequently, worm composters are incorporated into the kitchen fittings of some new homes as part of the recycling apparatus – the ultimate 'green' garbage disposal unit!

Everything I've described so far has been concerned with supplying the soil with bulky organic matter, like compost, manure and leafmould, so that it can be broken down and used as food by soil-living creatures, and because it improves soil structure. All such materials contain nitrogen and other plant nutrients to a varying degree – worm compost has far more than leafmould, for example – but this is not their key feature. They power the microbial life of the soil, which in turn provides the nitrogen and other nutrients essential to all plant life.

We can give nature a helping hand by adding concentrated nutrient sources, in the form of organic fertilizers. These can be of animal, plant or mineral origin and are mostly insoluble, so they can only be made available to plants through the activities of the soil micro-organisms already mentioned. This means that the goodness is released into the soil slowly, in some cases taking many years. So, like composts and other bulky organic wastes, organic fertilizers feed the soil and not the plant. But why are concentrated organic fertilizers needed at all? Well, it takes time to create a fertile and productive soil, and if land has been starved of organic matter or the soil is poor for other reasons – like the consolidated builders' rubble, overlaid with a smidgen of topsoil, to be found on new housing estates – it can need a little extra help.

Most animal-based fertilizers are derived from slaughterhouse wastes and have suitably lurid names, such as bonemeal, hoof and horn, or blood, fish and bone. The rise in vegetarianism, coupled with residual worries about the safety of slaughterhouse wastes in the aftermath of the Bovine Spongiform Encephalopathy (BSE) epidemic, has led to something of a decline in popularity of these traditional organic fertilizers. The current Soil Association standards adopt an overly cautious approach, in my view, in only allowing commercial growers to use such products in propagating composts. All contain some nitrogen, but hoof and horn has the most; whereas bonemeal is the richest source of phosphate. It's useful to know that, as a rough shorthand, nitrogen promotes the growth of shoots and leaves, phosphate helps root development, while potash is needed for flower and fruit formation. So, for example, it was traditional to add hoof and horn and bonemeal when planting fruit trees and bushes, to provide them with all they needed over the first few years while they were becoming established. And sprinkling hoof and horn will assist nitrogen-demanding winter brassicas, which spend a long time in the soil. Blood, fish and bone provides useful amounts of both nitrogen and phosphorus, and it's often used as a general organic feed in the vegetable garden, though it doesn't contain any potassium, so it's gradually being superseded by pelleted chicken manure, which has about 3 per cent potash. Wool waste, or shoddy, is another high-nitrogen source, though it's not that easy to get hold of nowadays, given that the wool textile industry has all but vanished. Nevertheless, you can still buy wool that has been shaped into flat strips of mulching material for use by gardeners. Placed under newly planted hedges, it simultaneously suppresses weeds and supplies the young saplings with nitrogen. One snag, though, is that it makes extremely desirable nesting material, so birds tend to tug at it.

Of the vegetable-based concentrated organic fertilizers available, seaweed contains a reasonable amount of potash and is therefore often used on tomatoes, gooseberries, peas and beans, and other potash-hungry crops. As you might expect, coming from the ocean, it's also rich in trace elements, and although it's usually bought as a dried powder, it can also be used fresh from the beach, either as a compost activator or lightly dug in. It goes without saying that seaweed should not be detached from rocks, and only material that has been washed onto the shore should be taken. Until relatively recently, growers in places like Cornwall, the Isles of Scilly and other coastal communities, relied on seaweed. You might think that there would be a problem with salt building up in the soil, but this doesn't appear to happen, even in places where it is used extensively. By far the best source of potash, however, comes from a by-product of the sugar beet processing industry known as kali vinasse, although it's usually marketed simply as 'organic potash'.

Mineral rock dusts make up the third category of fertilizer and are mostly used to treat specific mineral deficiencies. So, for example, ground rock phosphate is added wherever soils are lacking phosphorus, and dolomitic limestone (which comprises calcium and magnesium carbonate) is the organic alternative to hydrated lime in correcting soils that are too acid. Dolomitic limestone also supplies them with magnesium. In recent years more and more people have taken to 'remineralizing' their soils through the addition of finely ground granite dust or other crushed rocks of volcanic origin. Astonishing claims have been made for the gains in productivity that have been achieved as a result (Sir Albert Howard maintained that one of the reasons for the health and longevity of the Hunza tribesmen of northern India was that their crops were irrigated by the mineral-rich melt waters of the Himalayas). But the evidence is by no means conclusive and there would be an obvious environmental downside should rock dust ever be traded commercially on an appreciable scale in that the quarrying and transport use so much energy.

As I've already suggested, organic concentrated fertilizers are insoluble, in the main, and so the minerals they contain are only made available to plants slowly. This is in contrast to inorganic fertilizers (the ubiquitous NPK type of commercial product, eschewed by organic gardeners), which are extremely soluble and therefore very fast-acting. There are some rock-based products, however, that are highly soluble, including Chilean nitrate, and kainit, which is a crude potassium salt that also contains magnesium. Although it's fair to describe them as 'natural', in that they are simply dug out of the ground, their mode of action is indistinguishable from that of artificial fertilizers in that they feed plants direct, by-passing the soil's microbiological processes. Not surprisingly, arguments have raged in organic circles for years as to whether such products should be allowed to be used by commercial producers of organic crops, and the issue is still by no means settled.

A similar objection could be raised, incidentally, to wood ash, which for centuries has been used by gardeners, chiefly as a source of potash, although it contains a little phosphate and other minerals. It is also highly soluble, the timber having been reduced by combustion to its simple mineral constituents. Like chemical fertilizers, it gives an immediate boost to the plants and has traditionally been used to feed tomatoes and gooseberries, but the effect is short-lived and the potash quickly leaches from light soils. It's far better to store wood ash somewhere dry, to be recycled through a compost heap, where the potassium and other salts will be converted into more stable organic forms.

Liquid plant feeds might also appear to contradict the principle of feeding the soil rather than the plant, as indeed they do, but the justification (for organic gardeners, that is) is that they are used in artificial situations in which soil is usually lacking – for example, in pots, hanging baskets and grow-bags. Gardeners of old made their own liquid feeds by steeping a sack filled with manure or soot (the latter contains around 5 per cent nitrogen) in a tub of water, and then draining off the resulting liquor. Some gardeners still use this method today; others fill water barrels with young nettle leaves and extract a similar, nitrogen-rich feed.

But by far the best liquid feed, though, and the one we used mostly at Bocking, is made from comfrey. Its roots penetrate deep into the subsoil searching for minerals, and the leaves are especially rich in potash, having twice as much as well-rotted farmyard manure. Many organic gardeners grow comfrey to supply an extra source of green material for their compost heaps but, as we discovered on the trial ground, the leaves can also be turned into a potash and nitrogen-containing liquid plant food. One method is to soak them in water, as for soot and manure, but the smell given off by rotting comfrey leaves in water is definitely to be avoided. It's vile! It's far better to compress the dry leaves under a heavy weight to produce a concentrated extract. After various attempts at refining this process, we hit upon the idea of using a four-foot length of plastic drainage pipe, placed vertically, and capped at the base, into which comfrey leaves were stuffed. A litre bottle of water, tied to a length of string and lowered into the tube, provided the pressure, and the resulting liquid that dripped out of a small drainage hole drilled at the bottom was collected in a jug.

Of course, Jackie and I didn't know all these principles and practices of soil fertility from the word go. We garnered our knowledge gradually over the first couple of years at HDRA – not that I've mentioned everything there is to know on the subject, but the basic tenets, drummed into us by Lawrence, are the same. The main point to understand, he said, is that by taking advantage of nature's slow-release methods of recycling nutrients, via the soil's micro-organisms, we are able to grow plants in life-enhancing soil with a good, stable structure that is infinitely sustainable and non-polluting.

As an organization, HDRA always concentrated on promoting the positive benefits of organic growing, rather than highlighting the problems associated with chemicals, which, in general, we left to others. But we were, nevertheless, aware of the facts. In the Gulf of Mexico, for example, over 5,000 square miles of ocean become temporarily unable to support life each summer, due to the excessive amounts of nutrients from fertilizers and sewage that find their way into the Mississippi river, where they are washed downstream to nourish algae and other marine vegetation, to such an extent that when they die and decay the process uses up all the oxygen available for life in the Gulf.

If you combine this vast problem of eutrophication with the many other smaller, but nonetheless serious, examples the world over, and you take all the instances of soil erosion across the planet that I've already touched on, you can see why we, and so many other gardeners, are keen to adopt the organic approach to soil fertility.

Chapter Six

POISON-FREE PEST CONTROL

IN THOSE EARLY DAYS on the trial ground, Jackie and I witnessed a striking demonstration of organic pest control in action. We had read about Sir Albert Howard's and Lady Balfour's belief that soils that are well supplied with organic matter, and biologically active, will support plants that are better able to withstand attack from pests and diseases. Lawrence himself had talked about this, but nothing convinces you like seeing it with your own eyes!

Next to the Pye House, half way down the trial ground, two plots of broad-bean plants were growing side by side, separated only by a narrow, grass path. One set of plants was stunted and sickly, with almost no leaves, and it bore a miserable crop; the other was tall and straight, with bushy foliage, and laden with pods. This, apparently, was a long-running soil-feeding trial comparing chemical fertilizers with compost. Although the chemically treated plots had started off well, and had out-performed the compost-fed plots for a number of years, any initial advantage had long since disappeared to the point that, 13 years later, they were barely capable of producing a crop at all. But what was even more striking on the chemically treated beds was the infestation of blackfly (also known as black aphids) that completely smothered the plants. And yet only a light scattering of the pests coloured the tips of their neighbouring compost-fed plants, less than two feet away.

Such observations, we learned, are by no means uncommon – so what is the explanation for these differences? Plants grown using artificial fertilizers are known to have larger, thinner-walled cells than those grown on compost-treated soils. The weaker cell membranes are punctured more easily by greenfly and other sap-sucking insects, and the cells also contain higher levels of soluble nitrogen nutrient, which means that the pests reproduce at a greater rate. Fungal disease organisms, whose thread-like hyphae must penetrate the cell walls to reach the sap stream, also benefit from chemically fed plants for the same reason. Infestations of pests and diseases are the inevitable consequence of artificial fertilizers and, as a result, at some point the chemically minded grower will also reach for the pesticide sprayer.

Pesticide use soared after the Second World War, when chemists put their wartime discoveries to more peaceful purposes. Dichloro-diphenyl-trichloroethane (DDT), for example, a so-called organo-chlorine compound, had been invented as far back as 1873, but its insecticidal properties were not discovered until 1939. The military found that body lice, the infantryman's curse, could be eliminated by dusting soldiers' uniforms with DDT powder. It appeared to have no toxicity to humans but was deadly to insects and its effect lasted for many months. Another group of pesticides called organophosphates also had their roots in the Second World War, when they had been developed as part of Germany's nerve-gas programme. Not surprisingly, they are extremely toxic to humans and wildlife but, unlike the organochlorines, they don't persist in the environment and break down within a matter of months.

These remarkable new wonder chemicals were taken up eagerly by farmers after the war. But before long some alarming side-effects began to appear. The numbers of creatures at the top of the food chain, including the peregrine falcon in the UK and the bald eagle in the USA, were decimated, as many birds either died or were no longer able to incubate their eggs. When autopsied they were found to contain massive quantities of DDT. On further investigation, it was found that the deadly chemical had come from eating prey that was also contaminated with it – as were all the other creatures going down their food chain, right back to the insects at the bottom, which were the original organisms that had been sprayed. The effect of the DDT was magnified the further it passed up the food chain. Female birds of prey that weren't killed outright produced eggs with thin shells that broke prematurely. Numbers of raptors fell so dramatically that, at one point, it looked as if the bald eagle, the emblem of the United States, might join the dodo on the extinction list.

In 1962, this story, along with a litany of others in a similar vein, was published in Rachel Carson's book *Silent Spring* (see page 20). Carson prophesied that if nothing changed, we faced a world without birds and many other animals. Unsurprisingly the author was viciously assailed by pesticide companies calling for the book to be banned. Although one of the most eminent biologists of her generation, this didn't stop a mass of defamatory articles, written by industry-funded academics at American universities, from appearing in the scientific press. Despite this onslaught, the book survived and went on to become a world-wide bestseller, although, tragically, Carson herself died shortly afterwards.

Throughout the 1960s, evidence about the harmful effects of pest-icides on the environment piled up, and as DDT started to accumulate in the body fat of other creatures at the top of food chains, concern began to be expressed about the long-term future of humans. By the late-1970s organochlorine pesticides had been banned or severely restricted in most countries in the West, although this is not the case in parts of the Third World, where they are still being used today, resulting in traces continually showing up in our food.

As organic gardeners we avoid polluting the environment and our food by never using synthetic pesticides. But how do we overcome pest and disease attacks, apart from making sure that our plants have the best chance in life by growing them in a richly composted soil? We have a number of mechanical, biological and cultural tricks up our sleeves. In other words, we use barriers and traps, encourage natural enemies and introduce bio-controls; we also practise crop rotation and companion planting and grow resistant varieties. If all else fails, we turn to natural sprays.

It's a bit like solving a puzzle, Lawrence used to say. You look at the life cycle and behaviour of whatever pest or disease you are trying to stave off and then you search for areas of vulnerability. Sometimes a single measure will suggest itself; more often, a combination. And in any case it's always better to have some back-up strategies. It's rarely possible to obliterate every pest, and you shouldn't be trying to do that anyway. The general idea is to keep pests at a manageable level and damage to a minimum – this is all that's necessary.

Lawrence ran many different experiments to improve organic gardeners' chances of keeping pests and diseases at bay. A good example of one of these was the use of a physical barrier to control a pest called the carrot-root fly – the bane of carrot growers everywhere. Adult root flies have astonishing powers of smell and are able to detect a crop of carrots as much as three miles away. They home in to lay their eggs on the surface of the soil, attracted by the scent that's released whenever the foliage is bruised by thinning or weeding. Once hatched, the larvae burrow into the developing roots, ruining the appearance with their characteristic black tunnels and laying the carrots open to infection by disease. At Bocking we were aware that the carrot-root fly is an extremely poor flyer and rarely strays more than two feet above the surface of the soil. So, in 1978, when an HDRA member living in Manchester suggested growing carrots inside a low, wooden barrier, we thought it was worth a try. We constructed four rough, wooden frames, just over two feet high, the length and width of the carrot bed, covering the outsides with clear, polythene sheeting. Then we wired the frames together to create an impenetrable plastic barrier that ran around the perimeter of the carrot bed, leaving the top open to the air. It worked, and kept out most of the flies (although some braved the heights to hop over), so the damage was markedly reduced. We followed this up with a nationwide experiment by members, who gave the carrot-root fly barrier a resounding thumbs up. This approach to dealing with what is undoubtedly the worst pest of carrots has been used by countless gardeners ever since. Nowadays polythene has been displaced by fleece and other suitably fine-meshed materials, which let light and water through but keep pests out. Indeed, many gardeners prefer to take no chances, and cover their crops completely, from sowing through to harvest.

Fleece as a physical barrier has proved a godsend in the control of other pests. One of the worst is the flea beetle, which can reduce young cabbage seedlings to shreds. On the trial ground, well before the advent of fleece, the only non-chemical way of coping with them was to use a flea-beetle trolley. This may sound funny, but it works!

I'd encountered flea-beetle trolleys when I came across a photo in an old farming book showing 20 or so solemn-looking labourers walking in line across a turnip field (rather in the manner of policemen searching for evidence). Each was pushing a wheeled gadget made up of what looked like a broom handle attached to a small, rectangular, flat, wooden platform with four largish wheels, suspended a few inches above the ground. It was impossible to tell from the picture exactly how the trolley worked, but there was enough detail for us to be able to knock up a replica at Bocking. The crucial part was a length of wire in front of the contraption that gently brushed the soil surface whenever the trolley was pushed slowly forward over the crop. Any beetles that were feeding on the foliage leapt up in alarm, and were caught on the underside of the platform, which was smeared liberally with sticky grease – the large wheels stopping them from springing sideways. At certain times of the year, especially in hot and dry weather when the pest is most active, a single pass over a row of radishes resulted in a rich harvest of the wretched beetles.

The great thing about something like the flea-beetle trolley is that it's highly specific, so no other creatures are harmed. Pesticides, on the other hand, kill all and sundry, including the pest's natural enemies – the predators and parasites that occur whenever and wherever the pests congregate. These 'garden friends' are the very creatures that should be encouraged, but invariably they have longer life cycles and a much less prolific breeding rate than their prey, so their recovery rate after being sprayed is slower than the pests – their numbers are therefore not high enough to prevent plants from being attacked by new generations of faster breeding pests.

To add to the problem, pests gradually become immune to specific pesticides as time goes by. Not all of them are killed when a crop is sprayed; a few, which have a slightly different genetic make-up from the rest, invariably survive and are able to feed and breed in the absence of competition. This is 'natural selection' with a vengeance. Over succeeding generations this 'immunity' affects increasing numbers of offspring and the pesticide eventually becomes useless. The manufacturer then has to invent a new chemical to do the same job, and so the cycle repeats itself.

During the last 50 years or so, more than 500 species of insects, 100 diseases of plants and more than 270 different types of weeds have become resistant to pesticides. Many compounds have subsequently been discovered to be toxic to wildlife or humans and have been withdrawn from sale. Chemical sprays have been responsible for immense environmental damage, DDT being a good example. Surely it makes no sense to engage in this unwinnable chemical war, which carries the risk of poisoning humans into the bargain?

Nowadays, thanks in no small way to the work HDRA did at Bocking, there are many ingenious non-chemical methods available that organic gardeners rely on to prevent pests from getting to the crop. For example, you can buy or make paper bands coated with grease to tie around the trunks of apple trees in order to trap wingless female winter moths as they attempt to reach the branches to lay their eggs. Slugs and snails can be discouraged by receiving a mild electric shock from the static charge emitted by copper rings or tape placed around vulnerable plants. They are also put off by barriers made from anything abrasive to their soft underbellies – such as crushed eggshells, grit or even pellets made from wool. I know a couple of commercial organic growers who actually feed their slugs by strewing dead lettuce leaves between the rows, to divert them from the growing crop, taking advantage of the fact that slugs and snails are first and foremost scavengers. Our favourite trapping method is the 'slug pub', which relies on the mollusc's predilection for a boozy tipple. There are several proprietary traps on the market, but the 'pub' can be any shallow container, sunk into the soil and filled with beer. After a night out and 'one too many' the creatures topple helplessly into the liquid and drown. Dead drunk, you might say!

Having a healthy population of slug-eating predators in the garden also helps to keep these greedy gastropods in check. Slugs make up approximately a quarter of the diet of frogs (which is one good reason for digging a pond) and they also figure on the menu of toads, birds and predatory insects. Hedgehogs, too, enjoy the occasional slug, and so it pays to encourage them to take up residence. Lawrence was especially adept at devising over-wintering quarters for garden friends, on the assumption that it was never too early to have nature's unpaid pest controllers out and about in the garden. Hibernating hedgehogs love to eat slugs, and the wooden box he invented for them quickly became a favourite and has been widely used ever since. Described in the HDRA booklet, *Operation Tiggywinkle*, first published in 1970, it was little different from those on sale today.

The same is true for over-wintering homes for ladybirds, the designs for which have their roots in HDRA's 'Ladybird Hilton' experiments of the early-1970s. These familiar little beetles, with their shiny red wing cases prettily spotted in black, can eat hundreds of aphids each day, and the rather ugly looking ladybird larvae are also avid consumers of these ubiquitous garden pests. Having spent the winter months asleep under cover, they emerge from hibernation in the spring and start searching for food immediately. Since nettle aphids are among the earliest to appear, it's worth leaving a small patch of nettles in an out of the way part of the garden to provide a tasty snack for hungry ladybirds.

Ladybird beetles aren't the only creatures to prey on aphids – other species, such as lacewings and hoverflies, are also attracted to them. Adult hoverflies are drawn to the nectar sources of brightly coloured annual flowers, such as the poached-egg plant (*Limnanthes douglassii*), and their oval-shaped, almost translucent larvae have a seemingly insatiable appetite for a wide range of sap-sucking pests, including blackfly. So, if poached-egg plants, for example, are grown among broad beans, which can suffer badly from blackfly, the numbers of this troublesome pest can be reduced significantly.

The best way of attracting nectar-feeding beneficial species into your garden is undoubtedly to grow flowers that have wide open centres, but you can ensure that you get sufficient numbers of these and other predators by going one step further and introducing them yourself. Specialist companies have now been set up in many countries to provide gardeners with beneficial insects, including ladybirds and their young, and lacewing larvae, which are known, somewhat sensationally, as 'aphid lions' in the USA. Personally, I prefer to use larvae, placing them strategically among the pests, as there is always a risk that the adults might fly off! In the USA you can also buy praying mantis egg cases, each of which contains over 300 baby mantids. It must be quite a sight watching them hatch out and swarm over the enemy like an invading task force.

Introducing predators and parasites into the growing environment is known as biological pest control, and it is an advance on attracting natural enemies in the hope that they will turn up. One is not better than the other, however: the two techniques go hand in hand. When we first arrived at Bocking, biological pest controls, or biocontrols for short, didn't exist – not for gardeners, anyway. But they were being used commercially by glasshouse growers, who employed a minute parasitic wasp, the size of a pinhead, called *Encarsia formosa*, to control outbreaks of whitefly, and *Phytoseiulus persimilis*, a predatory mite, to deal with red spider mite. Both of these were (and still are) major pests of indoor tomatoes and cucumbers and had become resistant to a wide range of pesticides. Working with Bunting and Sons of Colchester, Essex, then one of the major suppliers to the glasshouse industry, we developed packs suitable for amateurs, which we trialled with HDRA members. We discovered that dealing with live creatures brings its own problems and requires very careful instructions on how to use them. It may seem hard to believe, but some people actually stored their insects in the freezer and were surprised to find them dead when they thawed them out!

Since those early days, the outlook for biological control agents has become even rosier. The declining effectiveness of pesticides, the cost of developing new products and getting them registered, plus an increasing awareness of the potential threat to human health and the environment, have all contributed to a changing climate. Seeing which way the wind was blowing, the chemical companies themselves moved into the biocontrol business – Buntings disappeared in 1992, swallowed up by the pesticide giant Ciba Geigy. Nowadays there are dozens of biological products on the market, including parasitic worms that control slugs, sex hormones that confuse apple pests, and a bacterial insecticide called *Bacillus thuringiensis*, usually just referred to as Bt, that kills cabbage caterpillars.

What about birds? Are they a gardener's friend or foe? Apart from some notable exceptions (one thinks of pigeons and crows), birds are welcome allies. At the trial ground we made a point of feeding them, providing nest boxes and generally trying to make the place bird-friendly. Each winter Jackie and I would suspend strips of bacon fat over the bush roses in Lawrence's and Cherry's garden – the fat was attached to string that hung from bamboo canes pushed at an angle into the soil. Only one blue tit at a time could feed from each cane, so the remainder would settle on the roses, pecking away at aphid eggs as they waited their turn. Result – fewer greenfly in the spring! Another satisfying winter job was to lightly fork over the soil in the orchard, exposing any soil grubs to the sharp eyes of the resident robins – winter titbits for these charming little birds and fewer pests for us! But in the summer when the fruit is ripe, birds change from being valuable orchard predators to becoming pests themselves.

This is why, not long after we arrived at Bocking, we embarked on a major effort to find a reliable and effective bird scarer. Radio cassette tape looped above vulnerable plants seemed to work well, humming and shimmering in the breeze – apart from on still days, when the birds would attack with impunity. They also seemed to have a complete lack of fear of scarecrows, no matter how scary they looked. To add insult to injury, they would use them as a sighting post from which to survey the choicest crops before swooping down to feed.

Next we had a go at simulating the hovering action of hawks. Anyone who has stood near a flock of free-range hens will have observed the panic that breaks out whenever a low-flying plane passes overhead. They are reacting to what they perceive to be a predator in their midst. So we devised our very own, 'Blue Peter style' deterrent, made from an empty plastic detergent bottle with wings taken from a pigeon carcase, lashed to three long bamboo canes and hoisted into position above the crop. At the slightest breath of wind our 'hawk' performed daredevil feats of diving and soaring, which fooled the birds at first, but within a couple of weeks it dawned on them that our fearsome 'hawk' was not all it was cracked up to be and normal pillaging resumed soon after.

We even had a go at using an inflatable snake, guaranteed by the seed company that supplied it to keep off birds. I've never really thought of snakes as bird scarers, even though they will take the eggs of ground-nesting species, so I didn't hold out too much hope of success. But it was worth a try, so we sent away for one. But when we unpacked the parcel, rather than the ferocious looking reptile that we were expecting, there was a pixillated polythene python with a cheeky grin. According to the instructions, we had to inflate it with a bicycle pump before placing it in the garden, shifting its position every day or two to give the impression of movement. Alas, the birds weren't fooled one bit and after a few weeks we gave up. As for our 'python', it re- mained in the garden, lurking unseen among the cabbages, until one day someone accidentally punctured it with a fork. Like a burst balloon it rocketed skywards, giving the birds a fright for the first and only time, before disappearing into a neighbour's garden, never to be seen again. So how did this story end? I wish I could say that we ultimately came up with the perfect bird scarer, but I'm afraid we never did. Until that happy day arrives, the only foolproof way of protecting your crops against birds is to net them.

The use of 'companion plants' as a way of controlling pests was very popular in the 1970s, but at HDRA we were less than enthusiastic. It's based on the idea that if one plant species is grown in close proximity to its so-called 'companion', it will thrive and be less troubled by pests than if grown alone. It's a seductive idea and one that you'll find in most organic gardening books, usually citing the same examples, invariably with frustratingly vague instructions. Place plant X near to plant Y, they may advise, but exactly how near is near you wonder? Is six inches sufficient, or should that be four? How about getting up companiably close at two inches; and will they still be friends at ten? More often than not, the books just don't say. Is the variety important – are some more effective than others? This sort of hard information is usually missing, but the devil is in the detail, as we discovered when we started doing companion planting trials of our own at Bocking.

In 1966, two Americans, Helen Philbrick and Richard Gregg wrote a book called *Companion Plants and How to Use Them*, which contributed to this confusion because the book was heavily plagiarised by other writers. The text is basically a distillation of advice taken from folk reminiscences, gardening books and 'old wives' tales'. Although the authors were at pains to point out that few of their suggestions have been subjected to scientific scrutiny and shouldn't be taken as gospel truth, such cautionary caveats were frequently ignored by the authors who borrowed their ideas. What to Philbrick and Gregg were just interesting speculations have evolved, over the years, to become statements of 'fact'.

There isn't the space here to go into detail about the many companion planting experiments we conducted, except to say that in almost every case the results were either inconclusive or showed no positive effects. On the whole, most of what you read on the subject should be taken with a pinch of salt. Notable exceptions are the flowers that attract predatory and parasitic insects into the garden, like the poached-egg plant mentioned earlier. And there are some other 'companionships' that do seem to work. Planting cabbages and French beans closely together, for example, will usually reduce the infestation of cabbage aphids. As they skim overhead, these pests are programmed to search for the rounded outline that cabbage leaves make against the background of the dark soil. The intrusion of the spear-shaped bean leaves breaks up the outline, so they fly on to search for food elsewhere. Growing onions next to carrots, as a way of fooling carrot-root flies by masking their scent, is perhaps the most quoted companion planting trick. This also works, after a fashion, but only if you grow four rows of onions to every one of carrots. That's an awful lot of onions! Unfortunately, the effect disappears once the onions start to bulb up.

Companion planting needs far more dedicated scientific research than it has undergone so far. It's only when you have proper experimental controls, and repeat the trial over a number of years, and at different locations, that you can begin to form a true opinion of what actually works. It would be great if universities and other research establishments were to undertake a rigorous study of companion planting, but there's little chance of that happening. Most research these days is part-funded by biotech companies looking to recoup their outlay with something to sell. You can't patent a planting technique, so we shouldn't hold our breath – which is a pity, because there is so much more to discover.

Earlier in the book I mentioned HDRA's work with another companion plant, the Mexican marigold (*Tagetes minuta*), which produces root secretions that have herbicidal properties that can kill potato eelworms. Like a number of other harmful soil-dwelling organisms, potato eelworm only becomes a pest if potatoes are grown on the same patch of land year after year. This ensures a permanent food supply for the pest, and so the number of eelworm cysts in the soil is constantly increasing. Breaking this continuity to prevent the build-up of pests and diseases is the principle behind what is known as crop rotation. This involves grouping vegetables into their botanical families and always moving them to a different spot in the garden the following year.

Clubroot disease of brassicas is one of the most difficult pathogens to deal with and its spores can remain viable in the soil for up to 20 years. The clubroot fungus invades the roots of cabbages, cauliflowers and other members of the brassica family, causing them to become 'clubbed' – hence the name. Because the roots are unable to search out nutrients the plants cannot grow properly and therefore remain permanently stunted. Prevention is the best tactic and if crops are rotated and limed (the fungus dislikes alkaline conditions), clubroot can usually be avoided, but once it has become established there is no cure. In recent years, however, plant breeders have made great strides in developing brassica varieties that are resistant to clubroot, and cabbages that can grow happily in infected soil are starting to appear on the market.

Other cultural, non-chemical ways of controlling diseases include practising good hygiene – for example, disposing of fallen leaves at the end of the season to prevent the resting spores from infecting plants the following year – and ensuring good ventilation (opening up the centre of plants like fruit trees and bushes by pruning, providing wider spacings between plants, for example) to minimize the creation of the still, humid conditions that most pathogens prefer.

One of the chief ways in which organic gardeners can combat diseases is to grow resistant varieties, which have been modified by breeding in various ways; perhaps by subtly altering the nature of the surface of the plant tissue so that it is harder for pathogens to enter, or by producing chemical defences which obstruct or destroy the disease organism. Resistant varieties are most useful in countering diseases that are weather-dependent, like potato blight, which can strike even the healthiest looking plants without warning after warm summer rains. Breeders have had a degree of success in coming up with blight-resisting cultivars in the past, but things have improved dramatically with the arrival of the Hungarian Sarpo varieties of potato. And there are also plenty of black-spot resistant roses for sale, with leaves that do not succumb to the rash of dark blotches that so badly disfigure susceptible varieties.

As you might expect, our time at Bocking was largely spent on learning about British pests and diseases and how to deal with them. We were also aware, from the various discussions we had had with overseas visitors, that organic gardeners elsewhere in the world suffer from some of our worst pests too, and the methods they employ to cope with them are, in general, similar to ours. For example, in the USA, the ubiquitous slug is destroyed by means of a slug 'pub', just as it is here; and cabbage pests, like the cabbage white butterfly, or cabbage worm as it is known there, are controlled with netting and with *Bacillus thuringiensis* (see page 81). Of course, different countries also have a number of ways of dealing with their own particular *bêtes noires.* Thank goodness, for example, that we don't have to cope with Colorado beetles here, as they do in mainland Europe and the USA. In the States they pick these 'pesky critters' off by hand – this is still the best non-chemical way of dealing with them.

Organic gardeners the world over must be tempted to spray at one time or another, and in the case of diseases, the allowable chemicals of choice are copper and sulphur. I've yet to meet an organic gardener who is entirely comfortable about using pesticides, even those approved by the bodies that regulate organic food production. It feels like an admission of defeat, somehow. Many of these products are derived from plants and they break down quickly in the environment – within a few days at most – so they pose little threat to wildlife. Even so, they are not without their side effects. Derris, for example, which is made from the roots of a tropical plant, is deadly to fish. Copper is even more troubling and can build up to dangerous levels, especially in the soils of orchards and vineyards, where diseases can be at their worst. Fortunately, another chemical, potassium bicarbonate (which is chemically similar to baking soda) has been found to possess fungicidal properties and may in time replace it.

Most organically approved insecticides work not by poisoning but by 'suffocation', blocking the pores, or spiracles, of insects, through which they breathe. In the UK we tend to use sprays made from potassium soaps or vegetable oils but on the Continent and in the USA gardeners also use diatomaceous earth, an extremely fine and abrasive powder derived from the fossilized remains of freshwater single-cellular plants. Because of their mode of action, which is essentially physical, it is extremely unlikely that insects will ever acquire resistance to these types of products. Perhaps the most exciting new pesticide to come onto the market is ferric phosphate. It was first approved for use against slugs and snails in the USA and Germany in 1997, but didn't arrive in Britain until 2004. Unlike existing slug pellets made from metaldehyde and methiocarb, which can kill cats and dogs, as well as any wild birds and hedgehogs unfortunate enough to eat poisoned slugs, ferric phosphate only harms slugs and snails.

Sprays do not always have to kill, of course (some simply deter pests like rabbits and deer), and there are a number of ingenious concoctions on the market. My favourite is 'Poss Off' from Australia, apparently aimed at repulsing possums, but which the manufacturers claim may deter rabbits and kangaroos as well. Reports of the success of pest repellent products vary, however, and it's as well to have some alternatives up your sleeve.

Biodynamic gardeners and farmers spray their crops with plant extracts made from garlic and horsetail weed, the theory being that they 'strengthen' plants, making it harder for aphids and fungal mycelia to penetrate the cell walls. There is some evidence to suggest that the plant growth regulators present in liquid seaweed foliar feeds produce a similar effect. So-called 'teas' extracted from compost, which contain parasitic fungi, are also showing promising anti-fungal properties and even more interesting research is focusing on the ways in which plants react to the threat of attack by emitting warning chemicals, which may yield valuable clues to future organic pest control. But innovations like these were just a dream, back in Bocking in the mid-1970s.

Chapter Seven

BRANCHING OUT

BY 1976 WE HAD SETTLED into our outdoor routines at Bocking, which were largely dictated by the seasons. On top of this, as well as improving the scientific methodology of the trials, Jackie had tried to apply some logic to the organization of the office-based activities and slowly but surely she licked areas such as the mail-order department into shape. She also tackled the somewhat chaotic way in which members' experiments were dealt with, coming up with detailed response forms for the members to fill in, to replace the hand-written letters they had been sending back. Although Lawrence saw the need for this more scientific approach, it was difficult for him to accept a change in the way he had always done things. In fact the sheets proved to be a great success and analysing the results became a lot easier, but they still allowed the members to contribute the sorts of penetrating insights and suggestions they had included before.

We had just about got the experimental plots under control when Jackie and I realized that we also wanted to set up some purely demonstration beds, to illustrate good organic gardening practice. Jackie, in particular, saw spreading the organic message to a wider audience as a priority. We knew that changing the trial ground to include demonstration gardens wasn't going to be easy because Lawrence would be unhappy about giving up some of the precious land that was being used for experimental work. But we were both determined to try to get him to change his view on this issue – we felt it was of crucial importance if the organization was to widen its influence. The thousands of requests for HDRA's leaflet *Dig for Survival* suggested to us that there was considerable demand for information about home growing, and the huge numbers who watched *The Good Life* every week (BBC television's gentle satire on self-sufficiency) also indicated this. Lawrence had been born into a time that was still rooted in the land, so cultivating your own vegetables was taken for granted and children learned how to grow things from their parents as a matter of course. It wasn't the same for us. Our 'baby-boom' generation was far more urban-oriented, so, unsurprisingly, most of us were clueless about producing our own food.

Things came to a head in the winter of 1976. Lawrence had just returned from a three-month tour overseas to look at various tree crops and how they might be used in drought situations, taking in India, Australia and New Zealand, finishing with a 1,000-mile whirl-wind drive down the western seaboard of the United States. Jackie and I had been left in charge of the organization while he was away, but we still found the time to draw up proposals for a redevelopment of the trial ground to include several demonstration beds. We showed these to Lawrence on his return, but he still wasn't convinced.

A few weeks later we got the opportunity to put our ideas to the HDRA Committee, its ruling body. 'What's the point of doing all this good work on organic growing if the world at large knows nothing about it?' Jackie urged. A point in our favour was the huge success of our first organic gardening conference, held at Ewell College in Surrey the previous February; over 200 people had attended, and the Committee was suitably impressed. Anyway, after answering several questions about the cost of our proposal, and other possible drawbacks, the issue was put to the vote. Although Lawrence and one or two others voted against the changes, the majority agreed with us, but they insisted that experimentation should still be the main focus of the trial ground, a point with which we agreed wholeheartedly. We'd felt bad about getting on the wrong side of Lawrence, because we were extremely fond of him and respected him enormously. Much to our relief, however, he accepted the situation with good grace. Now all we had to do was make it work! The first thing we did was to try to find a head gardener, but getting a professional gardener with organic experience wasn't easy. None of the country's colleges at the time offered courses in organic horticulture, and anyone conventionally trained was steeped in a culture of chemicals. The best we could hope for was someone with the right outlook and a willingness to learn. Eventually we settled on Roger McLennan, a wiry young man in his early 20s, who duly arrived from his native Cumbria accompanied by his wife, Christine, and their young twins. Roger proved to be good and hard working. He quickly found his feet and spent three productive years with us before moving on to become Head Gardener at the Centre for Alternative Technology in Wales, where he has remained ever since.

Our second task was to replace the main arterial grass paths with concrete to cope with the expected increase in visitors. As an ex-civil engineer I took on this responsibility – and I was in my element. Although not, perhaps, in quite the same class as motorways, I built brand new paths connecting all corners of the grounds and was subsequently rewarded for my heroic efforts with the soubriquet 'The Concrete King'.

Jackie's idea of welcoming the general public to the trial ground was all well and good, but she also wanted to come up with other ways of spreading the organic message; and then she hit on the idea of the Chelsea Flower Show, where we could put the organic case to the several hundred thousand keen gardeners who attended. Even though Lawrence had never considered the possibility in the past, he was delighted with the idea, but suspected that persuading the Royal Horticultural Society was not going to be easy as competition for stands was so stiff. But to our surprise we were granted space in the scientific section for an exhibit on our chosen subject of 'Soil Fertility, the Organic Way'. Jackie was thrilled and got down to designing our display with enthusiasm. In those days there were no computers to generate the graphics for the information panels, so every letter of every word, down to the last full stop, had to be individually applied by hand, using iron-on lettering. What would nowadays take a couple of hours took several days back then. Jackie wrote the text and I patiently made the boards, a way of working that was to become familiar as our lives at HDRA developed – she was the creative half, while I was the implementer. I had discovered that she wasn't content with just being a scientist, with a need for orderliness and efficiency, she was allowing her creative side to run full rein too, and she loved every minute of it. The stand looked good – it was devoted to composting and featured many different types of containers and examples of garden and kitchen waste materials that can be broken down by the process.

As it was HDRA's first Chelsea, we attracted a fair bit of publicity on Press Day, with the remainder of the week passing in a breathtaking blur. There's nothing quite like talking to a Chelsea visitor to keep you on your toes! Members of the Royal Horticultural Society (RHS) are among the most knowledgeable gardeners on the planet, and their penetrating questions came thick and fast. How safe is it to compost diseased plants? Exactly how much potassium does comfrey contain? It went on and on. When it came to talking about the organic philosophy in general, however, opinions were much more equivocal. The prevailing view seemed to be that chemical pesticides and fertilizers were here to stay, so organic gardening stood no chance of catching on. This didn't put us off at all, so convinced were we that our approach would win through in the end.

Our quest to promote organic gardening to a wider audience was also given a helping hand during 1976, when HDRA acquired its first very own local group, set up by Doreen and Alec Wright, two hard-working organic farmers in Hampshire. In next to no time they had attracted a healthy following and went from strength to strength by putting on a biennial conference and taking a stand at local shows. Their success inspired other members and within a year there were groups in places as far apart as Cornwall, Kent, Berkshire and Manchester. And we even had groups in New Zealand and Australia, thanks to Lawrence's round-the-world trip.

As we had predicted, all this additional activity led to a higher public profile for the organization, which in turn generated more members, so that by the end of 1977 membership numbers had passed the 7,000 mark. HDRA had become the largest organic membership body in Europe! At this euphoric time Jackie and I decided that we needed more help, and so in the following spring we advertised for a full-time research assistant. Pauline Pears, a post-graduate student of horticulture with several years' work experience with Fisons, applied and got the job. She had become convinced that conventional growing was fundamentally flawed and wanted to work for an organic organization, even if it meant earning less money. We couldn't have known it at the time, but taking her on was an excellent decision. Pauline would stay with HDRA for decades, becoming one of the most knowledgeable and respected organic experts in the UK, communicating her extensive experience to countless people through writing books and other literature, giving talks and answering thousands of questions over the years on behalf of the organization.

Pauline soon got down to work, taking over the running of the trials and dealing with the members' experiments. Meanwhile we were making the trial ground as visitor-friendly as possible, but even two years later, in 1978, we hadn't solved the problem of providing day-to-day catering. It fell to Jackie, by default, to provide refreshments for visitors at all hours of the day, on top of her other duties. Even when a coachload of students from the University of California turned up early one Sunday morning while we were having breakfast, she didn't bat an eyelid and offered to make pancakes and maple syrup all round, in our tiny kitchen. We found out during an amazingly rumbustious couple of hours with them, when they seemed to talk non-stop, that they'd been influenced by the raised-bed methods of growing pioneered by fellow American John Jeavons. His book, *How to Grow More Vegetables than you ever thought possible on less land than you could imagine*, apart from having what is probably the longest-ever gardening title, had been a minor publishing sensation in the States. On a tour of Europe they had specifically sought us out to learn more about organic gardening in Britain. As it happens, we already had a copy of Jeavons's book, and we had even set up some narrow, gently mounded beds on which the vegetables were planted very closely together to increase yields and suppress weeds, as per his instructions. It was interesting to see the surprise on the faces of our American visitors when they saw them. Clearly, they were impressed.

In the four years since we had arrived at Bocking the trial ground had been dramatically transformed. Gone were many of the older research plots, but land at the lower end of the grounds, which had previously been overrun with nettles and brambles, was back in cultivation. In pride of place, seen coming through the gate, was a large allotment-sized demonstration plot, showing just what a healthy and productive organic vegetable garden could look like. Next came the Survival Garden, where crop data (including spacing, varieties and yields) were carefully measured; and nearby there were other demonstrations of growing techniques, like raised beds, minimal cultivations and planting through clover swards. We had also established a small orchard on the far eastern boundary that featured mostly apples trees, along with a couple of pear and plum trees, as well as an extensive collection of soft fruit. Everything was designed to say to visitors, 'Look! All this has been grown without fertilizers and pesticides. Organic gardening really does work!'

Even if we could have afforded it, we couldn't have done a lot of advertising to promote the opening of the trial ground to the public because the visitor facilities were still inadequate. Nevertheless, we had a steady stream of folk most weeks, and we didn't turn anyone away who had made an effort to get there, especially if they were from abroad. Jackie was just frustrated because she wasn't able to look after them in a more professional way. But before she could even begin to think of how to change things for the better, circumstances overtook us.

A very sad event, which affected Jackie's close family, meant that she left HDRA and Essex for a short period. It was a depressing time for both of us, but it didn't prevent her from feeling part of the organization. She continued to air her views that the limitations of the gardens at Bocking as a demonstration centre were insurmountable and that we needed an additional, separate and completely new site in order to take the organization forward. In March 1982 this was discussed at a weekend conference, called by the HDRA Committee to discuss the long-term future of the organization. Much to our surprise almost everyone approved of her plan, and this time even Lawrence was in agreement because it would allow the land at Bocking to revert to being a purely experimental area. When the idea was put to HDRA members at the AGM in Bristol the following month, they were, if anything, even more enthusiastic, and there were several suggestions for possible locations. The most promising turned out to be the walled garden of Kingston Lacy, a stately home near Wimborne Minster in Dorset, which had recently been bequeathed to the National Trust. Although it would be several years before the house opened to the public, no decision had yet been taken on the future of the walled garden.

As it turned out, the garden was all that we could have wished for, with glasshouses complete with glass – unlike so many places where nothing but ruins remain – and not too many weeds. The access, however, was terrible – a winding, single-track road, with no passing places. Over the next few months we waited, while first the Wessex regional office of the National Trust, and then people at the headquarters in London, considered our proposal. At the same time we looked at a number of other properties that had been brought to our attention, including a garden in Northamptonshire, one in Derbyshire and another in Oxfordshire, but none of these was suitable. Kingston Lacy was without doubt the best of the bunch, but by Christmas it was clear that all was not well and progress stalled. We were told that improving the road would be far too costly, although it did cross our minds that the real fear among the upper echelons of the Trust was having an association with the organic philosophy, which at the time was still perceived by many as 'hippyish' and 'alternative'. Whatever the ultimate reason, after a few more months of prevarication, the Trust turned us down. We were intensely disappointed then, but in retrospect they actually did us a huge favour by saying no.

In the autumn of 1983 Lawrence said that he was going to increase my salary and, recognizing that we needed a strong team to move forward, he also persuaded Jackie to rejoin HDRA. He once described her as 'the most versatile of all our staff' and it's true that she only has to see that a job needs doing to get stuck in. At Bocking she was, at various times, a gardener, a research scientist, the laboratory manager, a library cataloguer, the office and mail-order department manager, the exhibitions and literature designer, caterer, book-keeper and overall business developer. She really was a 'Jack' of all trades, which was what an expanding HDRA needed, because the organization couldn't possibly have afforded to bring in all that expertise from outside. Over the years, both Lawrence and I greatly respected her commitment, bubbling enthusiasm and professionalism – even if I did find her difficult to work with sometimes! Her lateral-thinking type of approach is so unlike my own; a person describing our relationship once said that Jackie is the accelerator and I am the brake! People say we make a good pair because of this, but, my goodness, we've had some heated discussions along the way!

You can understand then, that by this time, her ambitions for the organization had moved on. Instead of having a separate demonstration garden, with all the attendant problems of management from afar, she wanted to move the organization, lock, stock and barrel. She envisaged a national centre for organic gardening, somewhere central, that would be easy to get to, where people from all walks of life could come to see organic growing at its best, and go away inspired to become organic gardeners at home. It would demonstrate the best ways of making compost, controlling pests without poisons, and showcase the huge diversity of different vegetables that it is possible to grow in this country. It had to be a place where visitors could observe and compare different organic gardening methods, like raised beds, or 'no-dig' plots. It would be unique, but not too 'way out', and would appeal to everyone, from all walks of life, and whatever their age. The prime focus of the gardens would be educational, but not at the expense of aesthetics. They would be well-tended, to a professional level, with trimmed lawns and weeds under control. She envisaged a place of beauty, with trees, flowers and shrubs to soothe the soul. And it had to provide a rich habitat for wildlife. We would also be as 'green' as possible, by using, for example, sustainable sources of timber and stone and choosing environmentally safe, water-based wood preservatives.

We both agreed that it was also essential for the organization to carry on doing scientific research and we therefore needed to set some land aside for experimental purposes – an area in which fresh ideas could be trialled and new organic growing techniques pioneered. A shop would stock a full range of organic gardening products as well as a wide selection of organic food and drinks and a café would champion organic wholefood cookery, using fresh, local ingredients. It would be nothing less than a centre of excellence for all things organic. That was the plan, anyway!

As the months dragged by it began to seem as if we had set ourselves an impossible task. There were plenty of farmhouses with several hundreds of acres for sale or, at the other end of the scale, large dwellings complete with a small paddock. But finding a place big enough for our new headquarters, but with a mere 20 or 30 acres of land, was far more difficult. We pored over hundreds of agents' details to no avail. Would we ever find the perfect place? Desperation drove Jackie and me to embark on a whistle-stop tour of the Midlands. From Northampton in the east, to Worcester in the west; and from Oxford in the south to Derby in the north; we ranged back and forth, calling at over 50 estate agents in our search for suitable properties. Absolutely nothing! One week, and 700 miles later, we returned to Bocking, dejected and defeated.

Throughout this period we had been conducting delicate negotiations with the Braintree planners because the project could only go ahead if we were able to get the top price for the sale of the trial ground, and that could only mean one thing – the land would have to be sold with planning permission for new housing. The architect had told us that the land, with planning permission, could be worth as much as £120,000. With what we expected to get for the house in Convent Lane, we would be well on the way to reaching the amount of money we needed to buy a property elsewhere, including a bungalow for Lawrence and Cherry. But this would leave HDRA with cash reserves of around a measly £50,000 to fund the development of the site. There was nothing for it, we would have to borrow the balance. One of our members told us about the Mercury Provident

Society (which was later to metamorphose into Triados Bank), a small, registered friendly society, based in Forest Row, Sussex, which specialized in lending to 'alternative' enterprises. Two of their directors, Ray Mitchell and Christian Nunhofer, agreed to spend a day at the trial ground, talking to us about our plans, and at the end of the discussions they went away, promising to ask the Mercury Board to back HDRA's project if we, in turn, could persuade HDRA members to become depositors. The upshot of this was that we were granted a loan of up to £100,000 to fund the development. Many of our members specified that their contribution should be interest-free, and when it was aggregated with the interest-bearing funds of other depositors, the average interest rate for the loan, in total, worked out at less than half the going commercial rate.

At the same time that we were finalizing our finances we found a suitable property. William Waddilove, an HDRA member for 15 years, posted us details of a place called Ryton Court in Warwickshire, approximately six miles southeast of Coventry, just outside the village of Wolston. It certainly seemed to fit the bill. Although the place appeared to be a bit run-down in the photographs, the more we considered it, the more we could see the potential. The access was excellent and it had exactly the right amount of land. It was surrounded by countryside but near a village, where we could recruit staff. The site appeared almost level, so far as we could tell, which made it ideal for our experimental plots; and although the office accommodation was on the small side, at £150,000 it was good value for money and only slightly over budget. We decided it was worth a look.

A few days later, Jackie, Lawrence and I, and William, were shown over the property. The 22-acre plot was roughly rectangular in shape, with one short side running alongside the road that connected the A45 to the village of Wolston. Standing at the entrance, looking south towards the farmhouse, we were struck at how open the site was, with a clear view all round. The plot was split into four large fields of about five acres apiece, separated by ranch-style wooden fencing that had originally been painted white, but was now peeling badly. In the distance a neglected hawthorn hedge, inter-planted with other native species, marked the far boundary with the neighbouring farms. We could see scores of huge stumps, spaced at roughly regular intervals, and we realized that they were the last visible remains of what had once been magnificent elm trees, their lives cut short tragically by Dutch Elm Disease, which had swept through the country in the late 60s and 70s. Now, only a handful of mature oaks and a couple of ash trees were left on the site.

The buildings comprised a four-bedroomed farmhouse, a stable block with outbuildings and a huge indoor riding school. A badly pot-holed, tarmac drive, 100 yards long, led from the main road through paddocks to the two-storey house, which backed onto a small, uneven, rectangular concrete yard, enclosed on three sides by outbuildings – brick loose-boxes along the left-hand side and going around the corner, and a hideous Dutch barn on the right. Towering behind them all was a massive steel-framed structure with breeze-block walls that had apparently served as an indoor riding school. It still had its sawdust floor, as if a troupe of horses was expected at any minute.

We dug a trial pit in the nearest paddock, which revealed a friable, dark, loamy, well-drained soil, but this was obviously lacking in fresh organic matter and didn't contain any earthworms. But this was something that we could rectify easily. We had already been told that the owners hadn't used agrochemicals on the land, which was a great point in its favour, and another nice surprise was the virtual absence of docks, the pernicious weed that usually infests land grazed by horses. From a strictly horticultural perspective, the property was better than many we had seen, and although the buildings were clearly suffering from neglect, there didn't appear to be any serious structural problems. A bit of DIY and a lick of paint would work wonders, we thought optimistically. Might our long search finally be over? All we needed was planning permission. The property was in the Green Belt so, ordinarily, any plans to build on it would have been met with resistance, but Britain was in the middle of a severe recession at the time, and with unemployment at an all-time high, we hoped our project might be viewed in a favourable light because it would bring jobs to the area.

Jonathon Horsfield at the Economic Development Unit at War-wickshire County Council couldn't have been more helpful. He and his colleagues offered lots of advice and encouragement, and it was through them that we made contact with the local Manpower Services Commission (MSC). To our delight we were promised a team of manual workers to create the infrastructure of the gardens. The planning officers at Rugby Council were enthusiastic, too – even about Lawrence's and Cherry's proposed new bungalow. All went well, and we subsequently sold the grounds and houses at Bocking to buy Ryton.

Our first visit to HDRA's newly acquired property early in January 1985 coincided with an unusually cold spell of weather, but Jackie and I had organized a packed schedule, visiting council officers and other government officials during the day, and returning to the bleak and draughty house that night to sleep on the floor. When we eventually arrived we found to our horror that water started to leak everywhere the minute we turned the heating on. In desperation we called in a local plumber who discovered 26 burst pipes. There was nothing he could do that evening, so we just turned off the water and snuggled up together to keep warm. We were prepared to suffer for the cause, but this was way beyond the call of duty!

We did what we had to do that week, eating very unhealthy food at a 'greasy spoon' café in a service station on the A45, and with the plumbing repaired and a new boiler installed, we returned to Brain-tree. Planning consent for Lawrence's and Cherry's bungalow came through and work began in earnest on the new site early in 1985. Jackie and I needed to buy a house and get a mortgage because there was no 'house with the job' anymore, but we'd been out of the housing market for so many years that the enormity of what we had to pay came as something of a shock. Nevertheless we bought a house in Rugby next to a park, which would be nice for Jackie's mum, who had come to live with us since her husband Steve, Jackie's much-loved dad, had died.

It occurred to us then that we should think about whether to have children. Midway through our 30s, we needed to decide, one way or the other, if we were going to take the plunge. On the one hand, we were both fully committed to our jobs, which we saw as a vocation, but on the other hand, if we had a baby, we would want to bring it up with one parent at home. Even with help from Jackie's mum this would be difficult, because we worked such long hours. There was another influence on our thinking too. Back in 1973, at the time of the oil crisis, as I've mentioned, we'd been heavily influenced by the book *The Limits to Growth*, which predicted a major environmental crisis in the mid-21st century (see page 29). The main reason we'd given up well-paid jobs and started to work for a struggling environmental organization was to try to help prevent this type of global catastrophe. The oil crisis had subsequently passed, and with it, the world's attention, but over-consumption, pollution and the destruction of natural habitats continued unchecked. If the book's predictions were accurate, at a time when our lives would come to an end we would be leaving our children in the midst of a devastating environmental crisis. It was a sobering thought, and one that contributed towards our final decision not to have children. Interestingly, several of our friends and members of our family made the same decision. too. A sign of the times perhaps?

Work on the farmhouse and new bungalow was completed by the end of June 1985, with help from several stalwart volunteers. Alan McCulloch, one of HDRA's most well-liked and respected committee members, and his wife Dorothy, for example, took it upon themselves to completely redecorate the interior, driving up from Bristol at weekends and 'camping out' in the same room in which Jackie and I had spent a shiveringly cold night, months earlier. They and the others did a superb job, saving us effort, and HDRA a great deal of money.

Back at Bocking, Jackie put all her experience of running the HDRA office to good use by writing out a detailed manual of all the office procedures – how to deal with subscriptions, mail orders and so on. She was also going to have the job of training the new staff at Ryton, to make sure that the transition from one headquarters to another went as smoothly as possible. The last couple of weeks were a sombre time, knowing that we would be leaving behind most of HDRA's staff. Thank goodness that at least Pauline Pears had decided to come with us. We wouldn't have wanted to lose her. Happily, Steve Gifford, the student gardener, was coming too. Even so, most of the old team had worked for the association for years, and all were friends, so it was hard to leave. We're pleased to say, though, that we still see Luci Sims, the then office secretary, who is a very good friend, and we also keep in touch with several of the others.

In June, we packed up our few belongings and said goodbye to the house in Convent Lane that had been our home for more than ten years, and the trial ground where we had been given a wealth of invaluable experience. The builders moved in soon after we left and within six months you would never have known we had been there, other than by the name of the new development – Doubleday Gardens.

Writing to HDRA members in the final newsletter from Bocking, Lawrence said: 'When I first wrote of our move I said that HDRA was like a squirrel jumping out of a tree – it had to hit the ground running. Jackie and Alan are the two squirrels who have been running the fastest of all to take HDRA on the road to our great New Adventure.'

As we watched the removal vans rolling down Convent Lane, carrying all HDRA's records, we closed the little metal gate to the trial ground for the last time and climbed into our car, hopeful that we'd made the right decision in deciding to set up Britain's first organic demonstration centre. It was big leap of faith.

Chapter Eight

SEEING IS BELIEVING

THE STAFF WE NEEDED at Ryton had been recruited shortly before we set up our new headquarters. We took on several people to work in the office and the mail-order department, and we wanted someone special for the post of Lawrence's secretary. Of all the interviewees, only one had stood out – a local girl called Chris Bailey who had spent the last few years bringing up two children but was now looking for work. She had fast and faultless typing and Lawrence offered her the job on the spot. Over the years she went on to justify the faith put in her in those early days. I'm pleased to say that Chris eventually became my PA too and was an invaluable asset to HDRA for almost two decades.

Back then, on Monday 15 July 1985, when we finally moved in and the staff arrived for the first time, the office was still nowhere near ready. We welcomed them warmly and apologized for the slightly chaotic look of the place. Jackie then went through her office manual with the new office co-ordinator and the clerical staff while I made my way to what had been the sitting room in the old farmhouse. It had been kitted out with racks of shelving for HDRA's flourishing mail-order business, and it also doubled as a 'shop' for the visitors to Ryton who wanted to pick up their books, seeds and fertilizers on the spot, rather than have them delivered by post.

Sorting out the seeds was the most fiddly job. As part of our ongoing crusade to safeguard traditional British vegetables, we had compiled a catalogue of 'heritage' varieties, with the help of Brian Haynes, the Managing Director of E.W. Kings Seeds of Kelvedon in Essex – one of the last of the truly independent seed companies left in the UK. Many of the varieties dated back to the 19th century, like the 'Czar' white-seeded runner bean (1896), the 'Egyptian Turnip Rooted' beetroot (1890) and 'Long Red Surrey' – a carrot that had been introduced in 1834. The collection had been launched a year earlier and had been a huge success, finding favour with old stagers and first-time gardeners alike, who appreciated the reliability and flavour of these old cultivars. If nothing else, it put the lie to the seed industry's claim that everyone wanted to grow F1 hybrids, not the old varieties, which had had their day. Filling the large, wooden rack of pigeon holes with packets of seeds – everything from artichokes to zucchini – took most of the morning, but it was a great way for the new staff to get to know the types and varieties of vegetables we sold.

The clerical and despatch functions took over almost the entire ground floor of the farmhouse; Jackie, Pauline and I had separate offices upstairs. While Jackie managed things in the office and Pauline started to organize her gardening advisory desk, I stepped outside to check on how the Manpower Services Commission (MSC) gang was getting along. In charge was 'Big' Dave Brownlee, a former car worker from the days when Coventry was the hub of Britain's flourishing motor industry. He led a team of around 15 workers, all of whom had been unemployed, which had been on-site since April. They had accomplished a great deal in a short space of time, concentrating mostly on infrastructure work, which included the erection of a rabbit-proof, wire-netting fence around the entire site and taking down the hideous Dutch barn. Several workers were keen to stay on after the project officially finished and we took them on full-time. Happily, some of them are still employed by HDRA to this day, some 25 years on.

The plans for the gardens had been drawn up by Sir Derek Lovejoy, one of the country's leading landscape architects and the brains behind the 1984 Liverpool International Garden Festival, which had been set up by the government the previous year to revitalize the economy of Merseyside. A friend of his, Mrs Elizabeth Waldron-Yeo, one of HDRA's long-standing supporters, had persuaded him to help us create the layout of the gardens at Ryton on an expenses-only basis, and he was given a list of the various displays and model gardens we wanted to include. There would be around ten acres for the gardens, including a visitor centre, shop and café, with the remaining twelve acres set aside for research purposes, storage and car parking.

Derek Lovejoy's plan looked exquisite on paper and his involvement and endorsement played well with the local planners. He had included all the elements we'd asked him to, and added a few of his own – various sculptures, landmark structures (including gazebos, pergolas and a campanile) and even a monumental fountain. It looked fabulous, but we very much doubted whether we could afford all the beautiful ornamental features.

All the work that had been done so far by the MSC team was on the infrastructure and they still had a long way to go. There were trenches to be dug for the hundreds of yards of plastic irrigation pipe, paths to be laid, and a myriad of other urgent jobs that took up most of the time between July and December. As a result, they hadn't even started gardening, which was just as well, because the Head Gardener wasn't yet in post. Because this was such a large, groundbreaking project with a lot of responsibility, we had reluctantly said goodbye to Patrick Hughes, our gardener for the past five years at Bocking, and appointed Sue Stickland to take charge. Sue, a physics graduate who had gone on to become an experienced, qualified horticulturalist and gardening writer, was working out her notice, but she eventually arrived at Ryton during the last week of July. She would have just twelve months in which to realize Lovejoy's design – any longer and we would miss next summer's tourist season. And if that happened we would run out of cash!

Christmas arrived, and although Sue and the team had managed to plant hundreds of shrubs in the long borders, she still had the top fruit and many more trees left to go in. More worrying still was the fact that money was getting tight, even with the Mercury loan. There was no way that we would have enough left to build the visitor centre, which was estimated to cost £150,000. In desperation, Jackie and I visited the headquarters of a Bedfordshire-based company called Potton, which specialized in timber-frame buildings. Jackie practically begged them to sell us something for under £20,000. Thankfully they responded enthusiastically, offering us a cheap and cheerful open-plan structure that could be adapted easily for use as a shop and café. The larger, smarter, permanent building would have to be put on ice.

It was at this stage that Jackie started taking charge of how HDRA appeared to the outside world, to give the organization a look that conveyed all of our passion, integrity and professionalism. I dislike the expression 'corporate image' but that would be what it's called now. She took responsibility for the overall appearance of the buildings, the colour schemes, the materials and fittings, and the signage. She also designed a new HDRA logo and all the association's literature. The overall look of the gardens fell within her ambit too and because she and Sue shared a love for the same gardening style, she was happy.

Early in the New Year a camera crew from Central Television turned up to film a programme for a series called *Getting On*. It was about coping with old age, and Tish Faith, the Director, was interested in how Lawrence Hills, a 75-year old man, with a 90-year-old wife, was dealing with the pressures of a new project that would be a challenge for someone half his age. This was her fourth visit in a sequence that had begun with our arrival at Ryton the previous spring and would end in July, with the official opening of the gardens. Along the way, the film would provide a unique record of the first steps in the transformation of a bleak corner of Warwickshire into what we hoped would become an internationally known centre of excellence for organic horticulture.

She had already gleaned that although Lawrence was nominally in charge, on a practical level he was no longer in the driving seat, having withdrawn from the day-to-day running of HDRA and all the planning and organization of the Ryton project. The Committee itself had recognized this late in 1984 when they appointed me Executive Director, in effect creating a dual leadership. Lawrence still wrote most of the HDRA newsletter, corresponded with members and handled the media enquiries, but the organization was bigger now and there were a lot more responsibilities. Several people, including one of the Committee members, Gerald Pearson, a great confidante of Lawrence and one of the wisest men Jackie and I had ever known, thought that it was the right time for Lawrence to retire. Gerald talked it over with him with great sensitivity and understanding, and Lawrence decided to step down. He became HDRA's Honorary President, having been the founder, and fount of all knowledge of the organization for many years. He was much loved and respected by all who knew him. But he wasn't just going to sit around and vegetate, he said; he would begin work on his autobiography. True to his word, this is exactly what he did, and the book, *Fighting like the Flowers*, went on to be published in 1989. After Ryton opened, he could often be found sitting at a table on the patio outside the café, talking animatedly to visitors, who obviously enjoyed the encounter.

Several months before the opening, just after Lawrence stepped down and Jackie and I had been given responsibility for running the organization, the weather took a decided turn for the worse. It was on the eve of a major planting programme, but for the next six weeks the ground froze solid and all work ceased. Then, when the thaw finally came, it brought with it the inevitable problem of flooding. The builders were forced to lay more drainage pipes, at considerable expense, and the vital planting was delayed for yet another couple of weeks. Only with great difficulty, and the aid of a battery of pumps, were they able to dig out the footings and pour the concrete floor of the new Potton building. At last, however, the weather improved and we calculated that if we worked seven days a week, we might just open on time.

By now Sue had reinforced her gardening team, appointing Bob Sherman as her deputy. Bob comes from a long line of military men – General Sherman, of American Civil War fame, whose name was also given to the Sherman tank, was a distant relative. Bob had been educated at the Royal Military Academy, Sandhurst, read Russian at university, and had served in the British Army, before 'dropping out' in the 70s to become a full-time gardener. I had only met him briefly before, when I had spoken at a meeting he had organized on behalf of the Cotswolds Organic Gardening Group, but Sue, who had previously worked not far from Stroud, knew him well as a committed and knowledgeable organic gardener, so she was pleased to have him heading up her team, and I must say that we liked the look of him too.

The final few days before opening were frenetic and we worked well into the evenings, taking advantage of the long daylight hours. Shrubs that had perished during the big freeze were replaced and others were planted. Sowing continued apace, the grass paths were mown and edged, the final few fencing panels were erected and painted, and paving slabs were laid. Labels and explanatory notices, written by Pauline, suddenly sprang up throughout the gardens.

The shop and café were the biggest worry because they were running horribly late. The last of the kitchen equipment had only just been installed and the shop was without half its shelving, so the boxes of gifts, gardening goods and food products selected by Jackie remained stacked up in spare corners waiting to be displayed.

On top of all this, we'd asked Jackie's talented brother, Graham, who produced films for a branch of the civil service, to make a video in his spare time that we could use to promote the gardens. It starred the well-known British comedian Jasper Carrott, whom we had met through Steve and Sue Hammett (HDRA's typesetters and the driving force behind the local Heart of England Organic Group). Also in the video was the actress Thelma Barlow – a familiar face to most of the country as 'Mavis Riley' in *Coronation Street*, Britain's longest running and most popular television 'soap'. She had been one of the first visitors to the site back in 1985 and was a staunch supporter of HDRA.

Finally, on 5 July 1986, we held the official opening. Everyone who had played a part in making Ryton happen – members, supporters, representatives from local authorities and government agencies – was invited. Guests had been arriving all morning, and it was proving to be a relaxed and informal occasion, with people sitting happily on straw bales to eat the buffet lunch, despite their formal clothes. The weather had been good to us and the sun was still shining brightly as our visitors wandered among the newly planted gardens. Shortly before 3 o'clock I gave a short speech of thanks and introduced Thelma, who cut the opening ribbon with a flourish using a shiny new pair of garden shears. Throughout the formalities the sky had been darkening steadily but now, as Lawrence stepped up to the microphone, it suddenly went quite black. A terrific clap of thunder rent the air, followed instantly by a torrential downpour, forcing everyone under cover. Afterwards, one of the visitors came up to me and said that it was as if the gardens had been baptized – for all the world as if God was bestowing a blessing on our endeavours!

Thanks to the hard work of HDRA's brilliant staff, Ryton opened to the public the following day and the publicity generated by Jackie resulted in over 2,000 visitors a month passing through the turnstiles during the remainder of the season. The British Tourist Authority even placed Ryton in its top dozen attractions in the 1986 'Come to Britain Awards'.

Although the gardens had been completed on time, we were not, alas, on budget, and Mercury stepped in again with emergency funding. Now this was a brave move for them – they weren't to know then that HDRA and Ryton would influence many millions of people over the coming years, persuading generations of gardeners to convert to organic methods.

Let me take you on a tour of Ryton as it would have looked to visitors shortly after it opened in the summer of 1986, so that you can get some idea of what they saw. We begin at a simple wooden building, which houses ticket sales and a bustling organic shop and café, the first of their kind in the UK. The aroma of freshly cooked food wafts over enticingly from the entrance. Jackie has given the kitchen staff a crash course in the art of wholefood cookery using her own recipes, and in just a few short weeks the café has acquired a formidable reputation, to the extent that a food critic has already made a secret visit, and the café will feature in the next edition of *The Budget Good Food Guide*.

Tempting as it is to linger on the café's sunny patio to enjoy a delicious meal and a glass of wine, we will leave the other diners behind and take a short stroll to the 'Soil Fertility Display', where a collection of different plastic and wooden compost containers is on show. In those days, manufacturers had barely grasped the commercial opportunities offered by composting and there was nothing like the number of models that are available now. Standing next to these is another, completely closed, wooden box containing hundreds of tiger worms, which are feeding on the remains of yesterday's café scraps. This is a worm bin and it is already turning out to be a great hit with children, who have to be restrained by anxious parents from plunging their hands deep inside. A sign explains that the waste is converted into nutrient-rich compost over a period of six weeks and a sample of the sweet-smelling, peat-like end product illustrates how it can be used as an ingredient in seed and potting mixtures. Other parts of the display demonstrate leafmould, the various uses of comfrey, and different types of green manures – and all the various ways that organic gardeners improve their soil. Nowadays, most people recognize the value of compost, leafmould and other organic fertilizers, so what I'm describing might seem a bit 'old hat', but in 1986 much of it was new, even to keen gardeners.

We're on the move again. This time it's a short walk to the herb garden, which is in a semi-circular formal design and yet looks pleasantly informal because of the sheer profusion of the herbs that spill onto the paths. Everyday culinary herbs are represented – including sage, mint, parsley and chives – along with others that are lesser known and have uses in medicine and dyeing. An intoxicating succession of wonderful smells follows you as you walk around the display, brushing against the various plants.

The 'no-dig' garden is next on the tour and, perhaps unsurprisingly, is already a firm favourite with visitors, who warm to the idea of eliminating what can be a back-breaking chore. The basic principles are described on an information board, but there is not enough room to go into detail. In fact, F.C. King was the first to advance this controversial idea in 1946, when he penned *Is Digging Necessary?*; this was followed three years later by A. Guest's *Gardening without Digging*. Both authors considered it a mistake to invert the topmost inches of the soil, where most of the beneficial micro-organisms live. They also pointed out that you get fewer weeds when you don't turn the soil because the seeds remain safely undisturbed below.

Dr W. E. Shewell-Cooper, founder of The Good Gardeners' Association (GGA) was the best known exponent of 'no digging', promoting what he called 'minimum work compost gardening' in scores of garden-ing books written over many years, which described this method of sowing seeds into a layer of compost that was spread every year over the entire garden. When we were still at Bocking, Jackie and I had been to see him at his ten-acre Arkley Manor estate in Barnett, Hertfordshire, and had been mightily impressed with the gardens, although he was obliged to make compost on a heroic scale. At its height in the mid-1970s the GGA had around 4,000 members, but a decade later, following Shewell-Cooper's death in 1982, membership had shrunk to just a few hundred and has remained much the same ever since.

Even the task of making compost was too much trouble for Ruth Stout, a quirky American who began writing about 'no-work' garden-ing in Rodale's *Organic Gardening* magazine in 1953. Her idea was to strew a thick layer of organic mulch over the ground – slightly rotted hay for choice – and then plant through it, emulating the way in which seeds in nature germinate under a blanket of fallen leaves. Over the years, in her garden in Connecticut, she refined what ultimately became known as the 'Ruth Stout method'. Lawrence had tried it at Bocking but had been unimpressed, finding that birds were forever scattering debris about the garden and he had a continuous problem with germinating grass and other weed seeds that were contained in the hay. And, as he acidly pointed out, lugging scores of heavy bales of hay each year hardly counts as 'no work'.

At Ryton, as visitors can see in pride of place on the no-dig garden, we have adopted the Ruth Stout approach for growing potatoes, plant-ing them into a shallow depression scooped out of the soil, surrounded with a shovel-full of well-rotted manure, and then lightly covered with straw mulch. When the first green shoots appear they are coaxed through the strawy layer, which is then added to by successive layers of straw throughout the season, to be finally topped up with dressings of grass clippings, to prevent light from greening the developing tubers. All we have to do when we want to pick potatoes is scrape away the mulch, take what we need and then carefully replace the straw to allow the plants to continue growing. It's not possible to avoid disturbing the soil entirely – for example, when making a seed drill, hoeing or incorporating green manures – but the aim is to keep it to a minimum, and it's interesting to see how many more worms there are in this patch of the gardens. They flourish in undisturbed land and the tunnels they make as they travel through the soil help to aerate and drain it.

By way of contrast, the soil in the adjacent demonstration garden has been dug deeply and shaped into six gently domed rectangular plots, each 12ft x 4ft; the plants are tightly packed so that weeding becomes unnecessary once the crop is established. This is the Californian 'raised bed' system, devised by the English gardener Alan Chadwick and popularized by John Jeavons. In 1967, with assistance from student helpers, Chadwick (then in his late 50s) had created a beautiful and productive garden out of a barren and rocky hillside at the newly built University of California campus of Santa Cruz, using an approach he called the 'Biodynamic/French Intensive Method'. His inspiration came from the skilful Parisian market gardeners who fed the capital at the turn of the 20th century using a combination of copious amounts of horse manure and deep digging. Chadwick took their techniques and combined them with those of Rudolf Steiner. The University of California authorities were suitably impressed and by 1974 Chadwick's original four-acre garden had evolved into a 17-acre experimental farm, with apprenticeships in ecological horticulture firmly on the curriculum.

John Jeavons had similarly been inspired by Chadwick and had worked with him at Santa Cruz, but in 1972 he moved to Palo Alto, a city at the northern end of Silicon Valley, to set up Ecology Action, where he began intensive cultivation of a small plot. Although closely modelled on the Chadwick approach, but without all of the biodynamic overtones, Jeavons was driven by the vision of maximizing food production from tiny plots of land. In 1982 he moved to Willits, also in northern California, where he has remained ever since, refining his techniques and spreading the message in countless lectures, workshops and revised editions of his book *How to Grow More Vegetables* (see page 92). Although Chadwick died in 1980, his work continued under the guidance of Stephen Gliessman, who set up the Agro-ecology Programme that same year. You can still visit the original Alan Chadwick garden today.

So which is best – raised beds or no-dig? People have strong opinions, but my own preference is a combination of the best features of both, growing plants intensively on beds and keeping soil disturbance to a minimum by avoiding deep digging.

At Ryton, in the distance, we can see a patch of pasture that is being cleared of weeds to make way for a demonstration allotment by covering it with several different materials – black plastic, flattened cardboard cartons and old carpets. This is a simple, if time consuming, way of getting rid of grass and other weeds, although nowadays we have learned to be wary of the pesticides that are routinely incorporated into woollen carpets to kill carpet beetle larvae, and of the synthetic dyes that are used – both of which can leach out into the soil. Because of this we tend to avoid carpets in favour of inert materials such as woven polypropylene weed-control matting, or natural substances like bark mulch. Mind you, we've spent the best part of two years trying to eradicate bulbous buttercups from the gardens, but unfortunately one or two keep reappearing. The trouble is, they love dry grassland, so the pasture at Ryton is ideal and all we can do is keep on digging them out. Annual weeds like fat hen and chickweed can be simply hoed out – the important thing is to not let them seed, as per the old adage, 'One year's seeding, seven year's weeding'. But even when they are pulled up, weeds can still shed seeds, so the compost heap with its fierce heat is the only safe place to put them. Perennial weeds, such as couch grass and bindweed, which possess a tenacious root system, are more intractable. Every scrap of root must be dug out carefully, for the tiniest remaining fragment will regrow; but perseverance usually wins through in the end. With weeds such as these, it's best to bake them in the sun before adding to the compost heap, just to make certain that they've been killed.

Next is the conservation area, which is split into three distinct habitats – a small patch of woodland, a large pond and a wildflower meadow.

Although we've tried to make every display garden at Ryton wildlife-friendly, this area is on an altogether bigger scale and its management is kept to a minimum. It's our small attempt to right some of the terrible damage that has been inflicted by intensive agriculture on the British countryside. Again, we don't have enough room on our explanatory sign to say all we'd like to about conservation, which is that British agriculture during the 1970s and 1980s was a time of utter madness. Farmers, urged on by tantalizingly generous subsidies, declared war on some of our most sensitive landscapes, even though there was no market for the extra food. Heathland was ploughed up, wetlands drained, woodland chopped down and hedges ripped out, in an insane quest to increase agricultural production. Meanwhile, the grain, butter, milk and other food produced as a result of this absurd policy piled up, unwanted and unused, in giant silos, warehouses and cold-stores across Europe. In 1983, the government's then nature watchdog, the Nature Conservancy Council, reported the destruction of 95 per cent of Britain's lowland herb-rich meadows, 80 per cent of lowland grasslands on chalk or limestone, 60 per cent of all lowland heaths, 50 per cent of lowland fens and 50 per cent of upland grasslands, heaths and mires. Ancient woodlands echoed to the ugly sounds of countless chainsaws, and almost half of them disappeared, along with over 150,000 miles of hedgerow. Is it any wonder that wildlife numbers plummeted?

It wasn't until the 1990s that the European Union (EU) seriously tackled the problem of food surpluses by, ironically, paying farmers not to grow crops on part of their land (a policy known as 'Set-Aside') and then, when it could no longer deny the harmful environmental consequences of its policies, ordering them to leave the edges of their fields uncultivated and unsprayed. Although this edict has had a beneficial effect overall, many species have continued their sad decline. Skylarks, yellowhammers, linnets and grey partridges have suffered more than most, while the tree sparrow, a bird once so common that every child could instantly recognize it, now stands at little more than 10 per cent of its numbers 40 years ago. During this same period, the number of bumblebees, nature's pollinators, has gone down by 70 per cent, as have most species of butterfly.

But habitat destruction is only part of the story – chemicals have also played a major role in this carnage. Although pesticides poison some creatures outright, they can be just as deadly in more subtle ways. For example, the newly hatched chicks of grey partridges are dependant on caterpillars and other creatures that live on weeds found among arable crops. Modern herbicides are so effective that the fields are weed-free. No weeds means no insects, and so baby partridges slowly starve to death. And it's not just partridges that suffer, all insect-eating farmland birds are at risk.

Artificial fertilizers have played their part in this tragedy. Wild flowers thrive in pasture when soil fertility is low and they are able to co-exist with slow-growing grass species. But most dairy farmers plant their fields with vigorous rye grasses, which perform best under a high nitrogen fertilizer regime, producing good crops of grass to make silage for the winter, and hence maximizing milk yields. Under these conditions of high fertility wild flowers are unable to compete and die out, along with the host of invertebrate species that depends on them.

Many of these problems disappear when land is farmed organically but, unfortunately, this only accounts for a small percentage of the total. And things are about to become worse, not better, now that the EU has abandoned the Set-Aside initiative. That's why it's so important for gardeners everywhere to do all they can to assist the wild creatures that live in their gardens. With more than half a million gardens in the UK, ordinary people can make a real difference, and in the conservation area at Ryton, and indeed on the rest of the grounds, we show visitors how it can be achieved.

We also have a small copse here, which has around 600 saplings – a mixture of typical Warwickshire tree species, including ash, field maple, wild cherry and oak. Young transplants, or 'whips', were chosen because they establish more quickly than older trees and are much cheaper. Each is spaced about six feet apart and is inter-planted with shrubby species, such as goat willow, buckthorn, holly and guelder rose. Dense planting like this helps to suppress weeds and provides protection from the wind, but in five or six years' time some of the trees will be removed and the shrubs thinned out to allow more room for growth. Nearest the road is a stand of fast-growing willow hybrids, planted through a sheet of black plastic. These trees started life as 'truncheons' – stout cuttings, the length and thickness of a broom handle. They really puzzled passers-by, who were curious to know what was underneath the sheeting that was held down by such large stakes! Eighteen months later most have grown at least ten feet. Approximately a third of the trees will be coppiced every year to provide poles for beans and other plant supports in the gardens.

The pond comes next. We had great fun excavating it mechanically using a large digger. The ground is not naturally water retentive and the pond had to be lined with a large custom-made butyl rubber lining, which took the entire MSC gang the best part of a day to manoeuvre into place. The pool, a habitat for frogs and other aquatic wildlife and a source of drinking water for many creatures, also acts as a reservoir for the irrigation system. In some parts of the country, agricultural 'improvement' has destroyed so many farm ponds that frogs have disappeared completely, and were it not for pools in domestic gardens, the common frog might have become extinct in some areas.

In its turn, the subsoil, taken from the pond excavations, was used to make the wildflower meadow. It replaced the topsoil, which was removed to a depth of 18 inches in order to leave us with a piece of ground having little or no fertility. Our flowery meadow looks best in the spring, when it's ablaze with species such as ox-eye daisy, yellow rattle, knapweed and field scabious. Only after the plants have finished flowering and dropped their seeds can the vegetation be cut with a strimmer. It will then be taken away to keep the fertility of the meadow artificially low.

A beautiful formal rose garden is the next stop on our tour, all the roses having been chosen for their resistance to diseases. They are edged with lavender and surrounded by a beech hedge in a precise geometrical design. This is completely different from the display garden next door, which is set up to show what a reasonably sized rear garden of a typical house might look like if managed organically. It's planted up to maximize food production but it still looks attractive. As you might expect, there's a lawn and patio, and there are attractive flower borders, a small wooden greenhouse and a vegetable plot, screened from the lawn by espalier apple trees trained along posts and wire. A six-feet-high boundary fence is clothed with elegant fan-trained pears and cherries, which are interspersed with honeysuckle, clematis and other decorative climbers. Vegetables, chosen for their shape or colour, like crimson lettuces and purple leeks, can be found growing among the flowers in the borders, potager style. In the furthest corner of the garden is a large New Zealand compost box, which recycles the weeds and other waste from the garden; a wire-netting container for dead leaves; and a worm bin for kitchen waste – all of which underscore the point that maintaining and improving the health of the soil are at the heart of organic gardening.

This informal plot was designed to show visitors that anyone can have an organic garden that is productive, beautiful and full of wildlife. It contains a pond, a wooden hedgehog box placed under the hedge as an over-wintering refuge, and several bird boxes. We go out of our way to encourage birds at Ryton and put out food throughout the year, ensuring that they also have a supply of winter hedgerow berries. The same applies to beneficial insects, and so the ground underneath the apple trees is planted with annual and perennial flowers to attract lacewings and hoverflies that have larvae that feed on fruit pests. Less sportingly, perhaps, a tent-shaped plastic trap dangles from the branches above, containing the synthesized scent emitted by female codling moths, to lure unsuspecting male codling moths to a sticky end, ensuring that the eggs laid by the female remain unfertilized and never develop into maggots. The wider message is don't just create a special area for wildlife, make the whole garden conservation-friendly.

We've reached the furthest point of the grounds and we begin our return, pausing first at the unusual vegetable plot to look at obscure roots like salsify, scorzonera and skirret, the towering cardoon (a relative of the globe artichoke), the fascinating ice plant with succulent dark-green leaves that are covered with what look like frozen water droplets, and many other little-known edible plants. It is such a shame that so many people never get beyond eating peas or cabbage – the display is here to encourage visitors to be more adventurous.

Next is a series of 'topic-led' pest and disease control beds, displaying barriers and traps, predator attractant plants, resistant varieties, crop-rotation groupings and other non-chemical methods – everything, in fact, to tell you how you can keep pests and diseases at bay in your garden – and all in a comprehensive assortment of practical demonstrations.

The bee garden that follows has been designed, and is maintained, by Edward Gough, an HDRA member who lives in Manchester. It is hexagonal in plan, mirroring the shape of a honeycomb cell, and planted up with flowers that provide good sources of nectar and pollen for bees throughout the year. A lych-gate-like structure with a tiled roof stands in the centre, sheltering an observation bee hive with a hinged wooden door beneath, which opens to reveal a scene of intense and purposeful activity. Visitors have to force themselves to stop watching this fascinating sight – it's not good for the bees if the cover is left open for too long.

Just beyond the bee garden is a large structure, circular in plan, constructed from six-feet-tall fencing panels, which has a double door entrance of the sort that you can often see at walk-in aviaries at zoos. The whole thing is completely covered with fine-mesh, black plastic netting, supported on a lattice of wires and has been designed to keep birds out. Why? Because this is the soft fruit display, in which every inch of available space has been taken up by one sort of fruiting bush or another. On the walls are a number of different types of blackberries, strange sounding hybrid berries, such as the medana tayberry, the jostaberry and the Japanese wineberry, and more familiar fruits like loganberries, and red and white currants. Raspberries, supported on wires, in shades of lipstick pink through to deepest orange, occupy the middle ground, along with different sorts of blackcurrants and gooseberries – all of which provide soft fruit for the Ryton café from early summer through to late autumn. It's all very tempting. Too tempting for some visitors!

Leaving the fruit cage behind, a path winds through newly planted fruit trees, mostly apples, pears and plums, laid out in a circular arrangement to show how the eventual size of a mature tree is determined by the rootstock onto which it is grafted, and how, through pruning and training, fans, espaliers and cordons, as well as traditional bush shapes, can be created. It's still early days and all the trees look much the same, but in ten years' time there will be significant differences among them.

You're on the home straight now and on your right is the new bungalow where Lawrence Hills lives with his wife, Cherry. They only have a small garden, with a sloping bank dedicated to alpines – Lawrence's first horticultural love. These have been planted through a weed-suppressing black plastic sheet, hidden beneath a layer of stone chippings. The plants appear to be enjoying the conditions and are growing away nicely. What is not obvious to visitors is the 'leaky hose' irrigation system on the surface of the soil under the plastic, which ensures that the plants are never short of moisture.

The long shrub border, which is the final feature of the tour, contains plants that have been chosen to provide colour and interest throughout the year – we want Ryton to be an oasis of calm and beauty, not just a learning experience. Right now the plants are suffering from the effects of the raw winds that cut across our empty acres, and although we have windbreak netting strategically placed, only time and maturity will bring about the true effects we are seeking. Before you head home you can treat yourself to a cup of tea and a homemade wholemeal scone – all organic of course. Then there's just time to visit the shop, where you browse among the gifts and books and seeds, hopefully buying something, because all the profits go towards HDRA's charitable activities. I hope you've enjoyed your visit!

If you go to Ryton Gardens nowadays you wouldn't recognize what's just been described to you. These days the grounds are mature and lush, amazingly productive and diverse. They are also unbelievably beautiful and, I'm convinced, would persuade anyone, however sceptical, that organic gardening works, and works well.

Chapter Nine

ALL MUCK AND MAGIC?

RYTON GARDENS HAD attracted thousands of visitors over the summer of 1986, but Jackie and I didn't expect anything like those numbers to come through in the winter, so we needed to think of other ways of attracting people to organic gardening. Then the perfect opportunity presented itself. Tony Holmes from the television company HTV West called us. I didn't recognize the name at first, but then it dawned on me that he'd contacted us three years ago, when we were at Bocking. Turning up unannounced, he'd spent the day looking at all the trials and the demonstration beds, with a view to making a film. Like us, he felt that a TV series with a fully organic approach was long overdue. Channel 4 would be our best bet, he thought, because it had a mandate to tackle subjects that weren't getting an airing elsewhere. Over the next few weeks there had been a flurry of letters and phone calls, out of which emerged a proposal for an eight-part series filmed at Bocking. Tony had sent it off to Channel 4, warning prophetically that their response might take some time. We'd waited and waited, but as the months, then years, slipped by, the memory of it dimmed, and with all the excitement of the move to Ryton we forgot about it entirely. Now, out of the blue, here he was again, desperate to make up for lost time.

After having waited for so long, it was ironic that Channel 4 wanted the series to be completed as quickly as possible. Apparently, Naomi

Sargant, the Commissioning Editor, had told him that it had already been pencilled into next year's early summer schedules, starting in June 1987. 'That means filming in the winter,' Jackie said to Tony with horror, when he arrived at Ryton. 'You can't make a gardening series when nothing is growing. Can't you get the dates changed?' He promised that he would see what he could do, but once the schedules were produced, he pronounced, that was usually it. We would just have to make the best of it.

There was a lot of excitement on the day that various members of HDRA staff were given a short screen test to decide who would take part. I don't know whether any of us was particularly outstanding – Lawrence ruled himself out completely by talking too fast but Jackie, Pauline, Bob, Sue and I must have been okay, because we duly went on to become the five familiar faces of *All Muck and Magic?*, the UK's first organic gardening series.

In those days the programmes were made using film rather than video cameras, which demanded an enormous crew, including a director, two cameramen, someone to carry the heavy camera and its tripod, two sound recordists, a production assistant and a researcher, plus an electrician, in case extra lighting was required. To those of us used to a more frugal existence, expenses seemed to be limitless. The crew stayed in the best hotels, and we joked with the Director, Sebastian Robinson ('Sebby') – a large, genial man with dark, twinkling eyes and a bushy, dark-grey beard – that he worked in television just for the gourmet lifestyle it gave him on the road. Joke or not, the perks weren't to last much longer – a new mood of austerity was soon to sweep through the television industry, bringing a halt to an era of unbridled excess.

The eight programmes that eventually materialized bore little resemblance to the original outline, but we were pleased, nevertheless, that they were full of practical organic gardening. Each one involved a number of themed items from Ryton, with a longer interview filmed off-site. Inevitably, given the seasonal weather restrictions and the immaturity of most of the plants, an embarrassingly large amount of footage was devoted to manure and compost! We also filmed organic vegetables in supermarkets, organic fertilizers in the shop at Ryton and organic seeds at a warehouse in Essex; anything, in fact, to disguise the embarrassing absence of impressive plants in the gardens! I remember vividly doing a piece to camera surrounded by seedlings that were only a few inches high. I waved an expansive hand over the crop, announcing confidently: 'And these have been grown entirely organically.' Even as I spoke the words I could imagine viewers peering incred-ulously at the tiny plants and saying to themselves, 'Well, if that's the best you can do, I'll stick with my artificial fertilizers!'

What struck Jackie and me about filming was how interminably long everything took. Brief and intense bursts of activity were sandwiched between tedious hours spent hanging around doing nothing much. We would start by having a discussion with the Director, telling him what we were going to say, and where it could be filmed. The cameramen would listen in, then go off to check out various locations and select the best camera positions. While all this was happening the sound recordist would 'mike up' whoever was taking part, clipping a tiny radio microphone to their shirt or blouse, with a cable connecting it to the battery pack which was kept in a back pocket. The idea was to make these devices invisible to the viewer, but this was impossible in reality and half the time we appeared to have a third nipple and a very bumpy backside! Next, when everyone was ready, came the rehearsal. This might be a two-person interview, or a 'walk and talk', or a practical demonstration, or a 'piece to camera'. All of us had obviously thought about what we were going to say, so there was a script of sorts, but at the end of the 'take' the Director would suggest any changes he wanted to make and ask us to do it all over again (and sometimes again and again) until he was happy with the result; so we had to be pretty versatile.

Eventually we would do it for real. At which point you could almost guarantee that something technical would go wrong, or a plane would pass overhead with a roar, so we would have to do it again. Then there were common faults, like stumbling over words or completely forgetting what you'd planned to say. And the more 'takes' you did, the more anxious you became. I'll never forget when I had to interview a commercial organic vegetable grower in a glasshouse at her farm in

Lincolnshire. She was an irrepressibly bubbly character and produced a near-faultless performance the first time round. But casting about for a more 'arty' shot, the Director, who was a bit of a perfectionist, asked her to do it again, with the camera outside the building looking in at us through a distorted pane of greenhouse glass. This involved us in having a strictly controlled walk, with our conversation timed accurately to end at a pre-designated spot. It took the cameraman three or four takes to get it right, by which time there was a palpable sense of nervousness in the air from my interviewee. From then on it was all downhill – all the spontaneity had gone. It is curious, but nonetheless true, that the more you repeat the same thing, the harder it is to remember. By the thirtieth 'take' the poor woman was in such a state she could barely speak. There was nothing to be done but to film the rest of the piece mute and add the soundtrack later as a 'voice-over'. So much for the pursuit of art!

Tony Holmes did eventually manage to persuade Channel 4 to delay the screening of the series by a few weeks, which gave us the opportunity to film vegetables that were more mature and took some of the time pressure off us. Finally the whole series was 'in the can' and we waited anxiously to see the results of our labours. The big screening day arrived at last when the first programme was shown on a Saturday evening early in July 1987. We wondered how it would be received, but we had nothing to worry about because the critics were kind, much to our relief. More to the point, lots of people wrote in for the booklet that had been written to accompany the series. Within three weeks all 10,000 copies sold out. It was reprinted with double the quantity and that sold out too. By the end of the summer, the figure rose to 45,000, and Channel 4 was so pleased with the audience figures that it commissioned a follow-up series.

Filming for the second series began in the spring of 1988 and this time it was less of a rush. The programmes wouldn't be going out until the following summer, so we had a year to do the filming – luxury, indeed. Sebby was tied up with a drama series, so we were assigned a new director, Trevor Hill. This was his first documentary series as a fully fledged director, so he threw himself into the role with energy and enthusiasm. The format was the same as before, but two or more items out of each programme were filmed in various gardens up and down the country.

Another nice little feature of the second series was a tiny garden, which we built on screen at Ryton. Measuring just 24ft x 15ft, it was designed to show that even the smallest of plots could be managed organically and would benefit wildlife. The transformation from the bare patch of turf to a fully planted garden was accomplished over six months and documented in each of the programmes. We erected fences, constructed a dry stone wall, put up a small greenhouse, built the ubiquitous compost bin and even managed to fit in a small pond, little bigger than a dustbin lid. But taking pride of place in the centre of the garden was a circular vegetable bed, partitioned into four equal segments. The wooden trellis fence was planted up with climbers to provide somewhere for birds to nest, and with berries for winter feed. To complete the design, a small herb bed flanked a gravel and stone patio. In the final programme Trevor thought that the viewers ought to see us christening the garden by having a mini party on the patio (such is television!). You could only fit three of us on it, and that was a squeeze. Being real troupers by now we pretended it was all for real, and I was filmed with a drink in one hand and a barbecue fork in the other to prod the sizzling sausages, while a bikini-topped Jackie, and Sue in summer shorts, were captured on celluloid enjoying a glass of wine. Well, there have to be some perks!

Life was certainly not all sunny skies and plain sailing then – we had a busy organization to run, on top of the filming. To make things worse, in the summer of 1988 an issue erupted over the implementa-tion of new pesticide regulations. Under the Food and Environmental Protection Act's Pesticide Regulations, 1986, only those compounds that had been approved by the Ministry of Agriculture, Fisheries and Food (MAFF) could be used on crops. On the face of it, this bill, which emanated from Brussels, had been framed with commercially available products in mind and was eminently sensible. Anything that improved pesticide safety had to be a good thing, but the Ministry decided to include traditional, homemade 'pesticides' as well, which was really going over the top. It was the usual story of over-zealous bureaucrats interpreting rules in a heavy handed and, frankly, ridiculous way.

Sprays made from natural products, which gardeners had used for centuries without any ill effects, became illegal overnight and anyone caught using them in their garden, or on their allotment, risked a fine of £2,000. The ministry was adamant – if gardeners wished to use sprays made from soapy water, infusions of nettles, or bicarbonate of soda, or anything else for that matter, they would have to submit them to an elaborate set of official tests costing hundreds of thousands of pounds. It was nothing less than a de-facto ban.

HDRA responded at once, setting up a Safe Spray Campaign. We urged our members to lobby their MPs, pointing out the stupidity of the new rules – after all, who doesn't use soap? Likewise, people have been making elderberry wine, using baking soda and eating nettle soup since time immemorial, so how on earth could sprays made from these same substances be deemed as dangerous? You don't need an official test to tell you that they pose considerably less risk to human health and to wildlife than many a chemical pesticide that has success-fully negotiated the government's screening process.

The gardening media picked up our campaign and had a great time poking fun at some of the sillier inconsistencies of the rules, which allowed nettles, for example, to be steeped in water to make a liquid feed, but banned them from being steeped in water in exactly the same way to be used to kill greenfly. And while it was acceptable to spray leaves with soapy water to clean sooty marks caused by moulds, it became a crime if any insect pests were accidentally killed in the process. As for using the natural, anti-fungal liquid that each of us produces every day (I'm talking of course about urine) to spray against apple scab disease, forget it! If it hadn't been tested, it was a crime to apply it.

As is usually the case with ill-framed legislation, nobody had con-sidered how the regulations would be enforced. Would a special police 'Spray Squad' be set up, with the authority to enter garden sheds in search of rhubarb juice or other illegal substances? Perhaps people would be expected to report on any neighbours seen carrying a

1. and 2. Jackie (left) and Alan (above) arriving at Braintree railway station in the early days of working for HDRA

3. Lawrence D Hills, HDRA founder and director from 1958 to 1986

4. RIGHT Jackie receives instruction from Lawrence Hills on the Bocking trial ground, 1975

5. ABOVE Alan and Jackie Gear at Ryton, not long after the gardens opened, 1987

6. RIGHT The Prince of Wales chats to Alan Gear during his first visit to Ryton Gardens, July 1989

7. BELOW Jackie Gear (left), with organic wine producer, Dr Huw Tripp, and Joanna Simon, *Sunday Times* Wine correspondent, at the first National Organic Wine Fair, July 1988

8. ABOVE Joy Larkcom at Ryton in the late-1980s

9. ABOVE RIGHT Keen organic gardener, Thelma Barlow, the popular actress from ITV's *Coronation Street*, 1998

10. Channel 4's *All Muck & Magic?* Britain's first organic gardening television series. Standing (from the left): Pauline Pears, Alan and Jackie Gear; sitting: Sue Stickland and Bob Sherman

11. The ever-popular composting display at Ryton, 1990

12. The Cook's Garden at Ryton, 1998

13. Dr Bill Blyth, HDRA Chairman from 1992 to 2004

14. RIGHT Commercial vegetable variety trial at Ryton

15. Community intensive vegetable growing in Cuba, 1997

16. The National Trust's Plot to Plate vegetable growing display at the Chelsea Flower Show, 2002

17. BELOW Potato variety display at Ryton Garden's national Potato Day event, 2002

18. Actress Susan Hampshire at the 2002 Chelsea Flower Show with HDRA gardener Rebecca Costello on the Alitex stand

19. Children at Howarth Primary School demonstrate their vegetable-growing credentials

20. ABOVE Garden Organic Vice President and keen organic enthusiast, celebrity chef Raymond Blanc

21. RIGHT Geoff Hamilton – one of the country's most popular TV gardeners of all time

22. BELOW Bird's-eye view of the Vegetable Kingdom, HDRA headquarters and part of the gardens at Ryton, 2008

chamber pot. Joking aside, it was pretty clear that this was unlikely to be a high priority for the police, or for anyone else for that matter.

Under public pressure, MAFF started to waver, stating that it would consider issuing a general approval to legitimize the use of homemade sprays if sufficient evidence could be produced in their support. Once again we appealed to our members to send in details of their own experiences. Alongside this we began an experimental programme with the Royal Botanic Gardens, Kew, to evaluate the effectiveness of a range of traditional substances. Not that any of this made a difference. Once the heat had died down, the ministry reverted to its original stance and nothing that HDRA said or did was able to change matters. And, incredibly, this is how the position remains today. Predictably, of course, gardeners up and down the land continue to make and use homemade sprays, just as they have always done, and most of them would be astonished to learn that they are breaking the law. No one has ever been prosecuted.

That July, Channel 4 repeated our first TV series, on Friday evenings – the traditional time for gardening programmes. Viewing figures were even bigger this time round and regularly topped three million. At HDRA we were delighted to be told that it was the fifth most popular show in Channel 4's Top Ten charts. Demand for the booklet also soared, to 60,000, no less. By the end of the run it had become the bestselling publication Channel 4 had ever produced. Not bad for a bunch of amateur presenters!

Around 50,000 people visited the gardens at Ryton that year, including Karin Mundt from Terre Vivante, a Parisian publishing company that produced the bi-monthly magazine, *Four Seasons Gardening* (*Les Quatre Saisons du Jardinage*). She was on a fact-finding mission to Ryton and the Centre for Alternative Technology in Wales with a view to setting up something similar in the southeastern corner of France. Jackie, Pauline and I helped her as much as we could with advice and information, and several years later the Centre Terre Vivante opened at Mens, a few miles south of Grenoble. It was modelled more on Machynlleth than Ryton, with examples of energy efficient buildings, compost toilets and water conservation, as well as the gardens themselves, which, at over 2,000 feet above sea level, couldn't have been the easiest of places to grow things. Today it's seen as France's most important 'green centre'.

We also welcomed Eliot Coleman from the USA, who was on one of his periodic study tours to Europe. Eliot is America's most celebrated organic farmer, having started in the 1960s on land purchased from Helen and Scott Nearing (see page 56). He subsequently moved to Four Seasons Farm at Harbourside in Maine, where, in 1989, he wrote *The New Organic Grower*, still the most useful book for aspiring commercial vegetable producers. Several years later, Eliot and his wife, Barbara Damrosch, a gardening writer, hosted *Gardening Naturally*, the US equivalent of *All Muck and Magic?*

Eliot was able to tell us that there was nothing quite like Ryton in the USA as most organic activities were run on state lines. In his own state, for example, there happened to be the most flourishing membership organization in the whole country – the several-thousand strong Maine Organic Farmer and Gardeners Association, which organized a highly successful Common Ground Country Fair each year, although it didn't operate any demonstration gardens. The Rodale Institute, however, an offshoot of Rodale Press, did have small demonstration gardens and a 333-acre research farm, near Kutztown in Pennsylvania open to the public. Like Haughley Research Farms before them, they had been running comparative trials between chemical and organic farming.

Other US initiatives, such as the New Alchemy Institute (set up by Nancy and John Todd, with their friend William McLarney in 1969 at a former dairy farm on Cape Cod, Massachusetts), were not organized to receive visitors on any scale, and unfortunately it looked as though the place would fold – which it did in 1991. But in its prime, the New Alchemy Institute was an inspiration to many of us here in the UK. It had pioneered solar greenhouses and aquaculture systems for rearing fish, using water from the fish tanks to fertilize intensive vegetable beds, and had developed novel ways of utilizing perennial food and tree crops – an early example of what Bill Mollinson in Australia called permaculture. We certainly enjoyed talking to Karin and Eliot about other organic initiatives taking place elsewhere, but we also met all sorts of other interesting folk who had come to Ryton as a result of watching *All Muck and Magic?*

Why were the programmes so successful? The series was as far removed from today's personality-led TV as you could get. It was real, down to earth, 'how-to' television, demonstrating techniques and putting over ideas that most people had never seen before. Too many programme makers these days assume, patronizingly, that viewers have the attention span of a gnat, so they sacrifice content for quick sound bites and gimmickry. These may look great on screen as they flash by, but there is not much solid practical information for viewers to get their teeth into. The 'dumbing down' process had not really begun then. The *All Muck and Magic?* programmes told it as it was, but, nevertheless it was gardening that anyone could understand and put into practice.

But that's only part of the reason for the show's success. The other ingredient was, perhaps, our naivety, freshness, enthusiasm and obvious commitment. Here were five young people who believed passionately in what they were doing and wanted to share their philosophy and knowledge with viewers. Without even realizing it we were saying, 'We may not be professional presenters, but please take the message to heart and garden organically in your homes,' which touched a chord with viewers everywhere.

Most of the location filming for the second series took place during the summer of 1988. Sue and Bob visited a community on the island of Mull, off the west coast of Scotland, where the islanders had transformed a barren plot using copious amounts of fresh seaweed. Meanwhile, Jackie returned to the country of her birth to film an enterprising businesswoman in West Wales who made a living making worm compost for sale to gardeners and commercial organic growers. Pauline travelled north, to Liverpool, to pick up tips from members of HDRA's local group on their communal allotments, and I visited Jim Hay, a keen worm composter, at his home in Lancashire.

Interestingly, the second series was shot using videotape rather than film, and we were amazed to see how the crew had shrunk in size accordingly. Most of the time only one cameraman, a sound recordist, a production assistant and the director accompanied us on our travels. The television companies had shed huge numbers of permanent staff, only to take back the people who had lost their jobs on a self-employed basis, as and when required.

One great advantage of video was that the director could see what had been filmed immediately, in a way that was not possible with film, which had needed to be sent away for processing. Consequently the whole process was speeded up. Whereas with film, 10 to 15 minutes of broadcastable material might have been the output for a day's filming, this increased three-fold with video. Nowadays, companies think nothing of recording two, or even three, half-hour programmes in a single day's shoot.

The accountants were also busy trimming the fat off the expense budgets all round and our accommodation on location was decidedly less luxurious than it had been before – a case of table d'hôte rather than à la carte! Even so, it was still a great treat, particularly as we were accustomed to living so carefully on HDRA's below-average salaries – Jackie and I rarely set foot in a B&B, let alone a top-quality hotel. For all the cost-cutting, however, the filming budget did run to a short visit for Jackie and me to the small town of Rouffach in eastern France to cover the annual Organic Food Festival. This attracted food producers from miles around who sold fresh fruit and vegetables, meat and dairy products, wines and other goodies – all produced organically. The visitors to Rouffach were ordinary folk who thought of organic food as being good quality rather than cranky. They belied the muesli-eating, sandal-wearing, bearded-hippy image, which was how most people in Britain viewed organic 'types' back then. I particularly enjoyed eating organic *poulet-frites* from a hot food stall that was doing a brisk trade among the many thousands of visitors. It was as far removed from a typical 'chicken and chips' takeaway in England as it's possible to get. On the following day we were filmed visiting a biodynamic vegetable grower who had a very impressive commercial market garden. He told us that he had no trouble selling his produce through local markets, and we could see why. It looked fabulous!

Of all the people we interviewed for the second series, perhaps the most interesting was a young man whom Sue went to interview at his one-acre plot in Norfolk. Vegetables and fruit were growing there in profusion, including all sorts of things you don't usually find in the east of England, such as exotic vegetables and fruits that were more suited to the tropics, growing inside polytunnels. Yes, this was the home of the well-known Bob Flowerdew, who appeared in *All Muck and Magic?* long before he became a celebrity. At that time he had more of a Beatles hairdo than the long pigtail for which he has subsequently become famous, but he surely knew how to grow his fresh produce! Sue discovered that before settling down to full-time gardening, Bob's career had been nothing if not colourful and had even involved stints as a nude model, a cook in a house of ill repute and a dog impersonator – whatever that is. Since then, of course, he has become one of the best-known panellists on BBC Radio 4's *Gardener's Question Time* and has written over ten books on organic gardening, including *The Organic Gardener*, *Bob Flowerdew's Organic Bible* and, most recently, *Grow Your Own, Eat Your Own*, published in 2008. And we have not lost touch with him at HDRA – he has been to Ryton several times, most recently in July 2008.

I appeared in the same programme as Bob, sitting in a barber's chair in Romsey, near the New Forest, Hampshire. Locals had discovered that the scent from human hair deterred deer from trespassing into their gardens. Being something of an entrepreneur, the hairdresser collected up all the clippings, stuffed them into net balls and sold them to gardeners to dangle from trees at the edge of their properties.

Which reminds me of a quick tip about how to deal with badgers, given to Jackie by Marguerite Patten, doyenne of cookery writers, when she invited her to Ryton to give a talk on preserving. Like deer, badgers can do an enormous amount of damage, digging up lawns and borders as they rootle about in search of worms and beetles. Finding that fencing is no deterrent (they either push through or burrow underneath), Marguerite feeds them instead! At first I thought she was joking, but she insisted that sandwiches were the answer – but they had to be made with peanut butter. I mentioned this a few years later to Craig Sams, founder of a wholefood processing company famous for its peanut butter spreads. Had he come across this idea of using peanut butter as a remedy for scavenging badgers? 'Oh yes,' he replied. 'But it has to be the smooth sort, they don't seem to like the crunchy variety for some reason.' So there you have it. An expensive pest solution maybe, but it is successful!

Tips like this had their own five-minute strand woven into every programme in the second series of *All Muck and Magic?* For the introductory music, Trevor had dug out a catchy little tune from the 1930s, with lyrics as follows:

> On useful garden tips and knowledge I will now expound
> Always plant rice pudding seeds a mile beneath the ground
> And there's one thing more I'd like to say while on this tack
> If your rhubarb's far too forward, simply bend it back!

The song was accompanied by a grainy, sepia film of Bob descending a ladder into a deep pit, clutching a bag of 'rice pudding' seeds. It was a nice touch, and Bob and his tips went down well with viewers when the programmes were eventually screened. Trevor, to our horror, was keen to inject more humour into the series and came up with a series of one-liners and visual gags, usually as links between items. So, for example, Pauline was asked to deliver her lines 'I'll shout it from the rooftops', sitting astride a ridge of roof tiles, 20 feet up. We all thought she was very game to go along with this piece of nonsense!

My own excruciating turn came when Jackie was filmed interviewing Jacques Aubrée, a handsome Frenchman who produced organic snails for export on his farm in Dorset. Jackie's piece went like a dream and she developed a good rapport with Jacques, who was keen to live up to the amorous reputation of his race, stressing the aphrodisiac qualities of his product by treating her to a candlelit meal (for the benefit of the cameras only, I'm pleased to say!). My role in all this was to don a pair of wellies, wade across a pond and then crawl towards a large, concrete gastropod on the island in the middle, turn to camera and say, 'And now for something completely different'. When uttered by the Monty Python team it sounds hilarious, but I just looked stupid, and I still cringe whenever I watch the clip.

By the end of autumn 1988 filming was over and all that remained was a couple of trips to Bristol to record 'voice-overs' for the edited films. Trevor was pleased with how the filming had gone and Derek Clark, the Executive Producer, opened negotiations with Channel 4 about a possible third series. Everything would depend on the audience reaction when the series went out the following spring.

Until then, it was back to the day job! Despite the substantial fee paid to HDRA for the use of the gardens and our TV performances, by far the biggest problem awaiting Jackie and me was a cash shortage. It had been another good year for visitors but the cost of servicing the original debt, incurred when the gardens were developed, still remained and we had to find some means of reducing the overall level of debt. Jackie thought that HDRA's members might help the organization out and she decided to send them a special printed appeal, but she was unhappy at producing what could be construed as 'junk mail'. Then it occurred to her that she could turn it into something with a practical use by printing it on plain brown kraft paper, with instructions on how to recycle it into paper plant pots. It was a great idea and, as we had hoped, the members responded generously, agreeing to donate over £120,000 to HDRA over the next four years. Apart from making a huge difference to our finances, that first appeal further helped to clarify how Jackie and I would divide our time in future. She enjoyed handling HDRA's public relations, marketing and fund raising, and became a skilled professional in these spheres. Her fundraising efforts alone raised many millions of pounds over the years for our campaigns and projects. Unlike Jackie, I was more comfortable looking after the administrative, financial and technical side of HDRA's work, so to reflect this, my job title was changed to Chief Executive, while Jackie became the Executive Director, with responsibility for all the developmental and commercial activities.

When the second television series was eventually screened, in April 1989, Trevor's optimism was fully justified. Audience reaction was even better than in 1988 with viewing figures exceeding four million during some episodes. HDRA did well in other areas too. At the Chelsea Flower Show in May our exhibit on organic slug control won a medal from the Royal Horticultural Society (RHS) and attracted a continuous stream of visitors. Ryton was busy all summer long, inspiring many people to go organic and join HDRA, so that by the end of the year membership stood at over 16,000. In the Advisory Department, Pauline Pears and her staff coped magnificently with a torrent of gardening queries, at a time when we had also teamed up with Search Press, a small publishing house in Kent, to produce a series of lavishly illustrated handbooks. Local HDRA organic gardening groups were also springing up like mushrooms throughout the country – 80 in total, from Cornwall to the Scottish borders. They were forever asking for speakers from Ryton who had appeared on television – a duty we were happy to fulfil.

That summer Naomi gave us the go-ahead for the third series, warning us at the same time that it would probably be our last, in spite of its runaway success. She was stepping down as Commissioning Editor at Channel 4 and implied that her replacement, Sue Shepherd, would almost certainly want to commission entirely new programmes of her own. With this in mind, changes were made to the format, including the introduction of a new presenter, Rebecca Pow, an in-house newsreader at HTV West. Much of the filming was done away from Ryton by Rebecca and me, with Jackie, Pauline, Bob and Sue also putting in regular appearances. This time we made ten programmes, rather than eight, and got the chance to interview more organic farmers and commercial growers. When the programmes were screened in 1990 the viewing figures were fine, but, sure enough, Ms Shepherd ended the run and came up with her own new gardening series. Such is life!

In any case, that wasn't the end of the story. The organic gardening philosophy, which we had aired in the late-1980s, inspired others, most noticeably Geoff Hamilton, the anchorman on BBC's *Gardeners' World*, followed by a succession of other TV gardeners. And although the *All Muck and Magic?* team didn't ever appear together again on television, we have collectively given hundreds of interviews on television and radio in our quest to persuade the whole of Britain to go organic.

Chapter Ten

ENTER THE PRINCE

In 1988 few people were aware that The Prince of Wales harboured a passion for organic growing. He hadn't made any major speeches on the subject, only the occasional statement about the problems of intensive agriculture. Nevertheless, word had got round in organic circles, much to our delight, that the garden at Highgrove, the Prince's home in Gloucestershire, had 'gone organic' and that the rest of his 1,000-acre estate might soon follow.

Knowing this, we had written to his office, sending him information about HDRA and had received a polite reply. And then one day in late summer the receptionist at the HDRA switchboard was startled to hear a caller say:

'Hello, Buckingham Palace here. I'd like to speak to the Director please.'

Fortunately, Jackie and I had just returned from a tour of the gardens and we were in my office when the call came through.

'This has got to be a joke,' I replied, when the receptionist said that someone from the palace was on the line. But, no, the receptionist was convinced that the call was genuine.

'Put them through,' I said, raising my eyebrows to Jackie who looked on quizzically. A soft click told me that the caller was connected and a beautifully modulated voice began to speak. The receptionist's instinct was right, this was definitely no hoax call. The speaker apologized for disturbing me and went on to explain that The Prince of Wales would be holding a 'horticultural lunch' at Highgrove in a few weeks' time and would like two representatives from HDRA to attend, before adding that there was no need to give an answer straightaway, as long as I let him know in the next couple of days. I put the phone down, turned to Jackie, and said, 'You're not going to believe this ...'

In fairness, Jackie and I should have gone together, but she thought that it was only right to ask Lord Kitchener to accompany me, as HDRA's President. Thus it was that, three weeks later, I was driving up the narrow lane that snakes round to the front of the Prince's Gloucestershire home. I now know that this is famously flanked by stunning wildflower borders, planted with the help of naturalist Miriam Rothschild, but then, that late in the season, only one or two poppies remained to give the briefest of hints of earlier glory. Among a group of people who'd already arrived I spotted the familiar face of Lord Kitchener, HDRA's Chairman, but the rest were complete strangers. One by one they introduced themselves – the director of the Royal Horticultural Society, the head of this or that research establishment, senior civil servants from the Ministry of Agriculture, Fisheries and Food (MAFF) – it was going to be an interesting lunch. All of a sudden, His Royal Highness appeared at the doorway and explained that lunch would be in about an hour, which, he said cheerfully, would give plenty of time for a good look around the gardens.

Twenty years on, my recollections of that first tour are not what they once were, having been mingled with memories of the other events that Jackie and I attended. I seem to remember, though, that the Prince took us first to the walled kitchen garden, where most of the vegetables for the Prince and his family are grown. When he bought the Highgrove estate in 1980 it was completely overgrown, having even been used as a piggery at one time. At just under an acre it was not especially large, as walled gardens go, but it looked absolutely charming. It was bounded by four tall, mellow red-brick walls of roughly equal length, which were generously planted with fruit trees –

including apples, pears and plums – that rubbed shoulders with ram-
bling roses and other decorative climbing plants. Alongside the walls,
beneath the fruit, were colourful borders planted up with flowers,
fruit bushes and herbs, growing in riotous profusion. These were
flanked by a gravel path that ran around the entire perimeter.

My eye was drawn along one of a pair of paths that crossed the
garden, one from side to side, the other from top to bottom, and broke
it into four separate, square vegetable beds. A row of closely spaced
cordon apple trees that grew over a discreet metal framework stood on
either side of the path that leads from the entrance gate, but at the time
of this first visit the trees were no more than waist high. As they have
matured they have been trained into a successive series of arches to
form a near-continuous tunnel of fruit – an enchanting leafy refuge on
a hot summer's day. Each of the vegetable beds was further broken up
into four individual plots, which were crisply defined by neatly clipped
box hedging laid out in the shape of either the cross of St George or
the saltire of St Andrew – two of each – giving square and triangular
plots respectively, a rather charming touch, I thought.

We were all, I think, interested in the vegetables, which are grown
inside the box hedging, and it was at this point that The Prince of
Wales first spoke to me personally. His Royal Highness had been
talking to the Director of the Royal Horticultural Society (RHS) since
leaving the house, with the rest of us following on behind, chatting
among ourselves. But as we passed a bed of carrots he stopped and
asked me which varieties we grew at Ryton, having already heard,
apparently, that we had some really unusual vegetables. I explained
that we did indeed have white, yellow and even purple types of carrot,
along with the more familiar shades of orange. Warming to my
subject, I said that it was generally believed that carrots had been either
white or purple originally, but Dutch breeders in the 16th century had
succeeded in creating roots with the deep orange colour with which
we are all familiar with today. I added that they'd been trying to
curry favour with their royal master, the Prince of Orange! The new
varieties quickly caught on throughout western Europe and most of
the alternatively coloured strains gradually died out, I went on. The

Prince was interested to know that we'd tracked down some of these long-lost cultivars, including one that was deep purple, which an HDRA member had discovered growing in the mountains of Afghanistan. They all shared a similar 'carroty' flavour, irrespective of colour, but some were tastier than others, I said. His Royal Highness commented that he would like to expand the range of carrots grown at Highgrove, and I promised to send him some seeds of the more unusual and historic varieties.

Moving on, we paused by a young crop of winter cabbages whose foliage was being reduced to shreds by scores of greenish yellow caterpillars. I wondered if the gardening staff knew about a biological pest control called *Bacillus thuringiensis* (Bt for short) that kills cabbage caterpillars but leaves everything else unharmed. Dennis Brown, the gardener who looks after the walled garden, was working nearby, so the Prince called him over and asked him what he was going to do about the infestation. Dennis, who'd been growing vegetables all his life, replied that he'd probably pick the caterpillars off one by one. It would be a time consuming task, he went on, which is why he hadn't got round to it yet. I explained about Bt, which he admitted sounded a much better bet, and worth a try, so I made a mental note to add a packet to the royal shopping list.

While Dennis was nearby I took the opportunity of congratulating him on the superb state of the garden which, minor transgressions on the part of the caterpillars apart, looked in tip-top condition. The Prince had told us that its design had been a joint effort be-tween him and the Marchioness of Salisbury. Although I hadn't met Lady Salisbury at that time, I knew that she was a keen organic gardener and that she had been a member of HDRA since the 60s. Her magnificent gardens at the Jacobean palace of Hatfield House in Hertfordshire were a marvellous testament to her creativity and skill, and an excellent advertisement for organic methods. It was she who had recommended HDRA as a source of technical advice, the Prince had confided.

Leaving the walled garden, our party strolled across the broad sweep of roughly clipped meadow which, we were told, makes a spectacular display of massed tulips in early spring, and then we arrived at the formal flower beds at the side and rear of the house. Lady Salisbury has had an input into the design process here as well, with a formal rose garden, but the influences of art historian Sir Roy Strong, who suggested the flamboyant topiary, and plantswoman Rosemary Verey, who helped with the cottage garden, were also in evidence. But the most striking feature of all, the thyme walk, which is the one that most people nowadays have come to associate with Highgrove, was nowhere to be seen in 1988. It would be another three years before the Prince would replace the long gravel path that connects the house with the ornamental pool with one made with stone and brick, planted up with every variety of thyme imaginable, creating a mesmerizing mosaic of subtly varying hues of mauve, yellow and green.

On that first visit, however, the tour of the magnificent garden over, we made our way back to the house and into the dining room. At table, I found myself sitting to the left of The Prince of Wales and felt quite disconcerted to be surrounded on all sides by portraits of his ancestors, who appeared to be gazing down with critical eyes. Fortunately, I didn't feel nervous for long because the Prince quickly put me at my ease, and we picked up the conversation where we had left off, then moved effortlessly from discussing old varieties of vegetables to alternative ways of dealing with pests and other problems that can trouble gardeners. All too soon, alas, the delicious lunch and the round-the-table conversation was over. We were about to leave when, without thinking too hard, I suddenly said that it would be a great honour if the Prince would agree to be HDRA's Patron. Much to my surprise, he said that he would and, true to his word, it was confirmed by letter not long after.

A couple of months on from that memorable trip I received another call from the Palace, this time from the Prince's Private Secretary, who told me that His Royal Highness had been invited to dinner by the Worshipful Company of Fruiterers, one of the City of London livery companies, and would be giving a speech. Would I be willing to provide some information for it? The request took me completely by surprise, and modesty made me ask if I could think about it. That would be fine, came the reply, but from the tone I got the distinct impression that I didn't ought to leave it too long. Jackie was in her office next door and I put my head around the door to tell her.

'The Prince's Private Secretary has asked me if I'll assist in writing a speech for him,' I said.

'I hope you said yes,' she replied.

'I said I wasn't sure and wanted to think about it,' I answered sheepishly.

'What!' Jackie yelped. 'Get back on the phone and tell him you've changed your mind and that you'll be delighted to help,' she said, astonished that I should even think of declining.

Now, as it happens, an important national issue concerning fruit was staring us in the face – the imminent closure of Brogdale, the National Fruit Trials in Kent, which had recently been announced by the government. So I picked up the phone there and then, dialled Buckingham Palace and asked for The Prince of Wales's office. When I was put through I said that I'd given it some thought and decided that I would like to provide some information for the Prince's speech. I explained about Brogdale, and asked if it would be acceptable to mention it. I was told not to worry because the speech would be checked thoroughly. Reassured, I began to state the case in defence of Brogdale, in the certain knowledge that the campaign to save it would receive an enormous boost if the Prince agreed to it.

Jackie and I knew Brogdale Farm well. It lies about half a mile to the south of the historic market town of Faversham and had been the home of the National Fruit Trials since 1952. The farm is a unique treasury of fruit – the apple collection alone, which comprises more than 2,000 varieties, includes the ancient 'Decio', which was brought to England by the Romans and is arguably the oldest apple in the world. There are also 500 different types of pears, 350 plums, over 200 cherries and countless soft fruit varieties – yet all this was about to be lost.

We were aghast that anyone would contemplate destroying such a precious genetic resource that stretched back for almost two millennia. It would be like torching the National Gallery or demolishing Stonehenge. And then there was the issue of climate change. Existing commercial varieties might suffer badly in the increased temperatures that we can expect as the climate warms. New pests and diseases will evolve. Hidden within the all-but-forgotten varieties might be the genes that can overcome these changed circumstances. Where would fruit breeders obtain grafting wood for new varieties if Brogdale closed?

But this was to be an after-dinner speech, delivered in the atmosphere of warm conviviality, so I cheekily suggested that the Prince might like to add that there had once been an apple named after an earlier Prince of Wales that has long since disappeared; even Brogdale didn't have one. Sure enough, 'Where is The Prince of Wales now? Last sighted in Belgium,' was jokily included in the draft.

The Prince had obviously also cared about this potential loss to our genetic heritage because the speech focused heavily on Brogdale. It was widely reported, and Baroness Trumpington, the minister responsible in the House of Lords, was actually a guest at the dinner. The public reaction was immediate and vociferous, demanding a reprieve for Brogdale, a sentiment that I fuelled by penning a hard-hitting editorial in HDRA's magazine. Gradually, the government began to change its position, and it looked as if the collection might be spared after all.

Throughout the summer I kept up the pressure, along with a group of people that had close associations with Brogdale. That autumn a small voluntary organization called Common Ground held the first ever Apple Day. The event was a huge success and attracted thousands of visitors who, for the first time, were able to compare the textures and flavours of non-commercial varieties with the bland offerings on sale in most supermarkets. But why limit it to one day a year, I thought? If Brogdale was open to the public, every day could be an Apple Day – or plum, pear or cherry day, come to that! Jackie thought it was a great idea too, and before long the idea of turning Brogdale into a tourist attraction began to gather momentum. A charitable trust could own and run the site, we thought, using the example of Ryton as a model. And there could be guided tours of the orchards, lectures and demonstrations, and a shop selling a fantastic range of fruit trees for gardeners to plant, along with the fresh produce itself.

But first of all we had to persuade government, and in January 1990 I was part of a small delegation who met with MAFF officials at their London headquarters to explore the possibility of buying the site. This turned out to be easier than expected, as the Ministry appeared to have already reached an in-principle decision to accept our proposals and it only remained to fix the price. The land and buildings had been valued at around three-quarters of a million pounds, which seemed excessive to me, but officials were unwilling to make any concessions. None of the buildings on site was really suitable as a visitor centre and at least another quarter of a million pounds would be needed to bring them up to scratch – that made a million pounds in total, an awful lot of money.

A public appeal was launched at once and I went on BBC Radio 4's *Farming Today* and the *Food Programme* to drum up support and ask for donations. Meanwhile, the Brogdale Horticultural Trust was set up and it applied for planning permission to develop the site into a visitor attraction – without this consent, nothing could go ahead. Fortunately the planning authorities could see how the locality would benefit from an influx of tourists and they gave the necessary approval. However, this turned out to be a double-edged sword, because once planning permission had been granted, the Ministry increased the price by another half-million pounds.

We were at a loss to know how we could find more money as Britain was in the middle of a deep recession and people were tightening their belts. Members of the Fruiterers' Company had been hard at work soliciting donations from City institutions, but with limited success – it was beginning to look as though we might fall at the final fence.

However, all was not lost. The Prince of Wales, through the Duchy of Cornwall, went on to offer the Brogdale Trust a mortgage on highly favourable terms, putting up three-quarters of the capital, with the local authority supplying the balance. It was an extremely generous offer and enabled the Trust to go ahead with the purchase later that year. At Brogdale's first major event – October's Apple Day – 5,000 people turned up to view a truly staggering display of more than 1,000 varieties. His Royal Highness visited Brogdale to see the collection for himself a few years later and was greeted with a rousing reception, in recognition of the crucial role he had played in getting the project off the ground.

When The Prince of Wales had said that he was willing to become HDRA's Patron I had little idea what it would mean in practice. As I had already seen, it involved the association in giving advice on technical gardening issues at Highgrove, as well as other responsibilities. Over the coming months we were contacted from time to time with minor requests for assistance – help with answering a letter from the public, an opinion on this or that individual or company, providing snippets of information, that sort of thing. None of these duties was onerous – on the contrary, they were always interesting and therefore a pleasure to fulfil.

Our contact at St James's Palace, the Prince's official London residence, was Commander Richard Aylard, who handled the Prince's environmental interests. Jackie and I found him engaging, friendly and direct. As we were to discover over the years, Richard was not unusual in this respect – none of the Prince's staff we encountered conformed to the buttoned-up courtier stereotypes of popular imagination. To us, the Prince's office appeared to be run in a spirit of informality and openness, yet it was equally sharp and businesslike. This continued after Richard left in 1996, when Elizabeth Buchanan took over as our new point of contact at the Palace. She invariably accompanied the Prince on functions that involved us and was formidably efficient, yet she always managed to spare her precious time to go over issues of etiquette or problems with the timetable. She is an extremely charming woman and we both became very fond of her.

For all that we were assisting The Prince of Wales here and there, this was nothing compared to how His Royal Highness was helping HDRA. Within a few weeks we had received a generous donation from one of the Prince's charitable trusts, and Jackie and I had been introduced to several other people who were able to help us with advice or financially. At that time, when the organization's finances were going through a bad patch, His Royal Highness's interventions couldn't have been more gratefully received. We also discovered that being able to state that the Prince of Wales was our Patron gave HDRA a gravitas it didn't have before.

But the most distinguishing feature of The Prince of Wales's first year as our Patron was his official visit to Ryton. I had mentioned the idea to him on my visit to Highgrove, and His Royal Highness had, amazingly, promised to try to fit it into his busy programme of 'Away Days', as his official duties around the country are known. Jackie and I had been cock-a-hoop at first, but then Richard had said that there was always intense competition for royal visits and so a lot would depend on whether other engagements, if any, were planned for Coventry and Warwickshire. As the weeks rolled by and nothing more was said, we accepted reluctantly that it had fallen by the wayside, until one dismal and grey morning in February, when a letter arrived informing us that His Royal Highness would be coming to see us in July.

Long before then we had to work out a programme in minute detail – the Prince's route through the gardens, what he would see, where he would stop, who he would meet, to name but a few considerations. We had been told that His Royal Highness would arrive mid-morning and leave after an hour and a quarter. Lawrence and HDRA committee members would be there, along with individuals who had helped the organization, but there were also our members of staff to consider and any HDRA members who would want to see him. We also had to take into account the fact that the Prince would be visiting when the gardens would be open to the public, so there were security implications to be considered.

Our plans must be detailed to the minute because by the time The Prince of Wales arrived, he would already have fulfilled two engagements that morning, and after leaving us would be going on to another three in the afternoon, finishing up with a reception and dinner in Birmingham in the evening, so there literally wouldn't be a minute to spare. We had asked Richard how he kept up this demanding timetable, and were told that it was pretty normal. Before the Prince became involved with HDRA, I'm sorry to say that, like a lot of people, we hadn't realized how amazingly hard he worked. If the media spent more time on covering the Prince's charitable activities and less time on the pointless 'lowest common denominator' trivia that absorbs so many pages of newsprint and hours of television, the world would be a better place. Sorry, but it does make Jackie and me mad!

When the big day finally came, His Royal Highness was due to arrive in a helicopter. Thankfully, it was a sunny day and the gardens were looking their best. Jackie and I had been up and about since early morning, and we had arrived at Ryton to find that Sue and the gardeners were already hard at work doing last-minute tidying up. The police had arrived shortly after, accompanied by a pair of ebullient spaniels, their trained noses tracing the royal route searching for suspect packages. Uniformed policemen would supervise the crowds, the plain clothes officers taking up more discreet positions, although all of this behind-the-scenes organization was not obvious to our guests, who had arrived on time and were waiting in a large marquee that we had erected. HDRA staff had time off to enjoy the occasion and were milling about outside, in the public area, while most of the gardens' visitors were clustered about the shop and café. No one had objected when we explained that on this very special day we were unable to allow visitors into the gardens while the Prince was there, so the majority had taken up a grandstand position outside on the café patio instead, happy to view him unexpectedly, from afar.

After what seemed like ages, Jackie and I heard a distinct, steady throbbing sound coming from the south and a shiny red dot appeared on the horizon travelling towards us, gradually taking on the familiar shape of a helicopter as it neared. As the engine cut and the blur of the rotors slowly subsided, The Prince of Wales, dressed in a pale grey suit, stepped down from the aircraft, to be met by the Lord Lieutenant, who ushered him to the waiting dignitaries. The Prince shook hands briefly with each in turn, exchanging the occasional word or two, working his way along the line until he came to Jackie and me at the end. Now it was up to us to ensure that his visit was a memorable one, introducing him to staff and guests, all the while keeping an eye on the clock.

I suppose, by rights, we should have been nervous, but anybody who has met the Prince, and there were plenty that day, will tell you that he has a knack of putting you at your ease, almost making you feel that it is you, and not him, who is the VIP. Happily, the visit passed off perfectly and the Prince appeared to enjoy seeing what had been achieved at Ryton in the three years since we had arrived. So interested was he, that the timetable went completely awry, with precious minutes being tacked on at almost every stop, so that by the time he reached the end of the visit he was half-an-hour adrift. All too soon it was over and we waved goodbye as the Prince took the controls of the helicopter to pilot himself to the next destination. Once airborne he performed a slow, lazy circuit of the gardens to take a final, lingering view before gradually disappearing.

Over the following 14 years Jackie and I were extremely fortunate to learn first-hand about the Prince's various passions and his commitment to organic gardening and farming in particular, and we were recipients of many invitations to royal events and meetings that would further HDRA's progress. One of the many ways in which The Prince of Wales helps to further his causes is to bring various interested parties together at Highgrove for informal talks, as was the case when I first met him. In 1993, His Royal Highness hosted an 'environmental' lunch there, to which Jackie was invited, along with representatives of environmental organizations, where he was able to encourage discussion among his various guests about organic growing and its important role in sustainability. Our organization and his other charities have every reason to be indebted to him.

And finally, a few words from The Prince of Wales himself, taken from the introduction to his book *The Elements of Organic Gardening*, which, to Jackie and to me, sum up the profound nature of the man:

We have, I suppose, become so used to the advantage of convenience in so many aspects of life that we have failed to realize how much we have abused Nature in the process. To go on doing so regardless cannot conceivably be sustainable in the long-term. If we are looking for technological 'fixes', then I happen to think they must be in *harmony* with the natural processes and, indeed, natural 'laws' – for organic gardening *does* teach you that there are certain 'laws' that need to be respected. The law of cause and effect is one of them. If we can reduce the causes – whether of pollution, waste or whatever – then we will reduce the effect they produce on us, on our garden, on the wider environment and, ultimately, on the entire planet. All is interconnected and interwoven; but we seem to have lost sight of this essential truth and have become ever more separated from the inherent rhythms that lie at the heart of Nature. We have been dancing out of time with the music ...

Chapter Eleven

♦

FOOD CHAMPIONS

On 20 September 1990, after a short illness, Lawrence D. Hills, the grand old man of the organic movement, died peacefully in his home at Ryton. During his final few days Jackie was constantly at his bedside, and along with representatives from the HDRA Council, we had been with him the previous afternoon, when the Vice Chancellor of Coventry University had awarded him its highest degree, an Honorary Doctorate in Science, in recognition of his towering contribution to organic gardening. As someone who had never passed an exam of any sort, nor even gone to school, Lawrence would have appreciated the irony of the occasion, but, lying in Jackie's arms, he was so near to death that he was barely aware of the solemn ceremony taking place around him. They had been such a remarkable double-act that Cherry's sudden death at the age of 93, ten months earlier, had hit him hard and although he'd tried to carry on as normal, writing his pieces for the HDRA newsletter and firing off occasional letters to the press, his heart was no longer in it. The two of them had been so close that his death, so soon after his beloved Cherry's, didn't surprise us. Lady Eve Balfour had also died earlier during the year, and thus the organic movement had lost the last of its trailblazers from the post-war years. They had kept the organic flame alive against all the odds, and had they lived just a little longer, they would have witnessed the vindication of everything they believed in. Thanks to the new generation of young and enthusiastic organic protagonists to whom they had passed on the baton, there would be a flowering of organic production across the world.

Lawrence had always led from the front and we had continued in the same vein. Not for us the interminable committee meetings that characterize many public and voluntary organizations, or the mindset that mere attendance at a meeting somehow constitutes 'action'. We knew what we wanted to achieve, and we got on and did it. Jackie and I held regular weekly get-togethers with senior members of staff, during which we heard their views and took them into account, and once a month I chaired an hour-long session to update everyone who worked for HDRA on the progress of current projects and the organization generally. This was also an opportunity for members of staff to offer suggestions and to ask questions about the running of HDRA and its finances. Summing up our management style in a nutshell, I suppose you could say that we would come up with ideas, listen to the staff, prepare a plan, devise an annual budget, put it before the Council and then let people get on with the job.

To Lawrence, nothing had been more important than scientific research into organic growing. It was at the centre of his life, so when we had begun planning what would happen at Ryton he was actively involved in the discussions about the various field trials that were about to take place in the Research Field – a four-acre block to the south of the main demonstration areas. Dr Bill Blyth, by then Vice Chairman, and other scientifically qualified members of the HDRA Council, including entomologist Dr Peggy Ellis, who specialized in biological pest control, were part of a scientific sub-group that oversaw the trials programme. This also included staff from nearby Coventry University – the Polytechnic as it was then. At first this was primarily a continuation of the sort of experimental work that had characterized HDRA's time in Essex, such as potato spacing trials, a comparison of the performance of different brands of grow-bags, investigations into non-chemical methods of weed control and the like. But with so much more land available – over twice the acreage that we had at Bocking –

new opportunities were opening up. In particular, we could now utilize HDRA's expertise to help the growing band of commercial organic vegetable producers who were sorely in need of technical assistance – something both Jackie and I were particularly keen on.

Organic vegetables are so commonplace these days that it hardly seems credible that as little as 30 years ago you would have found it almost impossible to buy a bag of organic carrots. Yet, at the end of the 1970s, only a handful of health food shops stocked organically grown produce and, to be frank, a lot of it was of fairly dubious quality. Limp lettuces, shrivelled spinach and careworn carrots were all too common – the result of a lack of professionalism, an erratic supply chain, inadequate storage and an understandable unwillingness on the part of retailers to throw away unsold vegetables that had lost their freshness. Many growers and shopkeepers had followed their hearts into a business that was new to them, so however hardworking they might have been, their inexperience sometimes showed. If organic produce was going to take off, then growers and retailers needed to 'up their game'.

The impetus had come in 1980, when one such group of young vegetable growers living in West Wales, most of whom had only settled there during the 'back to the land' exodus in the 1970s, formed the Organic Growers Association (OGA). Their de-facto leader was Peter Segger, who farmed a few acres outside Lampeter and, on his own admission, had known next to nothing about growing vegetables when he had started. He once told me that his first crop of carrots had been sown with a packet of seeds in one hand and a copy of Lawrence's *Grow Your Own Fruit and Vegetables* in the other! At the first National Conference of Organic Growers, held in January 1980 at Cirencester Agriculture College, which he organized along with ex-Bocking student Charlie Wacher and others, he made a powerful plea for greater professionalism, insisting that growers must improve the quality of their fresh produce and how it was packed, marketed and distributed.

This message became even more relevant when, in 1986, the supermarket chains J Sainsbury, Safeway and Waitrose dipped a tentative toe into organic waters, trialling a limited range of fresh vegetables at a select group of stores. Overnight, organic growers suddenly found themselves on the receiving end of the same demanding product specifications to which the supermarkets subjected their conventional producers. They were told to grow vegetables that were all alike in shape and colour to fit snugly into their pre-formed plastic packaging. It was a tall order, not least because most of the vegetable seed varieties then available commercially had been developed for chemical growers and they were bred to respond specifically to chemical fertilizers and pesticides. Whether these varieties would be suitable for growing organically was an open question. And it wasn't just an academic query – livelihoods depended on it. If a crop failed to meet the grade, super-market buyers would undoubtedly reject it, potentially plunging the organic grower into financial difficulties.

In July 1987 Dr Margi Lennartsson, a dynamic and talented young Swedish scientist with a passion for organic horticulture, who had recently completed her postgraduate studies at London University's Wye College, was appointed to lead HDRA's new research depart-ment. Among the first trials she instigated was one that compared different varieties of leeks, lettuces, Chinese cabbages and Brussels sprouts to discover which grew best under organic conditions. It was exactly the sort of information that growers needed. The work was a collaboration with the National Institute for Agricultural Botany (NIAB) and it was to become a lasting and fruitful partnership. As we'd anticipated, striking differences emerged among the varieties, some performing dismally without their chemical props. At the end of the season, our results, along with those from other NIAB test sites across the country, were presented at an Open Day for commercial growers at Ryton, setting a successful pattern for many years to come.

Also in July 1987, around the time Margi was starting her new job, the government announced the setting up of the United Kingdom Register of Organic Food Standards (UKROFS) to oversee the intro-duction of a Europe-wide regulation covering commercial organic crop production. This marked the end of HDRA's long involvement in setting organic food standards – an involvement that had begun in the late-1960s, when Lawrence Hills had been compiling *The Wholefood*

Finder, a consumer guide to shops selling organic wholefoods. His main concern then, apart from a dearth of entries, was to decide who qualified for insertion. Mary Langman, who, with financial support from Lord Kitchener, had opened Wholefood of Baker Street, the first store in London to carry a reasonable range of organic food, was facing a similar problem. In the absence of formal organic standards, who was to say what was organic and what wasn't? So Mary had come up with the first draft of a proposed definition, which she circulated to people within the Soil Association, to Lawrence and to other interested parties. Progress in turning this into a formal set of rules agreed by all concerned was slow, and it took until 1973 to publish the first British organic food standards, under the aegis of the Soil Association, and to see food carrying its distinctive logo appearing in the shops.

By 1980 a different set of organic standards was in operation, run by Organic Farmers & Growers Ltd (OF&G). David Stickland, its Director, had resigned from editing the Soil Association's magazine to set up OF&G as a marketing co-operative, selling organic cereals produced by his, mostly, East Anglian-based arable farmer members – a significant number of whom used animal manure obtained from non-organic sources. Many of us in the organic movement were opposed to using 'muck' from intensive livestock units on organic farms and we were also alarmed that the OF&G standards permitted other chemical inputs that were disallowed under the Soil Association's rules.

This was not just an esoteric dispute. Trading Standards Officers needed to know exactly what organic food was, and how it was produced, in order to protect consumers from any unscrupulous traders tempted to pass off conventionally produced food as the real thing. If the organic bodies couldn't agree on a definition, they said, how could they be expected to protect bona fide traders? It also worried officials at the Ministry of Agriculture, Fisheries and Food (MAFF), who let it be known that the organic movement should cease its continual squabbling, pointing out that a European regulation governing organic production was in the offing and that they required a draft they could take to Brussels that represented the British position. This concentrated minds wonderfully and led to the formation of the British Organic Standards Committee (BOSC), which had the job of devising a unified set of organic standards that could be applied nationwide.

Lawrence and I had both sat on the Committee, although later on, Pauline Pears often took Lawrence's place. Although HDRA was not directly involved in commercial organic production, it carried out scientific research to improve it and, in any case, the same fundamental principles applied, whatever the scale of production. We were also looking after the interests of our 6,000 members, many of whom bought organic food, so I suppose you could say that we were also an organic consumer organization. We therefore had to ensure that standards were not compromised by overtly commercial interests.

Our insistence on high standards was shared by our closest ally, the Soil Association, which was represented at the time by its General Secretary, Dick Widdowson, and we were both in general opposition to many of the views expressed by David Stickland. There were also other individuals sitting around the table, each of whom represented different strands of the organic movement and thought along the same lines as HDRA and the Soil Association. Two of the most vocal were Peter Segger, in his capacity as Chairman of the OGA, and Lawrence Woodward, Director of Elm Farm Research Centre (EFRC). Elm Farm had only come into being a short time before and was based on an organic dairy farm near Newbury, Berkshire. It was privately funded by David Astor, the wealthy former editor of *The Observer* newspaper, and had close links with the Institute of Biological Husbandry (FiBL) at Oberwil in Switzerland, which had been founded in 1973 and which, under its charismatic Director Dr Hardy Vogtmann, had already established an enviable reputation for its trialling work with different methods of organic cultivation and their effect on food quality. Hardy was also a trustee of EFRC and under Lawrence's outspoken and energetic leadership, Elm Farm soon became the undisputed leader of organic agricultural research in the UK.

Mary Langman was there too, representing the International Federation of Organic Agricultural Movements (IFOAM), an organization with which she had been actively involved since its formation

at Versailles, France, in 1972; she was therefore able to provide a perspective on what was going on in mainland Europe. Many European
organic farmers subscribed to the ideas of Rudolf Steiner and produced
crops and livestock to the biodynamic standard known as 'Demeter'.
There were only a few biodynamic farms in England, however, along
with a notable teaching institute at Forest Row in Sussex, and their
viewpoint was tenaciously advanced by David Clements, the redoubt-
able UK secretary of the Biodynamic Agricultural Association (BAA).

Joanne Bower represented the Farm and Food Society (FAFS) – a
body she had set up herself to campaign for the more humane treatment of farm animals. Organic farming, Joanne reasoned, was likely to
provide the highest welfare standards for livestock and she was there to
see that it did!

David Stickland had also set up the now defunct International
Institute of Biological Husbandry (IIBH) and Dr David Hodges
and Dr Tony Scofield, two scientists from Wye College, were its
representatives.

Although the issue that divided the Committee most of all was
whether to allow organic farmers to use manure from non-organic and
factory farms, there was no shortage of other contentious subjects.
What should our position be on soluble, potassium-rich rock-based
fertilizers, like Chilean potash nitrate, or kainit, for example? Both
were natural products mined from the earth, but their mode of action
was little different from that of artificial fertilizers. Mary informed us
that European farmers were adamant about their inclusion in their
standards, in contrast to the prevailing British view, which was to keep
them out.

There was also heated debate over pesticides. David Stickland
advanced the case for including a number of new synthetic pesticides
that he said were more environmentally friendly than the limited range
of 'natural' products then in use by organic farmers and growers. Here
we were on weaker ground, for as you've already read, copper fungicides and insecticides, such as derris, are not without their adverse side
effects. When Jackie and I discussed the issue of pesticides at home,
we didn't have any doubts. To us, any use of pesticides, even so-called

'safe' ones, was an admission of failure. Back at the meeting, however, it was agreed that organic producers should be allowed to use naturally derived sprays as a last resort. And rather than increase the number of permissible products, as suggested by David, the Committee decided that it would be far better if it were decreased instead.

Nicotine was one spray that stood out for discussion. It's a powerful chemical, effective against many pests, and is completely non-persistent. But it kills indiscriminately, decimating ladybirds and other beneficial creatures. Lawrence had used it at Bocking for many years, making it up from 'fag ends' scrounged from the local pub. He steeped them in water overnight and I can tell you that the resulting smell was disgusting. You had to take great care not to spill any of the liquid onto your hands, because nicotine is highly toxic and can be absorbed through the skin. It was a downright nasty substance that had no place in organic cultivation – a view with which the Committee concurred. So, thankfully, nicotine was given its marching orders.

By the spring of 1983 sufficient agreement had been reached for BOSC to publish its four-page *Production Standards for Organic Produce*, and from 1987 onwards this was further refined through the UKROFS Committee and adopted by MAFF as the British negotiating position at Brussels. As it happens, the European regulation took far more time to materialize than anyone expected, as member states vied with each other to ensure that the end result met with their approval. It had been a struggle in Britain trying to reach agreement with only two competing standards, so you can imagine the difficulties when the whole of Europe was given its say – in France alone there were ten different organic certifying bodies, each with its own set of standards.

Jackie and I remember this time as one of great trepidation. Until now the organic movement had been relatively small and self-contained – on continental Europe, as well as in Britain. In the main, it had been driven by idealists, who advocated organic farming because of its environmental and health benefits, rather than as a way of making money. Now that governments were involved, many of us thought that standards would be reduced to the lowest common denominator. So it was a huge relief to find that principles hadn't been compromised when the European regulation finally appeared in 1991. In retrospect, this can probably be put down to the absence of lobbying by supermarkets, food processors and representatives of industrialized farming – almost certainly because organic food represented such a tiny part of the market that they didn't think it was worth the effort. Trouble on that score would come later on, especially in the USA, when organic food became a force to be reckoned with.

Meanwhile, back at Ryton, we had other worries too. The state of the British economy, which in 1990 had been sufficiently rocky to torpedo Brogdale's fundraising efforts, continued its downhill slide into 1991 and persisted throughout the year. The weather had been abysmal that summer, and both visitor numbers and revenue were down substantially. HDRA's cash reserves – which were never great at the best of times – were at rock bottom and, to make matters worse, we were about to start work on a major building project to erect a conference and education centre, which Jackie felt was desperately needed. We had secured a substantial grant towards half the cost and Jackie had also obtained £50,000 worth of sponsorship in the form of building materials – bricks, tiles and concrete – from a company that had its national headquarters nearby. Despite this support, with inflation running at over 10 per cent, any extra pressure on HDRA's finances was the last thing we wanted. In the run-up to Christmas, much to our dismay, we were forced to lose a fifth of the staff, although judging by the fate of a great many other businesses in Britain, things could have been a lot worse.

We had discussed HDRA's deteriorating financial position at the previous Council meeting (the organization had changed its constitution when it moved to Ryton and members of the Committee, which was renamed the Council, were now elected from within the ranks of HDRA's members). Jackie and I always attended in a non-voting, reporting capacity. Our relationship with Council members was built on trust, and we invariably found meetings to be supporting and encouraging occasions. The Council was no pussycat, and members would expect to be given well-thought-out plans before agreeing to our proposals. But under the benevolent and wise chairmanship, first of Lord Kitchener until 1991, and thereafter Dr Bill Blyth, the Council never once failed to back us. Nor did its members ever attempt to involve themselves in day-to-day management – which in my view is the kiss of death for any organization. Over the years we got to speak to quite a few charity Chief Executives, many of whom, unlike us, had ruling bodies that insisted on micro-managing their affairs. Not surprisingly, they were extremely envious of the light-handed approach taken by HDRA. All I can say is that it worked for us, and was one of the main reasons why the organization was able to achieve so much.

At the following HDRA Council meeting, held at the end of January 1992, we reappraised them of the financial situation, which was so gloomy that we even offered to remortgage our house to provide additional funds. Bill Blyth wouldn't hear of it, but we insisted on taking a voluntary pay cut nevertheless, and implemented a pay freeze for the rest of the staff, which remained in force for the remainder of the year.

At this time of unremitting gloom the café, one of Jackie's responsibilities, was the only good news. Its reputation had carried all before it, and turnover had steadily increased throughout the recession. Although she had already made some improvements to the facilities, the kitchen was now wholly inadequate for the demands placed on it. Most of the equipment was in imminent danger of packing up, and at peak times the queues were horrendous. This was annoying enough for customers in fine weather, but when it rained they got soaked. The only realistic solution was to build a bigger restaurant.

In retrospect, even thinking about spending money we didn't have, in the middle of the worst time for business since the 1930s, looks like the height of folly, but at the time it seemed our only option. It was made possible by the Business Expansion Scheme – a new tax break that had been rushed out by the government in an effort to staunch the haemorrhaging of British industry. It was skilfully exploited on HDRA's behalf by Graham Dodd, its Honorary Treasurer. Jackie wrote a letter to potential investors explaining the scheme and within a matter of months the £150,000 needed to complete the conference and education centre, and build and equip a new kitchen and restaurant had been raised.

Throughout 1992 the gardens echoed to the sound of intense building activity, and the conference centre was completed by early July, just in time to receive The Prince of Wales on his second visit to Ryton to perform the opening ceremony. Delighted as we were with this royal occasion, there was no time to relax, because a few days later we hosted Britain's first National Organic Food and Wine Fair, a natural development of the annual Organic Wine Fairs, which we had been holding at Ryton each July since 1988. The fairs had been the joint idea of Jackie and Jerry Lockspeiser, the founders of Vinceremos Wines Ltd, the company that supplied the wines sold in the Ryton shop and café. It was conceived as a way of bringing organic wines to the attention of the public and the wine trade, and had been a great success from the outset. Tim Atkins, writing in *The Guardian*, described the event as 'combining the best elements of a folk festival, an English country fete and a boozy picnic, the fair is a splendid reminder that drinking wine is supposed to be enjoyable.'

In 1989, Jackie had obtained substantial sponsorship from Safeway (the supermarket chain that at the time was the most pro-organic of the multiple retailers), which continued for a further five years. The wine fair in 1991 had been hugely popular, in spite of the recession, and Sir Alistair Grant, Safeway's Chairman, had put in an appearance. That year, in order to inspire organic wine producers to improve the quality of their wines even more, we had also decided to hold an Organic Wine Challenge, presided over by Robert Joseph, editor of *Wine Magazine*, in which the country's top wine experts conducted blind tastings and scored the wines accordingly. Jonathon Porritt, the UK's best-known environmentalist, presented the winning trophy to Millton Vineyard, a small company from New Zealand that made an outstanding white wine.

By 1992 the event had become such a fixture that we could more-or-less guarantee several thousand visitors, but many of the organic food companies had suffered badly as organic sales across the country had plummeted in the recession and they were finding any sort of promotional activities difficult to afford. The public at large was very worried about bovine spongiform encephalopathy (BSE) at the time, so the big draw that year was organic meat, which was being promoted as a safe alternative by its producers.

Bovine spongiform encephalopathy had first been detected in 1984 on a dairy farm in Sussex, where a previously unknown and mysterious condition that damaged the central nervous system had suddenly appeared in one of the cows. The poor beast had developed head tremors and a total loss of co-ordination. The disease had spread slowly at first but then accelerated, peaking in 1992, by which time three cattle in every thousand were affected, despite the fact that in 1989 the government had put a stop to the inclusion of offal in cattle feed, believing it to be the source of the infection. British beef was banned from Europe and many farmers faced ruin.

A far bigger worry was whether the disease could be transmitted to humans – something the government of the day strenuously denied. However, in 1995 MAFF was forced to admit the existence of a link between BSE and new-variant CJD (Creutzfeldt-Jakob disease), a devastating and fatal new disease affecting the human brain. One hundred and fifty people in the UK have since died from it but, as the incubation period can last for many years, we have no way of knowing if this is the end of the story or just the beginning. What is not in any doubt, however, is the four billion pounds of public money that went up in the smoke of nine million incinerated cattle.

As far as organic meat was concerned, the Soil Association standards had banned offal from organic livestock feed for cattle and sheep in 1983, before the first case of BSE had emerged. However, organic farms had not escaped entirely unscathed, although only conventionally reared stock, brought in from outside, were affected. Out of the 180,000 officially recorded incidents of BSE, none had ever been detected in organic cattle that had been raised organically from birth.

The public's confidence in the safety of food was severely dented by the BSE debacle. It was one crisis too many after a decade of worrying reports about issues such as pesticide residues in food and salmonella-infected eggs. All these problems had finally got people thinking

e food they ate and how it was produced, and they
od they could trust. As a result, from the mid-1990s,
sales started to take off. Our Organic Food and Wine Fairs
ational focus for organic products on sale at the time. On the
ny summer weekend of the fair in July 1992, thousands of visitors
streamed into the marquees to taste and buy the wonderful range of
organic produce temptingly laid out before them. A corner had been
turned, and organic food was at last about to break out from its niche
status. As part of this nascency Jackie and I were co-authors, with
David Mabey, of a bestselling book called *Thorsons Organic Consumer
Guide*. Jackie went on to write a second volume, *Thorsons Organic Wine
Guide*, with Jerry Lockspeiser.

This time was a turning point in another way too. A couple of
months later, as interest rates briefly reached the dizzy heights of 15 per
cent, sending a shiver down the spine of anyone with a mortgage, the
government finally capitulated and decoupled sterling from the European Exchange Rate Mechanism, in preparation for the introduction
of the euro. It had been a disastrous economic flirtation with the proposed new European currency but, although at the time Britain
appeared to be on its knees, it did in fact mark the turning point in the
economic fortunes of the country.

Things started to pick up almost at once, and by April 1993 the
recession was officially declared over. Three months later, in early
July, Jackie finally moved the staff into the new restaurant. Now, thank
goodness, it could accommodate 80 customers indoors, with another
60 or so outside on the patio and in the permanent marquee. It was
four times bigger than our original café and the chefs had a much
larger kitchen. With supplies of organic meat becoming more readily
available, we also took the decision to put it on the menu, alongside
our vegetarian and vegan dishes. Although we finally had great facilities, what we didn't have was access to chefs who knew how to cook
with organic wholefoods. When Jackie had interviewed kitchen staff
she had explained why we only used organic ingredients, why we used
wholemeal flour and brown rice and why we didn't peel potatoes or
store them in water, ready for use the following day. She was invariably

met with looks of blank incomprehension. The concept of maximizing freshness, taste and vitamin content by preparing and cooking vegetables to order, appeared to be completely alien to most chefs, who seemed more at home with a microwave.

Another recurring problem was the cost of ingredients. Being all-organic they were more expensive and, due to the non-existence of other fully organic restaurants, catering-scale packs were unobtainable. Jackie's insistence on raw ingredients, instead of pre-prepared products, also upped our labour costs. This should have been reflected in higher prices to our customers, but because we didn't want to exclude anyone from eating on grounds of cost, we accepted lower margins instead. So, although business and turnover in the new restaurant shot up, it didn't make as much profit as it could have done. Jackie saw the restaurant very much as a showcase for healthy eating and organic food, and balanced the lower income by the substantial profit made by the shop, so the retailing and catering side of our work, taken as a whole, still contributed significantly to the charity's funds.

Not only was organic food everywhere more expensive, it was also extremely difficult to source locally – something that we felt strongly we should do. Because we were concerned about wasting the world's finite fuel resources, we didn't want to import organic vegetables that could easily be grown in this country. In 1994 the government also came to terms with the fact that most of the organic food consumed in Britain came from abroad, where financial support for producers was substantially more generous. We were pleased, therefore, when an Organic Aid Scheme was introduced that would help farmers through the crucial first two years of 'conversion'. During this period their crop yields fell, as chemicals were withdrawn but the land hadn't had time to restore to organic health. To make matters worse, farmers couldn't sell their 'in-conversion' produce as fully organic, so they couldn't charge more. Before the Organic Aid Scheme they just had to take the financial 'hit' on the chin.

MAFF also put more money into organic farming research, though the total still only represented less than a paltry 1 per cent of the overall agricultural research budget (a proportion that is little different today). Some of this extra money was allotted to horticulture, and Margi Lennartsson and I duly made the most of what was on offer.

As well as carrying out the vegetable variety trials I've already mentioned, our other main avenue of research at that time involved selecting possible plant species to extend the season for sowing over-wintering green manures. MAFF saw that this could benefit commercial growers (as it would gardeners) and, in 1991, awarded HDRA its first publicly funded research contract in its own right. Many more were to follow.

The previous year, the horticultural industry's use of peat, which had been largely responsible for the wanton destruction of Britain's last few remaining lowland peat bogs, had caused an outcry, and a campaigning group made up of ten conservation bodies was formed to counter it. HDRA joined the alliance and provided technical assistance, publishing a giveaway leaflet, *Alternatives to Peat*, while Margi and her research team began work formulating new seed and potting 'composts' made from such diverse materials as brewery waste, chipped bark, and composted 'green waste' from local authorities. Although stimulating, it was difficult work, not least because, unlike peat (which is virtually inert, and acts as a carrier for chemical fertilizers), most of the alternatives contained variable amounts of plant nutrients, which differed significantly from batch to batch, making it extremely hard to produce the uniform product demanded by professional growers. And whereas growing media designed for chemical-using growers could be made with precise amounts of artificially derived nitrogen and other elements, organic growing media relied for their nutrient sources on natural products like dried blood, which themselves varied in nutrient quantity and availability. Not surprisingly, Margi's team met with quite a few failures, but by the mid-1990s it had succeeded, mostly using coir, the dust residue from coconut processing, as the base of choice. It was not ideal, however, because of the environmental costs associated with shipping it all the way from Sri Lanka. With this invaluable experience gained, however, the research department would go on to become highly skilled, and respected, in the world of recyclables.

During this period, the UK branch of the International Wool Secretariat (IWS) approached us looking for novel ideas for using wool, the price of fleeces having fallen dramatically in recent years. Over lunch, Jackie was able to come up with several suggestions, including hanging-basket liners and a weed-suppressing mulch – both of which have since been developed – and Margi was asked to look into it as a possible basis for a potting compost.

By 1987, the tenth anniversary of the founding of the research department, around 30 scientists were working on more than 20 separate research topics, the majority of them funded by MAFF, that dealt with a wide spectrum of subjects, from the econo-mics of commercial organic horticultural production to the storage of organic crops. Most projects involved collaboration with one or more other institutions – usually Elm Farm, or the government-run vegetable research station, HRI Wellesbourne, nearby, where we ran a 30-acre experimental commercial vegetable-production unit on their behalf. At that time HDRA, either directly or indirectly, was a partner in more organic research projects than any other academic or research institute in the UK.

We had also become heavily involved with local authorities, advising them on all aspects of composting – from encouraging more home composting to helping to promote best practice procedures for the large-scale conversion of putrescible household and garden waste into a useful compost end-product, as an alternative to incineration or burying it in landfill. The education centre at Ryton was in regular use as specialist conferences, aimed at commercial growers and other professionals, were held by us, and by outside organizations, to disseminate research results. It was also routinely used to host practical organic gardening and food courses for amateur gardeners.

During the 1980s, through many different areas of its work – the Food and Wine Fairs, the shop and café, the conference centre, the publication of books, the many television and radio interviews and articles in the press, and the scientific research – HDRA had helped to promote organic food, to improve its quality and to protect organic consumers in a significant way.

Reflecting on these times in his book *Highgrove: Portrait of an Estate,* co-written by The Prince of Wales and published in 1993, Charles Clover commented:

> Looking back on the 1980s ... 'organic' lost its cranky associations. No one can say how much of this was the hard work of the talented populists at the HDRA, how much a result of The Prince of Wales's interest in organic methods and how much the increasingly environmental mood of the times. What can be said is that it was the gardeners who made the organic movement popular.

Chapter Twelve

THIRD WORLD GROWING

THE AGRICULTURAL POLICIES adopted by most Western governments since the end of the Second World War have enshrined the
principle of 'cheap food' for all, and for my generation food has been
plentiful and relatively inexpensive. But is all that about to change?
The last few years have witnessed eye-watering increases in food prices
due to a combination of events, including a general expansion of
population, rising global demand from newly industrialized countries
such as India and China, a sequence of poor harvests and vast areas
of land being taken out of production to grow biofuels. At the same
time, high fuel costs, linked to the price of oil, which has doubled,
have left many people on low incomes with the unwelcome decision
of whether to heat or eat – an unenviable situation, especially for
the elderly.

Unfortunately it's a choice that's all too familiar to people living
in the Third World. General research statistics, representing the
Third World as a whole, indicate that one in every three children is
malnourished and around 850 million people exist in a precarious
state of perpetual hunger. The agricultural model that has kept the
populations of the West well fed for so long is clearly failing to deliver
food for all – although, to be fair, this has as much to do with global
poverty, war and corruption as it has with the failings of farmers.

Sufficient food does exist, for the present at any rate, but the problem is that many people in the Third World simply cannot afford to buy it. However, it's an inescapable fact that increases in food production have failed to keep pace with the growth of human numbers, which rise by more than 70 million every year – over 90 per cent of them in the Third World. Global food shortages are, therefore, understandable.

Until the late-1990s it had appeared that the spectacular improvements in agricultural productivity in the West since the Second World War would always be able to keep pace with the growth of population. This new technology, which was based around high-yielding varieties of rice and wheat, chemical fertilizers and pesticides, was exported to many parts of the Third World (with the significant exception of Africa), in the form of the so-called 'Green Revolution'. As a result, from the 1950s onwards there was a doubling and tripling of crop yields. Yet in spite of all this plenty, conditions for the vast majority of small peasant farmers actually got worse. Unable to afford the new miracle seeds, and the fertilizers and pesticides that were needed to grow them successfully, they were bought out by larger farmers and agricultural corporations, who were able to buy the tractors and other heavy machinery that came with intensive methods of cultivation, doing away with the need for labour. Landless, and without any prospect of work, a bleak future beckoned for the dispossessed in the swollen slums of the big cities.

By the mid-1970s, the crop yields of the Green Revolution strains of cereals, which had been planted across the globe, continued their dizzying climb, and it must have seemed a resounding vindication of the new technology. But problems associated with it were starting to accumulate too. As in the West, the pests and diseases of the Third World soon developed immunity to the new pesticides and the artificially fed soils that had been deprived of manure began to degrade. Also, the watercourses became polluted with the chemical run-off from fields and, as a result, farmers had to compensate for declining soil fertility and heavier pest infestations by applying even more fertilizers and pesticides. And because Green Revolution varieties require more water than traditional seeds – typically three times the amount – their drinking-water supplies were adversely affected by the extra irrigation needed. In the Indian state of Punjab, for example, often cited as the Green Revolution's greatest success, the water table dropped alarmingly, and many boreholes had to be abandoned.

Fifty years on, the situation is desperate for many previously successful Third World farmers. Each year they spend more on fertilizers and sprays, but with resulting static or falling harvests, their income drops. In 2005 the Punjab State Council for Science and Technology warned that farm incomes were insufficient for a decent living, and it commented ominously that if this were allowed to continue it could foster outrage, social tension and political instability. What actually happened was far worse, because many debt-ridden small farmers committed suicide – and to this day, every 30 minutes a farmer in India takes his own life. It is now abundantly clear that the astonishing increases in food production brought by the Green Revolution in the last century were achieved at an unacceptable cost to social stability and the environment, and that unless policies radically change, colossal areas of land will have to be abandoned.

Elsewhere in the Third World, in places that the Green Revolution passed by, the environment is also under threat from different yet equally unsustainable farming practices. The fate of the all-too-many attempts to farm in the tropics is depressingly familiar. Forests are chopped down and burned to provide land for agriculture. Crops thrive initially, on the fertility released by the burnt vegetation, but yields quickly tumble, and before long the soil becomes worked out. At this point people then pack up and leave, to begin laying waste to the land elsewhere. This type of shifting, or 'slash and burn', agriculture only works when the number of farmers involved is small and they are relatively scattered, and there is a plentiful supply of virgin forest. In this situation, after they have moved on, the forest gradually recovers, trees colonize the bare ground and the soil slowly heals. Decades later, when the people return, the land will again be capable of providing them with food. Unfortunately, population pressures now force people back onto land before it has had time to recover fully, and they remain on it longer than it can properly sustain them. More and more trees are sacrificed to provide fuel for heating and cooking. The result is catastrophic. With the protective green canopy gone, the naked land is at the mercy of fierce tropical downpours, and the precious topsoil is washed away each time it rains. Logging companies and large scale agri-industrialists, who clear land to make way for plantation crops, exact an even greater toll on tropical forests, leaving behind only worthless scrub, which quickly turns to desert. Each day more than 200,000 acres of tropical forest are destroyed, and if this continues at the same rate, over three quarters of what remains will have gone by 2020.

But it's not just forests that suffer at the hands of humans. Vast tracts of grassland are stripped of vegetation as nomadic people graze their cattle and goats, leaving behind bare soil vulnerable to wind-blown erosion. In the Sahel, a vast swathe of sub-Saharan Africa straddling the continent, from Ethiopia in the east to Senegal in the west, land is being lost on a 3,000-mile front, as the desert advances remorselessly at over five miles a year. The problem, yet again, is that there are now too many people and not enough land for this traditional way of life to be sustainable.

★　　★　　★

Lawrence Hills had always been well aware and deeply concerned about what was happening in the Third World and this gave HDRA a global outlook. After all, the principles of organic growing are the same for Third World farmers as they are for farmers and gardeners in the West. As I've mentioned, Lawrence had stated, 'I don't want to die rich, I only want to change the world.' This philosophy had chimed in perfectly with our own idealism of trying to make a difference for the common good and it was one of the main reasons we'd decided to work with him.

During the 1950s and 1960s Lawrence had pinned his hopes on comfrey as a new high-protein food crop, picking up on Henry Doubleday's belief that it would provide cheap and nutritious sustenance for humankind. He persuaded growers in Africa to try it, and remarkable yields had been achieved, but unfortunately they found that the crop needed more water than the thirsty continent could spare, so it was eventually dropped in the early-1970s. Then, as an alternative attempt to help, Lawrence turned his attention to researching ways of restoring land in the tropics that had been degraded by deforestation and over-grazing. This, he believed, was one of the greatest challenges facing humanity. What interested him was whether certain trees, those that appeared to be able to survive on virtually no water, could be the key to reclaiming deserts. Lawrence was unable to do much of a practical nature about this until 1976 when, on his round-the-world trip, he stopped off in California and Mexico to take a look at some desert-living trees that the locals called mesquites (with the scientific name *Prosopis*).

There are around 45 species of *Prosopis* in the world, all of them very similar. The timber is hard and dense, like ebony, making it ideal for construction and furniture and for burning as firewood. Leaves and branches provide fodder for goats, and the large seed pods, which taste of caramel and have a pleasant, nutty texture, can be eaten by humans and livestock. Most originate in the Americas, but a few species are native to Africa and southwest Asia. Like peas and other leguminous plants, their roots co-exist with beneficial bacteria, which provide the trees with a regular supply of nitrogen. What makes *Prosopis* such an extra-special tree, however, is its ability to withstand drought. Its extensive rooting system penetrates up to 100 feet in search of water; above ground, the trees absorb moisture through their foliage. When months can go by without any rain, its ability to exploit the dew that condenses on the leaves is a powerful tool for survival.

On his return to Essex, Lawrence began to correspond with experts from around the world in an effort to seek out other trees with drought-resisting capabilities. One such example is *Gleditsia triacanthos*, or the honey locust. It has sweet, edible pods and is frequently grown as an ornamental tree in British gardens. Another is *Ceratonia siliqua*, the carob, a desert-living species found throughout the Mediterranean and Middle East, which, confusingly, is also known as the honey locust. Then there are fodder-producing shrubs belonging to the *Atriplex* family, many of which can go for long periods without water and survive on land that has been contaminated by salt.

Lawrence was particularly intrigued by the almost heretical suggestion that certain desert plant species might be capable of 'reverse transpiration'. It is universally recognized that transpiration occurs by water in the soil travelling upwards through the plant and evaporating through the pores in the leaves. The idea that water might flow the other way would seem inconceivable. Could these desert plants really take in water through their leaves and then pump it out into the soil through their roots, to gain access to soluble nutrients, or simply to use later? If so, that same water could theoretically be exploited by food plants growing nearby. The concept of trees and food crops growing in harmony was exciting, and Lawrence was anxious to explore its possibilities. Writing in the HDRA newsletter, therefore, he appealed for funds to investigate 'Leaves that Drink'. Perhaps members thought that the work was insufficiently practical because, whatever the reason, he only received enough money to pay for a couple of brief studies. On those slender resources, he continued to investigate the subject of drought-resistant trees throughout the late-1970s and early-1980s as best he could. Then, in December 1984, Africa was thrust into the media spotlight as the world woke up to the humanitarian catastrophe unfolding in Ethiopia. Thousands of men, women and children appeared before cameras in situations of acute distress as the drought that had gripped the Sahel region for almost 20 years extracted its grim toll. Unburied corpses lay all around – silent witnesses who touched our hearts. Bob Geldof captured the public's urge to do something to relieve the awful suffering – his song *Do They Know It's Christmas?* sold by the million, raising much-needed funds for famine relief.

Seizing his opportunity, Lawrence wrote to the press, pleading for a long-term solution to Africa's crisis, as well as emergency relief, and proposing that a proportion of the donated funds should go to research into reclaiming the desert. One of Britain's national newspapers, the *Daily Express*, picked up the story and asked Geldof to comment. He was unimpressed, commenting tartly, 'If I give £50,000 to research that means 50,000 starving people go without food for a month.' But Lawrence's appeal didn't fall entirely on deaf ears. Barbara Lowcock, an *Express* reader living in Bridport, Dorset, and a keen knitting fan, wrote in offering to donate the income from the sale of her teddy bear pattern to Lawrence's 'Drought Defeaters Fund'. It was just the sort of thing to appeal to the tabloid, which ran a full-length feature on the retired nurse. Cheques were soon pouring in and, with nearly £1,000 in the bank, a smiling image of Lawrence clutching two teddies, and a report of his campaign, appeared in the members' magazine. At which point HDRA's Third World research was given an astonishing boost.

In the past we had been the grateful recipients of the occasional large cheque from the Sunderland Trust, a charity run by the artist Leslie Marr who, at the time, lived with his wife on the Isle of Arran in Scotland. Leslie had inherited a considerable fortune from his grandfather, but rather than spending it on himself and his family, he'd chosen to give it all away. When he read about the Drought Defeaters project in the newsletter he made the momentous decision to donate all the Trust's income to HDRA, setting in train a close collaboration that was to last for more than 20 years, with his support for our overseas work totalling over half a million pounds.

At that time we were in the middle of relocating the organization to Ryton, where we soon established a fruitful partnership with nearby Coventry University. Two members of the Department of Biological Sciences at the university were to have a significant influence on HDRA's future. One was Dr Phil Harris, a lecturer in plant science, whose responsibilities included devising research topics for students in the final year of their degrees, and the other was Dr Bill Bourne, his boss. Both were interested in our research in the Third World and, as a result, Bill made the necessary administrative arrangements that enabled Phil to join us at Ryton as HDRA's Third World Projects Co-ordinator on a year's secondment, using the Drought Defeaters work as a rich seam of potential projects for his students. Little did we realize then that Phil would stay with us for almost a decade.

Leslie's funding, coupled with Phil's initiative and drive, brought immediate results. Meanwhile, at Durham University, botany lecturer

Dr Phil Gates, assisted by a Coventry student, began testing a wide range of pot-grown desert trees for signs of water uptake through their leaves. Scientists in Chile had claimed that *Prosopis tamarugo*, which is able to survive on less than a tenth of an inch of rainfall a year in the Atacama Desert – the driest place in the world – releases water from its roots into the soil during the cold nights and re-absorbs it, along with mineral salts, the next day. If they were correct, this would be the first firm evidence for the phenomenon of reverse transpiration in *Prosopis*.

In Coventry, Phil had constructed an aluminium greenhouse on the roof of one of the polytechnic's tower blocks and filled it with a small forest of young *Prosopis* seedlings to see if they could be 'micro-propagated' – a way of reproducing plants swiftly, in a test-tube. From observations in the wild, he knew that there were huge differences between trees of the same species – some grew as short, bushy shrubs, while others developed into tall, straight trees. Being able to select, and then quickly multiply, those with the most desirable traits, was a top priority. However, there's only so much that can be learned from laboratory research. The acid test occurs out in the field, where the vagaries of nature can overturn the best-laid plans, so we needed our own patch of arid land. And in 1987 this fell into place too, as a result of collaboration with the government of the Cape Verde islands, which allowed us access to a field station par excellence.

Lying 400 miles off the coast of West Africa and 1,000 miles south-west of the Canaries are the nine small, inhabited, mountainous islands that make up the territory of Cape Verde, with a total area roughly the size of Cornwall. The name, coined by the Portuguese colonists who arrived in 1462, implies that the islands were originally clothed with forests, but 500 years of felling and agricultural exploitation have taken their toll and few trees remain. The islands achieved independence in 1975, and the population, which was mainly descended from Africans and Portuguese, set about trying to repair the environmental damage caused by centuries of neglect. Their task was not helped by a severe and protracted drought, which limited rainfall to less than eight inches a year – much of it falling during a few sharp bursts in the summer. Most of the islands' steep slopes were badly eroded, with few plants being able to tolerate the extreme conditions. It was a perfect situation in which to try out *Prosopis* and other drought-resisting species.

Dr Horatio da Silva, President of the Cape Verde Agricultural Research Institute, had heard about Lawrence's interest in *Prosopis*, and in December 1984 invited him to participate in the islands' research. Lawrence responded by sending him seeds of some of the more promising species, but he had to turn down Dr da Silva's offer due to lack of funds. The Sunderland Trust money changed all that for the better. Phil flew out to Santiago, the largest of the islands, in January 1987, and immediately set about establishing field trials. The next few years were a whirlwind of activity as a succession of HDRA researchers planted tens of thousands of young trees at widely contrasting locations throughout the islands. Only the toughest specimens were exposed to the meagre soils, stinging salt spray and fierce winds of the barren headlands; others were given the luxury of sheltered positions in the valley bottoms, where the risk came from browsing goats rather than nature in the raw. But most plants were destined for the steep mountain sides, where they were placed along contour-hugging rows, in shallow depressions scooped out of the thin and hungry soil, with only a single watering at planting time to see them through the next twelve months without rain.

In spite of an apparent lack of water, whether they were reverse-transpiring or not, the young trees grew strongly under the hot, tropical sun. Seen from the air, the once dull-grey appearance of the slag-hill-like islands was magically transmuted into a pastel shade of olive green. After five years many trees had put on ten feet of growth and, with branches as thick as a man's fist, they were big enough to be harvested for firewood and to provide useful amounts of leaves as fodder for cattle and goats. Moreover, the force of the rainfall, when it came, instead of pounding into the ground and running to waste, taking the soil with it, was softened by the canopy of foliage and directed gently onto the roots below. Best of all, between the rows of trees grew crops of maize and beans, thriving in the shade and shelter they afforded. Only the rocky coastline stubbornly resisted the green invasion, where just the Chilean *Prosopis tamarugo* and the saltbush, *Atriplex*, hung on grimly.

We gradually learned more about the trees in our care and experimented with an ever-greater range of species, grown from seeds sent in by collaborators from around the world. Propagation experiments at Coventry University were also beginning to bear fruit, and the team there became skilled at taking cuttings, opening up the prospect of being able to select the most promising specimens, just as every Cox's Orange Pippin apple tree is ultimately descended from cuttings taken by retired brewer Richard Cox, from the seedling he originally found growing in his garden.

As news of our work spread, other aid and development workers began to request seeds and ask questions. We did what we could to help, but it was not until 1990, when Jackie obtained funding from Comic Relief, and Phil was granted funds from the Overseas Development Administration, that things really began to take off, with the launch of HDRA's 'Trees for Africa' project.

By now we had accumulated seeds of more than 70 desert tree and shrub species – sufficient to plant three million trees. We knew enough about each of them to be able to offer advice on planting, cultivation and aftercare. When someone wrote in giving details of their soil type, geography and climate, and why the trees were needed, we were able to come up with a list of appropriate species and supply the seeds. We contacted development agencies, church groups, agricultural projects and other aid workers throughout Africa, with an offer of free seeds to all. The response was phenomenal. Requests poured in from all corners of the continent, from South Africa to Morocco and from Burundi to Gambia. In a single six-month period, seeds were despatched to 53 projects in 25 countries, including a group in the Ethiopian highlands who received enough seeds for a million trees. With help from Bill Bourne, Phil's sabbatical was hastily extended and more staff were taken on to assist him.

Many of the seeds were sent to agricultural researchers who were keen to develop new methods of integrating trees with crops.

Although a relatively new concept in the tropics, agroforestry, to give it its formal title, has an honourable pedigree here in the UK, where food production, usually involving livestock, has long gone hand in hand with cultivating trees. Pigs scavenging for beechmast in deciduous woodland, sheep grazing under poplars or geese feeding on grass and gulping down windfall apples in traditional orchards, are all examples of agroforestry in action. The practice almost died out during the last century, but with an increase in public concern for the welfare of farm animals, and the shift to outdoor, free-range pig-keeping, it is once again experiencing a resurgence here.

The most popular tropical version of agroforestry is known as 'alley cropping', in which the alleys are strips of land between parallel rows of trees, cultivated to grow crops. The chief role of the trees is to stabilize the soil, particularly on bare hillsides that are vulnerable to erosion, as in Cape Verde. Once the trees are established, crops can then be planted beneath them, safe in the knowledge that the trees will protect them from strong winds, provide shade from the intense sun, and trap rainwater. Some tree species, like *Prosopis*, are multi-purpose. Branches can be cut to provide fuel for heating and cooking, for example, and leaves can be fed to livestock, or else they can be used as mulch around the crop or they can be composted to improve soil fertility. Many species produce edible seeds that can be eaten by live-stock and humans. Dried *Prosopis* pods can even be ground into a sweet, gluten-free and protein-rich flour, low in fat and cholesterol – Africa's very own 'superfood'. Other products derived from trees might include medicines, gums, resins, charcoal or honey. And to this impressive list of benefits you can also add the equally vital contri-bution of ameliorating climate change.

Alley cropping and other tropical agricultural systems involving perennial plants are examples of truly sustainable farming. The crops don't need artificial fertilizers because all the nutrients that the plants require come from green manures, composted animal manure and the nitrogen that is biologically fixed by leguminous trees. As I've explained earlier, the principles of organic cultivation are the same wherever they are put into practice. Soil fertility gradually improves and yields increase. Best of all, the trees are ridiculously cheap to establish – no small consideration in a world in which over two billion people exist on less than a dollar a day.

But it was not just aspects of tropical agroforestry that concerned our correspondents in Africa and elsewhere in the Third World. HDRA had built its reputation on providing gardeners in the UK with reliable information on organic growing. Now, it seemed, we were going to give the same sort of advice to growers in the tropics. Termites, African army worms and spear grass became the tropical equivalents to our slugs, caterpillars and bindweed!

Using information taken from the most up-to-date scientific literature we could find, results from our own research on Cape Verde and elsewhere, and enlisting the help of African organizations such as the Kenyan Institute of Organic Farming, we began to produce technical leaflets that covered the most commonly asked questions.

The 1990s was a period of intense growth in the work of HDRA's Overseas Department and we took on extra staff accordingly. We were fortunate to establish dedicated employees like Nick Paciecznik on Cape Verde, and Stephanie Woods and Esther Roycroft at Ryton. Esther ran the Tropical Agriculture Advisory Service and Steph oversaw the despatch of almost 100 million tree seeds around the globe, drawn from stock of over 200 different drought-resisting species, including the most comprehensive collection of *Prosopis* cultivars anywhere in the world. At one time, HDRA staff could be found working in Africa, India and even as far away as the barren salt flats of the Yellow River Delta in China.

Our next major initiative occurred in 1995, when we helped to found the Ghana Organic Agriculture Network (GOAN) by bringing together what had previously been a number of independent scattered groups to set up organic demonstration farms and gardens throughout this vast West African country.

For the next eight years we supported the GOAN central office in Kumasi, Ghana's second city in the tropical heartlands, and it proved to be a reliable and useful partner. Much of the information that found its way into HDRA's expanding output of data sheets originated with the practical experience picked up from Ghanaian farmers. We, in turn, were able to pass on research findings from other parts of the world for trial on the GOAN demonstration plots.

We were also pleased to be working in collaboration with Cuba. Like many places in the tropics, Cuba's agriculture was built on exports. Ever since the revolution that brought Castro to power in 1959, the country had supplied the Soviet bloc with its sugar, tobacco and citrus crops, and in return it had received wheat, beans and the fertilizers and pesticides needed to grow them. Then, suddenly, in 1990, the Soviet empire imploded and Cuba found itself without food overnight.

Faced with the prospect of hunger on an unprecedented scale, the Cuban authorities acted quickly and decisively. Workers in the cities were ordered to grow fruit and vegetables – and as there were no fertilizers or pesticides they had little choice but to do it organically. Long, concrete troughs, formerly used for hydroponic cultivation, were filled with soil and converted into raised vegetable beds. Land next to schools and factories was commandeered and dug up to supply canteens with food. And individuals were encouraged to take on allotments to grow fresh fruit and vegetables for their families.

At first, yields were poor, as people who had never grown anything in their lives before struggled to learn the rudiments of gardening. Visiting in 1997, the HDRA group encountered widespread ignorance of even the most basic organic techniques. But as experience grew, so did output, and from a standing start urban food production in Havana rocketed to over 115,000 tons in just six years. By 2002, across the country as a whole, a mere 35,000 acres of urban gardens were producing 3.4 million tons of food – the equivalent of almost 90 tons an acre.

Out in the country, the agriculture might best be described as low-input, with some chemicals being used, though far less than in Soviet times. Biological pest control has replaced pesticides, and vermiculture units have been established throughout the island, producing over five million tons of worm compost a year. As a result, Cuba is now not only completely self-sufficient in fruit and vegetables but also produces most of its other food staples. Compared with the Soviet era, the country now uses 90 per cent fewer fertilizers and has achieved a staggering 93 per cent reduction in pesticides. Diesel consumption has halved, in part due to a return to oxen-drawn equipment. Happily, taken as a whole, crop yields across the island are steadily increasing year on year.

It is a fantastically heartening story, and all the more encouraging because it shows how much can be achieved in a relatively short space of time if there is a will to do it. Cuba also provides a powerful alternative model for countries in the Third Word that have been sold the lie that the lives of ordinary people can only be improved by unfettered global trade, involving environmental absurdities like the air-freighting of perishable, out-of-season produce, such as Kenyan green beans, to the West.

And there were other exciting organic developments in the Third World. In 1980 Father Henri de Laudanie, a Jesuit priest working with poor farmers in Madagascar, hit on a revolutionary way of cultivating rice. Instead of transplanting seedlings into flooded paddy fields when they were a month old in the normal fashion, he planted them out two weeks earlier, into soil that had been merely moistened, delaying flooding until after the rice plants had flowered. The plants were also much more widely spaced, necessitating less than a tenth of the amount of seeds. On poor soil, and with no artificial fertilizers, pesticides or high-yielding seed varieties, he achieved yields that were four times the average for the area. At first, Father Henri had applied chemical fertilizers, but when he tried compost instead the results were far better. Since then, the System of Rice Intensification, or SRI as it's usually known, has been trialled in most rice-producing countries of the world, and in almost every case has demonstrated equivalent results. Needless to say, it has been stridently opposed by Green Revolution scientists and the agrochemical industry, but the results speak for themselves and it's now being taken up widely across the globe.

In October 2008 the United Nations Environment Programme (UNEP) issued a report on 114 agricultural projects in 24 African countries, which showed that crop yields had more than doubled when organic methods had been used. Achim Steiner, the head of UNEP, was quoted as saying, 'the potential contribution of organic farming to feeding the world may be far higher than many had supposed ... this report suggests it could make a serious contribution to tackling poverty and food insecurity.' Six months earlier, a massive four-year study into global agriculture, sponsored by the World Bank on behalf of the UN and involving 400 scientists drawn from international agencies, governments, non-governmental organizations (NGOs) and industry, had recommended small-scale farming using organic methods as a key policy option for the future. To the fury of the biotech and agrochemical industry it also cautioned against genetic engineering, saying, 'the use of GM [Genetically Modified] crops is much more contentious.'

Throughout the Third World peasant farmers are turning their backs on the discredited chemically oriented methods of agriculture, which have been so destructive in so many ways. They are turning instead to cheap and sustainable non-chemical alternatives. Jules Pretty, Professor of Environment and Society at the University of Essex, who has made a lifelong study of the subject, said in 2002, 'There really is no alternative to the radical reform of national agriculture, rural and food policies, and institutions. The need is urgent and this is not the time to hesitate. The time has come for this next agricultural revolution.'

Looking back over the 20 years of HDRA's active involvement in the Third World, thanks to Leslie Marr and the staff of HDRA's brilliant overseas department, it has made a real difference. The organization remains the world's leading authority on *Prosopis*, and through its pioneering work on Cape Verde and elsewhere, has demonstrated that even badly eroded land can be restored and need not be written off. Small-scale organic methods of food production are being adopted throughout the Third World. HDRA's technical advisors are still providing invaluable help, which is available in easily downloadable versions via the internet. Long may they continue.

Chapter Thirteen

❧

VANISHING VEGETABLES

MANY TRADITIONAL BRITISH vegetable varieties were almost wiped out in the 1970s and 1980s as a result of draconian seed laws. Now, however, they are enjoying something of a renaissance due to a tenacious campaign by HDRA to save them.

The problem began in 1973 when, in response to an edict from Brussels, the British government enacted the 'Seeds (National List of Varieties) Regulations', outlawing the sale of any vegetable varieties that were not included in the *UK National List* or a Europe-wide *Common Catalogue*. Seeds of hundreds of traditional varieties suddenly became proscribed overnight, including some that had been grown for more than a century. A £2,000 penalty was the punishment awaiting anyone who sold even a single packet of outlawed seeds.

The chief reasons put forward by the authorities for such severe legislation were that it would protect seed breeders from piracy and, through a system of royalty payments, reward them for their efforts. Human nature being what it is, unscrupulous seedsmen have always pirated seeds from their rivals, buying up the bestselling varieties, growing them to produce supplies of their own and then selling them under a different name. The practice was especially rife in the 19th century, when popular Victorian varieties would frequently acquire multiple synonyms. Proving the thefts was another matter, however, and there was little a plant breeder could do to stop a dishonest seedsman from poaching his best varieties.

On the surface of it, the aims of the 1970s seed regulations were unexceptionable. However, the rules were drafted solely with the needs of plant breeders and commercial growers in mind, and didn't consider their impact on the wider issue of plant genetic resources. And gardeners were ignored completely, even though the qualities they look for in a variety are invariably at odds with those sought by commercial growers, whose top priority is to produce uniform-looking produce for their supermarket and food processor customers.

Considerations of taste are secondary to commercial growers. And although taste is highly subjective, there can be no denying the blandness of many of the vegetables on sale today. Gardeners, on the other hand, appreciate vegetables that have taste and flavour. They also value other properties, such as extended ripening, so that they can harvest their produce over as long a period as possible – unlike commercial growers, who desire crops that can all be picked on the same day by machines. In addition, gardeners want varieties that are adapted to life in a humus-rich soil and that withstand the vagaries of our increasingly uncertain climate. Varieties that only thrive when subjected to an intensive regimen of synthetic fertilizers and pesticides, and fail when conditions are harsh, are of no use to them at all.

As a result of the limited, short-term thinking behind the seed regulations, gardeners lost out badly when many old favourites were dropped from the market. One of the main reasons for their disappearance was the crippling cost of getting a variety onto the *UK National List*. Before it can be included on the list, a variety has to undergo a minimum two-year trialling process to ensure that it is 'distinct, uniform and stable'. In the 1970s it cost more than £1,000 just to register a single variety; now the price has more than doubled and there is an annual maintenance charge of several hundred pounds as well, just to keep it there. It doesn't take a genius to see that you have to sell a lot of seeds to justify the registration costs, and that the more specialist and unusual varieties had little hope of survival.

But it wasn't just the high listing costs that signalled the demise of traditional vegetable varieties – many failed the uniformity test. The new F1 hybrid seeds favoured by commercial producers guarantee uniformity, whereas heritage varieties are nowhere near as reliable. This doesn't bother most gardeners, who are perfectly happy to put up with crooked carrots or the occasional misshapen marrow – in fact, it's one of the things that makes growing vegetables so fascinating.

The loss of these traditional, 'open pollinated' seed varieties also meant that gardeners could no longer save their own seeds because F1 hybrids don't breed true, and gardeners must therefore buy fresh stocks each season, a point not lost on the seed trade.

In anticipation of the legislation, seeds were submitted for testing from the early-1970s onwards, and out of this came the original 1974 *UK National List* of approved varieties, together with the names of all the varieties that could no longer be sold. Notice was given in the same publication that six years from then, on 30 June 1980, a further 1,500 traditional 'synonyms' (said to be identical to existing but differently named varieties) would be deleted from the list.

Lawrence Hills was apoplectic when he first saw the *UK National List*, with so many outstanding old varieties due for the chop, for reasons, it seemed to him, that were based on appearance only. Flavour, nutritional content, and anything else that was difficult or costly to measure, were simply ignored. It was so much cheaper and easier to assess the curvature of a cucumber or the colour of a carrot than to analyse a lettuce to find out how much vitamin C it contained, let alone to investigate whether a particular variety contained genes for pest and disease resistance, had the ability to withstand drought, or contained more cancer-protecting properties – qualities that might be of immense importance to plant breeders in the future. Almost casually the fruits of centuries of plant breeding were being cast aside for reasons of commercial expediency. Madness!

Lawrence had heard about the conservation work that Kew Gardens was doing at Wakehurst Place in Surrey, saving seeds of rare flowering plants. Scientists there had developed techniques to preserve seeds for decades by deep-freezing them at -20°C (-4°F). These cryogenic seed collections, known as gene banks, were operating elsewhere in the world for other crops: there was one for rice in the Philippines and another for potatoes in Peru. Why not establish one here in the UK for vegetable seeds, he thought?

So in 1974 Lawrence decided that HDRA should mount an intensive campaign to 'Save our Vegetables' and began by firing off a letter to *The Times*. This was followed by other letters to the press, taking part in radio interviews and urging HDRA members to lobby their MPs. After undertaking detailed research into those synonyms that were due to be axed six years hence, we discovered some glaring inconsistencies. Far from being identical to the approved varieties, as the authorities claimed, over 60 per cent were found to be unique in one way or another. Let me illustrate this with 'Bedfordshire Champion', one of Britain's best-known onions. Although superficially similar to another onion called 'Up-to-Date', the two had long been recognized as different and distinct varieties. Now, with the publication of the first *UK National List*, 'Up-to-Date' was suddenly reclassified as a synonym of 'Bedfordshire Champion'. The interesting point here is that in the Ministry of Agriculture's own trials, carried out in 1948, 'Bedfordshire Champion' was found to be one of the varieties more susceptible to two serious fungal diseases (white rot and downy mildew), whereas 'Up-to-Date' was the most resistant. So how could both varieties be the same? By deleting 'Up-to-Date' from the list, without making any arrangements for its survival, plant breeders would be denied the opportunity of making use of its disease-resistant genes in the future. Whatever its present commercial viability, commonsense taught thatit ought to be safely tucked up in a gene bank, where it would bepreserved for all time.

Other supporters began to take up the cause, among them Professor Jack Hawkes of Birmingham University, one of the leading academic lights in the world of crop plant genetic resources, and Brian Walker, Director General of Oxfam – both recognized that the future of world food security was at stake. Walker agreed to pay for the construction of a deep-freeze seed store and its running costs for the first seven years, if the government agreed to pick up the tab thereafter. Thus it was, in October 1980, that Britain's 'Vegetable Gene Bank' was officially opened at Wellesbourne in Warwickshire. Performing the opening ceremony, Brian Walker paid a fulsome tribute to Lawrence, and to HDRA's efforts, without which, he acknowledged, the project might never have got off the ground.

This was all well and good, but the gene bank could only be used by plant scientists and wouldn't help amateur gardeners to get hold of seeds of their old favourites. We knew enough about the obduracy of Brussels bureaucrats to realize that any campaign to change things was likely to be long and arduous, with little hope of success – something drastic was needed right then. Our priority was to save those varieties that were due to be dropped from the list within the next few months. It was time to take a closer look at the fine print of the regulations. To our surprise we discovered that we could buy up threatened varieties and even grow them for their seeds, provided we didn't then sell them. We also learned that it was perfectly legal to give seeds away for the purposes of experimentation, under a clause that allowed companies to test their new varieties before submitting them for official listing. If they could do it, so could we, using HDRA's experimenting members. But when we approached the Ministry of Agriculture, Fisheries and Food (MAFF) to gauge their reaction we were warned that a scheme that involved the deliberate marketing of 'illegal' seeds would be sailing close to the wind. This left us feeling decidedly nervous. HDRA wasn't well off, so the prospect of a court case, with expensive legal costs, and heavy fines if we lost, was frightening. On the other hand a David and Goliath contest, pitting the might of the Ministry against a small, penniless charity, would result in enormous publicity. It was a difficult decision, but doing nothing was not an option as it would spell the end of hundreds of excellent old vegetable varieties. We had to take a chance.

During 1976 and 1977 we acquired as many seeds as possible. Some seedsmen gave us varieties they could no longer sell. Others were donated by HDRA members. One of the most exciting discoveries came from an elderly lady called Miss Rhoda Cutbush, who sent us an envelope containing a handwritten letter and half a dozen broad-bean seeds. She told us she had grown and saved the seeds of this crimson-flowered variety for most of her life, carrying on a tradition begun by her father who had received the seeds when he was a young man in the 1890s, but ill health had forced her to stop gardening. We were very excited because although beans with striking red flowers were known to exist in Elizabethan times (modern varieties have flowers that are black and white), we had assumed they were now extinct.

Another contributor was His Grace the Bishop of Bath and Wells, who gave us some Martock beans, which he said had been grown continuously in the kitchen garden of the Bishop's Palace since the time of the Tudors. It appears that this inauspicious-looking small brown bean is a direct link with the fare of our medieval ancestors who would have used it as a source of protein in pottage or thick soup. I can't describe how privileged it felt to open these wonderful little packages containing a part of our history, sent to us by people from all walks of life, from all over Britain.

Both these varieties and many more were grown at Bocking, until we had sufficient stocks to launch the 'HDRA Vegetable Seed Library for Research and Experiment' in February 1978. Since numbers were scarce members were limited to three packets of seeds apiece and were charged a small fee to cover postage and packing. Each member was asked to note down as much information as possible about how the plants grew, what they tasted like, and so on, the implication being that we were collecting data that could be used in an application for official listing. And while it's undoubtedly true that we wanted to know more about the varieties in our care, the unstated reason for this request was to avoid the prospect of prosecution.

One of the biggest frustrations of those early years was not having enough staff or land at Bocking to enable us to look after all the varieties in the collection. We solved the problem of staff shortages by inviting members to be responsible for maintaining individual varieties, bulking up our supplies, by becoming 'Seed Guardians'. This started in a small way at first but as the library grew, so did the number of volunteers and by the early-1980s Seed Guardians were providing significant amounts of seed.

The problem of land shortage was overcome similarly when Lawrence dreamt up the concept of having 'Vegetable Sanctuaries' in stately homes and other historic properties. It was a wonderful idea, which resulted in Sir Michael Hanham, a member living at Dean's Court, Wimborne in Dorset, offering some of his land to create the first sanctuary.

It was all very well coming up with a safety net for seeds that had already fallen off the *UK National List*, but something else was needed to help those that were still clinging on. We reasoned that if we could create publicity for varieties that were in most danger, people would buy more and they would be less likely to be dropped. *The Vegetable Finder*, a booklet that listed every variety on sale in Britain, with the emphasis on the older varieties, was our first stab in this direction. It was launched at the Chelsea Flower Show in May 1977, with a print run of 10,000 copies and within six months it had sold out. This made us wonder about setting up our own seed company selling heirloom varieties. Unfortunately, it was beyond our capabilities at the time, but we did eventually go on to achieve it, launching *The Heritage Seed Catalogue* in 1984, our final year at Bocking.

HDRA's seed-saving efforts were put somewhat on the back burner during the first couple of years at Ryton because we had to concentrate our energies on getting the new demonstration gardens up and running. However, the mail-order company forged ahead, and with the added attraction of the seed collection, we found that within a few years we were suffering from an acute shortage of warehousing space. Unbeknown to us, our main competitor, a company called Chase Organics Ltd, was facing similar problems. Chase had been founded in the early part of the 20th century and was originally known for a small portable glass cloche it manufactured for market gardeners, but the company had long since diversified into making and selling a range of organic fertilizers derived from seaweed extracts. By the late-1980s it also had a range of vegetable seeds not unlike our own.

I can't remember whether we made the overture to Chase or whether they first contacted us, but some time early in 1990 Jackie and I sat down with Richard Rixon, Chase's Managing Director, to discuss the possibility of working together. The outcome was the publication in 1991 of *The Organic Gardening Catalogue*, which was an amalgamation of the mail-order catalogues from both companies. Thereafter, Chase handled all the mail-order business while HDRA checked out new products and provided technical support. The relationship worked well from the start and is still going strong today, although Richard has now retired, leaving the company in the capable and enthusiastic hands of his long-time deputy, Mike Hedges. Over the years it has contributed significant amounts of money towards HDRA's charitable work, so the amalgamation was a shrewd business move as well as a good means of popularizing our precious threatened seeds.

In 1990, with the gardens at Ryton reasonably well established, we at last had the time to revive the original Seed Library. We were especially fortunate when Matt Dunwell, an organic farmer and seed-saving enthusiast, offered to support the library for the next three years. Around the same time we also struck lucky when Dr Jeremy Cherfas, a talented biologist and science writer, agreed to run it, assisted by another horticulturalist with a passion for seed-saving, Simon Hickmott. Jeremy joined the team at Ryton in the spring of 1991, settling with Simon into a somewhat cramped, makeshift office next to Margi Lennartsson and her researchers, in one of the several second-hand portable buildings we had installed in the courtyard.

Our 'Vanishing Vegetables' stand at the Chelsea Flower Show in May 1992 caused something of a stir, especially the striking display of Rhoda Cutbush's 'Crimson Flowered Broad Beans' and the handsome obelisk of tall Victorian peas, which fooled quite a few people into believing they were sweet peas. The RHS awarded us a bronze medal for our efforts and we were rewarded with a continuous stream of visitors. Because we wanted to make the project financially independent when Matt's funding ran out, we had dropped the idea of asking for donations and opted for a fixed membership subscription instead. Although this was a more commercial arrangement than the one we had originally talked over with MAFF, and therefore carried a greater risk of prosecution, we had little choice. By the end of the week the library had several hundred new members, and Simon and Jeremy had talked themselves hoarse, without, thankfully, having to also justify the new set-up to the authorities.

As news of the project grew, people began to send in seeds, just as they had done in the early days of the seed library. One morning, as he was checking through his mail, Jeremy came across a large, padded package that was giving off a suspiciously sulphurous smell. Inside he found two turnips, each bearing a delicate flower stalk, carefully wrapped in a plastic bag, along with a note from the sender, Tom Cleghorn, explaining that they were a variety called 'Laird's Victory' and that they came from the garden of his recently deceased 90-year-old neighbour, Mr Alec Donaldson, who had kept the variety going since the end of the First World War. For all we knew these may have been the last 'Laird's Victory' plants in existence, so Simon immediately dug two deep holes and watered the plants in well. I'm pleased to report that the flower buds continued to develop and later in the year he was able to get a fine harvest of seeds.

Many of the varieties in the collection come with similar stories attached, but none is as heartbreaking as the tale of a small black bean called 'Cherokee Trail of Tears'. This used to be grown by Cherokee Indians on their ancestral lands in the southern Appalachian Mountains, until, shamefully, they were forced out by European settlers. In 1838, the entire nation, including women and children, was sent hundreds of miles on a forced route-march to a reservation in Oklahoma – a journey that took them over high mountains in the depths of winter. Thousands of people died and hundreds were left unburied where they fell. The bean, which many had taken with them, became known as the 'Trail of Tears'. What gives this story an almost unbearable further poignancy is that when the Cherokee people, who had survived this atrocity at the hands of the white man, heard about the Great Potato Famine of 1845, they were sufficiently moved by the plight of the Irish peasants to send them food parcels, including some 'Trail of Tears' beans. And it was from an Irish gardener, almost 150 years later, that we received our own gift of these truly historic beans.

The Irish Potato Famine is a graphic example of what can happen when a crop depends on too narrow a genetic base. No-one is certain when potatoes first arrived in Britain, but they probably came from

Spain in the 1590s, having originally been brought from Peru. Within two centuries they had become the staple diet of the poor. By the early-19th century every European potato variety could be traced back to just two original introductions, neither of which had any natural immunity to late blight, a devastating fungal disease that was brought to Europe from Mexico on a consignment of infected potatoes in 1845. The fungus spread rapidly across the European mainland and crossed the Channel to England that same year.

The most popular potato variety in Ireland at the time was called 'Lumpers', because of its knobbly shape, and most peasants either grew it, or another sort called 'Cups'. Both were highly susceptible to the new disease and in the wet summers that marked the late 1840s the fungus spread like wildfire. Overnight, potato foliage blackened and tubers rotted into a stinking mush. The mass of the people, who relied on home-grown potatoes as their staple food, were left with nothing to eat, and up to one million people died, and a further million emigrated, during what was the worst famine in Ireland's history.

In Mexico, peasant farmers overcome the problem of blight by planting their fields with up to 30 different potato varieties, each displaying varying degrees of blight-resistance. That way they can always be sure of harvesting some potatoes, even though part of the crop is likely to be struck down. You might think that we would have learned some lessons from the dire consequences of monoculture, as witnessed in the Irish Potato Famine and, like Mexican farmers, also hedge our bets by planting up a mixture of varieties. Yet in Britain today almost a quarter of the commercial potato acreage is planted up with a single type – 'Maris Piper' – and fewer than ten make up the rest of the national crop. None is resistant to blight, so farmers must use fungicides to keep the disease at bay, spraying up to 18 times in a season. Unsurprisingly, the disease has developed a resistance to the chemicals and in 1981 potato growers were alarmed to discover that one entire class of products, the phenylamides, no longer worked. Even more worrying is a new and aggressive strain of 'super blight' that has recently arrived from Mexico and is capable of cross-breeding with the existing fungal strain, which raises the prospect of even more virulent forms that can defy all fungicides. In which case, we could be in real trouble from now on.

In the decades that followed the Irish catastrophe, Victorian plant breeders turned their attention to developing improved potato varieties and, before long, farmers had a far greater choice at their disposal. Most seedsmen listed scores of varieties, although none could match the selection on offer from Bliss & Co., which in 1877 brought out a catalogue containing 500 different sorts. A Suttons Seeds catalogue in the HDRA library from the inter-war years boasts over fifty types, all beautifully photographed in sepia. However, by the late-1980s few garden seed catalogues listed more than half a dozen varieties; some listed none at all.

This massive reduction in the choice of potato and other vegetable varieties was mirrored in the seed trade itself from the mid-1970s onwards, with a startling collapse in the number of small, independent concerns. Companies had been quick to spot the commercial opportunities opened up by the new seed regulations and had swallowed up their smaller rivals with unseemly haste. Suttons Seeds, for example, was taken over by its French rival, Vilmorin-Andrieux – a seed firm dating back to 1727 – which in turn was devoured by Limagrain, an even larger French company that had begun life as a farmers' co-operative. Today it is the world's largest supplier of seeds to the home gardening market.

But it wasn't just seed firms that were getting in on the act. The Swedish car manufacturer, Volvo, joined in the acquisitions game and by 1989 had become the sixth largest global seed company. Not for long though, as chemical giants like ICI scrambled to control the world's seed supply. During a 20-year period beginning in 1970 more than 500 seed companies were bought up and the consolidation has continued apace ever since. Currently, the largest ten seed corporations have carved up 60 per cent of the global commercial seed market, the biggest being the biotech giant, Monsanto. Right from the start these huge transnational companies have ruthlessly pruned out open-pollinated varieties, replacing them with agrochemical-dependant F1 hybrid seeds, their ultimate goal being genetically modified varieties that are programmed to respond only to their own proprietary products. In the drive for ever-greater corporate profits the genetic resources of the world are being decimated and its food supply imperilled.

Nevertheless, in spite of the best efforts of the seed giants to close down the industry, back in the early-1990s you could still get hold of unusual potato varieties if you knew where to look. The biggest private potato collection in Britain was held by Donald MacLean and his wife Margaret and at their farm in Crieff, Perthshire, these avid enthusiasts grew more than 400 rare and unusual varieties. One or two small provincial seed companies that had somehow managed to slip under the radar in the takeover blitz also carried a respectable range. But potatoes were also covered by the same European Union (EU) regulations that governed trade in the seeds of other vegetables, so many slow-selling varieties were at risk.

Jackie decided that the best way of drawing attention to the plight of potatoes was to have a special day just for them – National Potato Day. It would be held at Ryton and would include fascinating talks from potato experts, cookery demonstrations, tastings from famous chefs and tips on cultivation by well-known gardeners. But at its heart would be a massive display of as many different seed potato varieties that we could muster, which would be available, by the tuber, for visitors to buy. We had the precedent of Apple Day, which had been running successfully at Ryton for several years and had always attracted large crowds – but that was in early autumn. Would people really turn up in February, the traditional time for buying seed potatoes, when the weather was at its worst? Jackie was convinced they would and turned for help to Alan Wilson, who at that time was senior vegetable buyer for Waitrose, one of Britain's high-end supermarket chains.

We already knew Alan, having met him in the summer of 1993 when he needed advice about publishing his book, *The Story of the Potato*. A great potato enthusiast, he had contacts with almost everyone in the trade, including Alan Romans, a fellow fan from Scotland, who agreed to obtain seed potatoes on our behalf from Donald MacLean and other Scottish growers. Jackie had fixed the date for National Potato Day at the end of February in 1994, in the hope that the worst of the bad weather would be gone by then. But as the day grew near our hearts sank with the Met Office forecasts for strong winds and wintry showers. Not that the bad weather deterred the 700 stalwarts who braved the conditions and travelled from as far away as Cornwall, Wales and Lancashire to join us.

Alan Wilson gave a talk about the history of potato breeding and had his newly published book on sale, while Jeremy passed on cultivation tips. Ryton's chef excelled himself with a culinary potato bonanza, starting with potato soup and bread, followed by an assortment of potato dishes to accompany the main course and finishing with apple pie made with potato-flour pastry. But the seed potatoes were the real stars of the show. Alan Romans had managed to winkle out more than 60 different varieties, from old favourites such as 'Duke of York' to the completely obscure 'Bishops Choirboys'. Each was displayed in an open cardboard box, with tubers priced at ten pence each, so for just six pounds visitors could buy one of every variety. Amazingly, by the end of the day more than 20,000 individual tubers had found new homes!

Potato Day attracted a huge amount of publicity, as Jackie hoped it would. This included a ten-minute broadcast on Radio 4's *The Food Programme* by legendary presenter Derek Cooper, who came to Ryton to interview Jackie and the chef and to sample some of our unusual potato dishes. Publicity tends to feed on itself and for the rest of the year a week rarely went by without a journalist or two contacting HDRA looking for a story. But all this was nothing compared with what we would experience in 1995.

Early in the spring of that year news came through from St James's Palace that The Prince of Wales would make another official visit to Ryton, this time to view the work of the Heritage Seed Library. We had been supplying the Prince with unusual carrots and other vegetable varieties to grow at Highgrove since he became HDRA's patron and we knew that he was interested in this side of our work. By now the collection had expanded to 600 varieties and the library itself had 5,000 members. Over 200 were active 'Seed Guardians', while others were 'Seed Sleuths' who spent their time combing libraries and

second-hand bookshops for old seed catalogues, searching out information about varieties from the past. Everything appeared to be
fizzing along just fine, but in reality things were far from rosy because
our seed-saving equipment and storage facilities were hopelessly inadequate. Even though we had converted a small room in the stable
block into a seed-cleaning room, it wasn't really big enough. A cash
injection was needed, and quickly.

His Royal Highness's visit would be a great time to launch an appeal
and Jackie knew exactly what to do: she would invite people to 'Adopt
A Veg'. It was a quirky idea and a few weeks later she'd designed
and produced a large, round leaflet in the shape of an onion, with
the words 'Do you know your onions?' emblazoned on the front. It
'unpeeled' to tell the story of our threatened veg, listed the 'orphans'
in our collection and finished with a plea for adoption. The Prince
himself readily agreed to adopt the 'Rat's Tail Radish' – a rather
strange looking vegetable with edible pods rather than the usual pink
fleshy root, and one of our more unusual accessions. It made a great
story when he visited in July, and unleashed a torrent of publicity.
Every national daily ran with it and even *The Times* carried the story on
its front page, thereby guaranteeing radio and television coverage.
Over the next few days Jackie was rarely off the telephone, talking
to journalists and giving 'down-the-line' interviews to radio stations as
far away as New Zealand. In all, her 'Adopt A Veg' appeal generated
around 100 articles in the press, as well as countless TV and radio
interviews. I appeared on television too, with the by now famous 'Rat's
Tail Radish' and several other vegetables that had been adopted by
celebrities, including the 'Poppet Pea', chosen by actress Thelma
Barlow and the 'White Belgium Carrot' picked by comedian Jasper
Carrott. I persuaded the show's hosts to adopt the 'Table-Talk Pea'.
Members of the public were equally generous in their support and by
the end of the year the 'Adopt A Veg' appeal had received substantial
funding.

Our third National Potato Day, held on 10 February 1996, was the
best so far, even though the weather had again turned against us,
depositing a thick blanket of snow over the whole of Scotland and

making life extremely difficult for Alan Romans, who had to negotiate his lorry through ten-foot drifts. At Ryton, people queued outside in the freezing cold for up to an hour before the doors opened, fortified by free helpings of hot toddy, which were passed down the line. Patricia Gallimore – who plays Pat Archer, the wife of the organic farmer in the famous BBC radio drama *The Archers* – opened the event, as more than 1,200 people surged past, in true Harrods Sale fashion, to be first into the seed-potato marquee.

Potato Day was undoubtedly one of the most successful events we ever held and it is now a bit of an institution for any keen vegetable grower. Like all good ideas it has been widely copied the length and breadth of the UK. Each year over 20 potato events are put on around the country by garden and community groups and go-ahead garden centres. As a result, seed companies have taken note and now offer a far greater choice of potato varieties than they did in the past. Thompson & Morgan, for example, publishes a separate potato catalogue with almost 80 varieties, including rarities like 'Shetland Black' and 'Burgundy Highland Red'. Tuckers of Devon goes one better, listing a staggering 120 different cultivars.

HDRA's Potato Days also inspired other vegetable-focused events, such as the hugely successful annual chilli and tomato festivals run by our old friends Jim Buckland and his wife Sarah at West Dean Gardens in West Sussex. The more the merrier as far as we're concerned – anything that promotes the conservation of genetic diversity in vegetables is good news.

For almost 20 years HDRA had been a lone voice in Britain, making the case for older varieties of vegetables, but at last the tide was changing and in 1996 we were even able to set up Heritage Seed Library gardens at historic properties around the country, which gave a modern twist to Lawrence's original Seed Sanctuary idea. In the north of England, Sir Thomas Ingilby, the owner of Ripley Castle near Harrogate, set aside a small part of his kitchen garden for heritage vegetables. Meanwhile, over on the other side of the Pennines, Quarry Bank Mill, at Styal in Cheshire, displayed some of the varieties that its cotton-weaver workers would have grown back in the 19th century.

This industrial theme carried through to a seed library garden in Wales at Drenewydd Museum, near Merthyr Tydfil.

But by far the most impressive seed-saving organization in the world is the Seed Savers Exchange (SSE), which was started in 1975 by Kent and Diane Whealy at Decorah Farm, Iowa, USA. Its enormous collection now runs to over 25,000 varieties and it co-ordinates the seed swapping activities of 7,000 members across the USA. It has also inspired initiatives such as Seeds of Diversity, formerly the Heritage Seed Program, set up by Canadian Organic Growers in 1984, and the Australian Seed Savers Network, founded in 1986 by Jude and Michel Fanton. European initiatives include Arche Noah (Noah's Ark) in Austria, and ProSpecieRara in Switzerland, which also conserves rare livestock breeds and fruits. During the past few years vegetable seed swapping by independent gardening groups has started to take off in the UK and a number of 'Seedy Sunday' events now take place across England.

In the USA, gardeners can choose to buy from more than 2,500 (mostly American) varieties of vegetables, herbs and flowers listed by Seeds of Change. This seed company was started in 1989 by Howard and Nancy Shapiro, but it really took off after Stephen Badger, a scion of the Mars family, joined in 1992. The business was subsequently sold to the confectionary giant, which re-launched it selling pasta sauces, soups and other organic convenience foods. Seeds of Change is the biggest of a number of seed companies offering heirloom seeds that have sprung up across North America in recent years. Jackie and I met Howard some years ago and he looked just like an archetypal US 'old timer' with long flowing white hair, an even longer beard and a passion for conserving heirloom varieties.

In the UK, where once there was only HDRA's seed catalogue trading in heritage varieties, there is now an ever-increasing number of small, specialist seed companies that have sensed a distinct lack of enthusiasm on the part of the authorities to prosecute and are cheekily marketing non-listed seeds. In the UK, for example, if you pay a penny to join 'Ben & Kate's' seed club, you can buy from their *Real Seed Catalogue*. Or if your taste runs to the faux Gothic, how about ordering from Thomas Etty Esq., who 'begs, most respectfully, to bring to the notice of the Nobility, Gentry, Clergy & Others, his annual specialist seed catalogue'?

Not so amusing, however, is the reaction of the French authorities, who convicted the tiny, Auvergne-based seed company Terre de Semences (Seeds of the Earth) of selling unlisted seeds, forcing it to close down in 1998. The company resurfaced the following year, as Association Kokopelli, but Dominique Guillet, its outspoken and passionate leader, continued to ruffle feathers and it was hauled before the courts again in 2007 and 2008, presumably in an effort to silence him for good. This time the fine was a massive 28,000 euros. We can only hope that this heavy handed French reaction is an exception, and not the start of a coordinated attack on unconventional seed savers.

These grassroots and voluntary initiatives are unlikely to give the chief executives of transnational seed companies any sleepless nights, but they do represent a victory, nonetheless, for an individual's right to decide what to grow in their own garden. They also stand as a warning that people are becoming increasingly alarmed by the threat to the world's genetic diversity posed by giant corporations. We are not prepared to stand idly by.

Chapter Fourteen

DESIGNED TO BE GREEN

THERE USED TO BE A feeling among many people that the organic approach to horticulture belonged in the kitchen garden rather than among the flowers. And I suppose that at HDRA we were, to some extent, also guilty of fostering this impression because for most of our history we'd been concerned primarily with growing fruit and vegetables.

In the early-1990s Ryton was still young, as gardens go, and didn't possess the mature trees and plantings you find in long-established gardens. In addition, most of its displays veered towards the utilitarian, so the grounds were woefully short of colour. Sir Roy Strong, the garden designer and former Director of the Victoria and Albert Museum, had visited Ryton not long after it had opened and had written enthusiastically about it in *Country Life*, saying, 'Everyone should have a Ryton near them. So far unique, one of these is needed within reach of everyone in every part of the country.' But, unsurprisingly, he had not been knocked out by the layout, commenting that, 'The various demonstration areas were punched out of field turf almost haphazardly. This was certainly no design paradise.' In all fairness, he couldn't have known that Sir Derek Lovejoy had planned a more ambitious ornamental scheme, which we couldn't afford to create – hence the blocks of carrots, cabbages and compost containers!

In the spring of 1990, Bob Sherman, Ryton's Deputy Head Gardener, travelled to Kent to film an interview with an organic fruit farmer called Donald Cooper for our third television series, *Loads More Muck and Magic*. As Bob toured the orchards, chatting to Donald and his wife, Pixie, he suggested casually that they might like to see Ryton. And so it was that on a warm summer's day a few months later, Jackie and I took them on a tour of the grounds. We got on well and Donald was evidently impressed because over tea in the café he announced, 'I'd like one of these on my farm and I'll give you ten acres. What do you say?'

Now, the idea of setting up a garden in the south of England had long been a dream of ours because it would reach out to the millions of people living in the sprawling conurbations of London and the southeast who had a long journey to Ryton. It was a wonderful offer, but Jackie and I knew that we couldn't accept it unless we could somehow lay our hands on the substantial amount of funding that would be needed to turn the dream into reality. Thanking him profusely, Jackie explained that when creating a new garden it's not so much the land as the cost of construction, planting and staff that eats up the money. Creating the gardens at Ryton had cost HDRA almost £300,000, she added candidly, so we would need at least that much money and the land as well. She paused.

'Okay. What if I give you the land, and £300,000? Now will you do it?' Donald replied. And before we had time to get over our astonishment, he added, 'But you have to raise at least £50,000 of funding as well.'

'No problem,' said Jackie, quick as a flash. And it wasn't.

Two years later, in October 1992, we were standing in the middle of a flat, open field on the edge of the village of Yalding, among the hop gardens and oast houses of rural Kent, poring over a set of plans. This time round we had an attractive design that was affordable and that we would stick to, come what may. Seen from above, Donald's ten acres resembled a swollen teardrop. Five acres were destined to be turned into gardens open to the public, while the remaining land would be used for trials and car parking. Jackie's overall concept centred on a

'Green History of Gardening', demonstrating how organic gardening has its philosophical roots in the practices of earlier generations but also looks to the future, using modern science to help decipher the complex world of soil–plant relationships. Learning from the early days at Ryton, this time we were determined that the garden would be beautiful – a feast for the eyes and food for the soul.

With us on that October day was Bob Sherman, who had taken over from Sue Stickland as Head Gardener at Ryton when she left the previous year. He would be closely involved with the project, as would Peter Bateman, a new member of staff who was to be in charge at Yalding. Peter had, until recently, been Head of Horticulture at Moulton College, the Northamptonshire County Institute for Agriculture, but had become frustrated at what he saw as the 'dumbing-down' of higher education in the pursuit of ever-greater numbers of students. With our help he had devised the first accredited organic gardening qualification in the country, but he was ready for a change and when we offered him the job of managing Yalding he jumped at it, even though it meant a considerable drop in salary.

We all met at the site and studied the plans, looking around to envisage what would go where. The master plan had been drawn up by Stella Caws, a landscape designer from Wales, who had impressed us with her work and seemed to understand intuitively what Jackie had in mind. The main feature was a vast circular pergola in the centre, 150-feet wide, made from weathered Kentish hop poles, which supported roses, wisteria and other elegant climbers. Radiating off this were a number of themed 'historical' gardens, which were individually designed by a friend of Bob's, garden historian Caroline Holmes. They began with the sort of apothecary garden you might have found at a 13th-century monastery and then progressed, through Tudor times, with an elaborate, formal knot garden, before moving on to a reconstruction of a typical cottager's garden dating from around the time of the Battle of Waterloo (1815). A late Victorian town garden and Gertrude Jekyll-inspired Edwardian long border brought this historical excursion into the 20th century, which ended with the sort of 'Dig for Victory' allotment that was commonplace in Britain 60 years ago. You could say that this final plot was there to represent the nadir of eco-friendly gardening, with gardeners piling on the fertilizers and dousing the garden with lethal pesticides, without a second's thought (although we would manage it non-chemically, of course).

The remaining plots were all set in the present, and demonstrated organic techniques of composting, safe pest control and suchlike, acting as a guide to good organic gardening practice. Those were the delights, at any rate, that we could look forward to, as we stared at the featureless turf before us and imagined Stella's beautifully coloured plans brought vividly to life.

We desperately wanted this project to get off to a good start but hadn't reckoned on opposition coming from a voluble minority of Yalding villagers, who were determined to halt the development, fearing the extra traffic the gardens would bring. At a noisy public meeting, organized by the parish council in the village hall, one man stood up and shouted, 'I don't bloody care if it's the Garden of Eden. I don't want it in my village!' Thankfully, the planning authorities saw things differently and eventually gave us permission to go ahead. In order to secure her matching funds Jackie had sent out an urgent appeal to HDRA members and they had rallied round generously, as usual, donating sufficient money to hit Donald's target.

We didn't underestimate the challenges Peter faced at Yalding because they were similar to what we had encountered at Ryton – fencing the land to keep out rabbits, planting thousands of trees and shrubs, installing irrigation, laying paths and so on. The big difference this time around, however, was the absence of the 30-strong team of government-funded workers that had been critical to our success in Warwickshire. Peter had managed to recruit half a dozen school leavers as part of a 'work experience' programme and there were enough funds to employ a full-time gardener, but otherwise we were totally reliant on volunteers. He had put an appeal for help in the newsletter, and over 100 HDRA members had replied, but less than half had actually turned up on the first day and most had subsequently dropped away. Now, only a hard core of a dozen or so remained, and the most reliable was David Holman, a retired electrical engineer from

Medway, who had worked with Sue Coppard in the early days of WWOOF (Working Weekends on Organic Farms) and who would go on to become the secretary of the Kent organic gardening group.

At the time there were around 80 local HDRA groups, and we saw them as playing an important role in persuading people to 'go organic', especially as most groups usually had a fair sprinkling of experienced gardeners who could pass on sound practical advice. In 1991, Sue Chadd, a member of the Yorkshire Dales group, wrote to Jackie, suggesting that HDRA members could open their gardens to the public, emulating the successful open days organized by the National Gardens Scheme. Jackie thought it was a great idea and, knowing that generating good publicity would be the key to making it a success, she established Britain's first National Organic Gardening Weekend – a focal point in the gardening calendar that she was sure the media would promote. We knew that many of our members' gardens were colourful and attractively designed places. Now we had another chance to show the public that organic gardening didn't mean untidy vegetable plots. It would also counter any lingering perception that organic gardeners were superannuated hippies!

And so it turned out. On that first weekend in August 1992 over 100 HDRA members invited people into their gardens. Their hard work was rewarded by more than 6,000 visitors, with another 2,000 coming along to the Organic Gardening Weekend events that we had organized at Ryton. Twenty-two local groups took part by supporting members in their area – doing last-minute tidying up, serving teas and generally helping to make the garden visits quintessentially English occasions. Some groups were already running their own local organic demonstration gardens, but they also supported the national event by participating under the National Organic Gardening Weekend banner over the two days. There was a first-rate allotment in Bath, set up by Tim Baines, Veronica Phillips and others; another in the Wirral, Cheshire, organized by Audrey Sharples and her friends; and yet a third in Halifax, managed by members of Calder Valley Organic Gardeners.

Organic Gardening Weekend was such a huge success that it was repeated the following year, this time over one weekend in June and another in August, to allow for climatic differences between the more advanced gardens in the south and the later-developing gardens in the north and Scotland. Another 50 gardens took part and, in all, around 10,000 visitors were attracted. This set the scene for the next decade, during which time the event raised over £50,000 for HDRA.

On these occasions Jackie pulled out all the stops on the publicity front and as a result Geoff Hamilton regularly plugged the event on BBC Television's *Gardeners' World*, much to her delight. Not that she had needed to twist his arm, because he was already a committed organic gardener by then. Geoff had begun to drop hints about his organic leanings soon after joining the *Gardeners' World* team in 1979. This was something new for the BBC's flagship gardening programme, which until then had been fiercely pro-chemical. Lawrence had often joked that the show's first presenter, Percy Thrower, scattered so many artificial fertilizers about his garden that the chemicals crystallized on his boots. Ironically, Percy was summarily sacked by the BBC in 1976 after appearing in a fertilizer advert on its commercial rival, but his successor, Arthur Billet, and other gardening personalities at the time, like Peter Seabrook, were equally enthusiastic about using chemicals. Despite the fact that we were all scientists at HDRA, carrying out bona fide research, the chemical opposition always tried to paint organic growing as old-fashioned and 'anti-science'. Not that this worried us, of course, but we could see that 'coming out' as organic was a big step for other well-known personalities such as Geoff.

Geoff had, in fact, devised an organic trial on three small vegetable plots, not long after he had bought the Victorian farmhouse and five acres at Barnsdale, in the heart of rural Rutland, which went on to become so well-known to millions of viewers every week. One plot was managed entirely organically, a second used only artificial fertilizers and sprays, and the third was treated with compost and chemicals. I'd been invited onto *Gardeners' World* a year later to discuss organic crop protection and had taken along a length of polythene sheeting and some stakes to erect a carrot-fly barrier. During the interview Geoff mentioned that the organic plot had performed well in its first year – I replied that I wasn't surprised and that he could expect it to continue to get better as the years went by. The trial ran for three years, by which time Geoff had become even more inclined towards organic growing, although he was still careful to present a 'balanced' approach on screen. But by the end of the decade all restraint had disappeared and he would often look straight into the camera, with sparkling eyes and a big grin, and say, 'Now as you all know, I'm an organic sort of a chap ...'. Geoff's *Organic Gardening*, published in 1987 and still in print today, remains one of the best books on the subject.

Geoff wasn't able to visit the garden at Yalding, but I'm sure he would have loved it. An acute shortage of staff had meant that work was progressing more slowly than we would have liked, but Peter and his team managed to complete most of the infrastructure work by the summer of 1993, including the large, central hop-pole pergola, which stood out from the surrounding landscape like a garlanded and wooden equivalent of Stonehenge (though not, perhaps, on the same scale!). But that still left the planting of the individual gardens, which took up the whole of winter and the following year.

Back at Ryton we were also about to improve the infrastructure by laying a block-paved path linking the conference centre with the new restaurant, and another one that reached out towards the rose garden. I like block paviour paths because they're attractive to look at and virtually maintenance-free – that is, as long as they are laid properly. The odd weed might occasionally take root between paviours but it can usually be easily pulled out or destroyed by a quick burst of heat from a gas-powered flame gun. Until now we had only been able to afford hard-standing paths within the individual display gardens, where the space for walking was narrow and so visitors had to travel between gardens over broad sweeps of lawn. In most years this was fine, the turf standing up well to the relentless passage of thousands of feet, but during prolonged wet weather, and in the winter, the grass could be slippery and uncomfortable.

Like everything else at Ryton, the grass is managed organically, without using any weedkillers or other chemicals whatsoever. When it is cut the clippings are usually left on the surface (apart from the first clip of the season, when the grass is longer than usual) so as to return fertility to the soil. Nobody is ever going to confuse the Ryton sward, which is a mixed community of grasses, clover, daisies and the occasional dandelion, with the immaculately striped turf of Wembley Stadium, but nonetheless it looks handsome enough most of the time. And in periods of drought, when other people's lawns are browned and bleached, ours at Ryton stays resolutely green, prompting many envious questions from visitors about the reasons for our success. The simple fact is that most people trim their lawns far too often and keep their grass far too short. This seriously undermines the grass plant's ability to photosynthesize, thereby weakening it. The problem is compounded when lawn feeds are also applied, which encourage shallow rooting, whereas the roots of organically grown grass penetrate deeper into the soil, where there is a greater likelihood of water. The Ryton lawns are clipped when they are about one-and-a-half inches tall, reducing them to about an inch, and are fed but rarely, although they are occasionally dressed with seaweed meal or another type of organic fertilizer in the early spring, if the sward shows symptoms of weak growth.

On the far southern boundary at Ryton, where fruit trees caress the research plots, yet another interesting feature was being created, this time by an HDRA member, Jane Powell, and a team of volunteers. It was a forest garden, and we were hoping that it would be not only ornamental and productive but also the most naturalistic garden we had ever planted. Forest gardens are an example of 'permaculture', or permanent agriculture, a design philosophy that imitates natural ecosystems. It was started in the 1970s by two Australians, Bill Mollison and David Holmgren, and is a broad ranging and ambitious concept that can be applied to all types of food production, the objective being to devise low input/high output systems that are ecologically sustainable. Permaculture is remarkably non-prescriptive – it doesn't insist on a rigidly organic approach or indeed on any other particular style of growing, although techniques like mulching and no-digging are commonplace. According to those who practise it, each situation should be carefully assessed on its merits and the design adapted accordingly. In the case of a forest garden, the philosophy is to mimic the many-layered ecology of woodland, using only edible plants. Tall trees shelter smaller ones, with bushes and herbaceous plants below these, ground-cover plants at soil level and, finally, perennial root crops underground. The garden becomes almost self-sustaining when it has matured and, apart from weeding now and then and a once-a-year trim, needs little maintenance. That's the theory anyway!

In our case several sweet chestnut and walnut trees constituted the upper storey, with smaller fruiting trees below, including apples, pears and quinces, along with a number of lesser known species like the azarole – a type of vitamin C-rich hawthorn found in North Africa. Redcurrants, hazels and other bush fruits and nuts jostled for space underneath, among a carpet of herbs such as comfrey, lemon balm, sorrel and Good King Henry, along with nasturtiums, strawberries and other ground-cover plants, and various perennial roots, such as horseradish. Jane had also optimistically planted a grapevine, in the expectation that it would clamber energetically through the storeys.

The design owed a lot to Robert Hart, a man who had spent much of his life promoting and experimenting with forest gardens. I visited him at his stone farmhouse on Wenlock Edge in Shropshire a few years before he died and he showed me round the quarter-acre garden that he had made out of an old apple and pear orchard. There could be no doubting the lushness of the planting, and I believed him when he told me that he rarely did any work in the garden, but I had my doubts as to how much food it was capable of producing. The herbs and other perennial plants would doubtless produce a regular, if limited, supply of bitter and peppery leaves for a salad. But without netting to protect it from the birds, the fruit would provide easy peckings, while I could imagine squirrels having a grand old time feasting amongst the nuts. I also wondered about some of the other tree species he was growing, which normally had their home in warmer climes. Would they even fruit in Britain and, if so, how long would it be before they began cropping? What works for Bill Mollison in sun-kissed Australia, where there are far more fruiting species from which to choose, is not necessarily going to translate to the much duller and wetter climate in the UK. Nevertheless, we were prepared to give it a go.

For the first year or two, looking after the garden at Ryton took a fair amount of time and involved quite a lot of weeding, even though the ground was heavily mulched with straw. Shading from the taller trees also inhibited the bushes and plants underneath. But it settled down eventually and began to provide us with fruit, nuts, berries and leaves. Most yields were pitifully small, however, and a decade later the decision was taken to abandon the under-storey planting and convert the area into an ordinary patch of woodland. And I never did get to taste an azarole!

In 1996 Ryton celebrated its tenth anniversary. By now the gardens were a lot more mature, especially the plants in the shrub borders and down by the pond, where the trees were finally beginning to resemble a proper copse. Overall though, the grounds still lacked colour, so in the winter we embarked on an ambitious ornamental planting scheme that would transform the entire entrance area from the conference centre to the kitchens, and reach deep into the gardens.

The designers we chose for the commission were Tim Rees and Brita von Schoenaich, who were the leading exponents in Britain of a way of planting called the 'new perennial' style. It had been pioneered at the Bavarian State Institute of Horticulture at Weihenstephan, near Munich, where Brita had studied, in response to a request from the municipal authorities for public planting schemes that look good all year round, can be managed without using weedkillers and require minimal maintenance. A tall order indeed! Their approach is based on the fact that the nearer you can approximate a plant's growing conditions to its natural habitat, the better it thrives. Most garden flowers have their origins in the wild species that were brought here by intrepid plant collectors of earlier centuries who travelled far and wide to search for new species. The plants they discovered came from very specific environments, be it the sandy shores of some distant lake, the rocky slopes of a high mountain pass or the swampy fringes of a tropical forest. These habitats could not be easily recreated away from their natural home, but fortunately most plants are extremely forgiving, and will still grow under less exacting conditions. The German specialists at Weihenstephan wanted the plants to be as robust as possible, and so they took this detailed knowledge of plant habitats and used it to devise appropriate combinations of herbaceous perennials and tall flowering grasses. And by planting closely, in continuous drifts, the problem of weeds was greatly reduced.

Tim's and Brita's design for Ryton was created in the spring of 1997 and by mid-summer was provoking many admiring comments. A gravel mulch was used initially to keep weeds under control, but as the plants filled out this became unnecessary. And we found that we did indeed have a superb display, which flowered for months on end and needed very little work to keep it under control. Over the years it has just got better and better and it even looks fantastic in winter, especially on a crisp sunny morning, after a hard frost, when the grasses stand sparkling white and ramrod straight. It was so beautiful that four extremely large, stunning photographs of it were later featured, alongside a portrait of Jackie, in Tessa Traeger's and Patrick Kinmonth's exquisite book, *A Gardener's Labyrinth: Portraits of People, Plants & Places*. The National Portrait Gallery in London had commissioned Tessa to photograph Jackie for its permanent collection and for use in a major exhibition in 2000 entitled *Escape to Eden*, which traced the lives and careers of the most important women in the history of horticulture over the last five centuries.

The 'new perennial' movement soon caught on and spread to other countries in mainland Europe. In Holland, for example, garden designer Piet Oudolf became its leading advocate and created a superb garden in Britain at Pensthorpe Waterfowl Trust in Norfolk, where a quarter-acre bed provides a dramatic backdrop to a lake. More recently, in 2005, he teamed up with a British designer Tom Stuart Smith to transform a massive 37-acre plot at Trentham Gardens, Staffordshire, which has also been winning rave plaudits.

While all this had been going on at Ryton, work had not stopped at Yalding. The gardens finally opened to the public in 1995 and The Prince of Wales visited the project a year later. Unfortunately, Peter Bateman decided to move on. His place was taken by Sue Turner, a young gardener from South Africa who had been his deputy. She continued to develop the gardens, planting up additional flowerbeds around the pergola, and in 1996 turned her attention to improving the look of the 19th-century labourer's cottage garden. This was called the 'Cobbett Garden' for short, after William Cobbett, the radical, political commentator who had travelled widely and written passionately about farming and the plight of farm workers. His *Rural Rides* was a well-deserved classic (see page 2), but one of his lesser-known publications, *Cottage Economy*, written in 1822, might justly be described as the earliest practical work on self-sufficiency. In this book he urged labourers to grow their own fruit and vegetables, keep chickens, rear a pig or two and make their own bread and ale, as a means of staving off destitution. Our little garden at Yalding was designed to illustrate some of Cobbett's ideas, but you had to exercise all your powers of imagination because a woven willow fence, which was all we had been able to afford at the time, stood in for a wattle and daub cottage. But in 1997, thanks to a small grant from a charitable trust, we were able to make the garden a lot more authentic, constructing a replica 'cottage' – a timber-framed façade at any rate – complete with brick oven, mock well-head, a cosy pig-sty and even an outdoor privy!

In late August a local thatcher put the finishing touches to the 'dwelling' and a few days later on the bank holiday weekend Jackie organized a William Cobbett themed party for the members and visitors to celebrate its completion. Thelma Barlow came along to read passages from Cobbett's books, accompanied by her stage partner from *Coronation Street*, Peter Baldwin, and there were demonstrations of thatching, blacksmithing and other traditional crafts. Jackie had really gone to town with the catering. She'd researched and commissioned special organic Cobbett pies and loaves and had even persuaded the local brewery to brew a Cobbett Ale, making sure that all the ingredients in these special refreshments were authentic for the period. And for once, in defiance of all the traditions of an English Bank Holiday weekend, it didn't rain!

Our only regret that weekend was that Geoff Hamilton would never be able to see the Cobbett Garden, for he had died quite suddenly the previous August while taking part in a sponsored charity bike ride. Geoff had become a good friend and, as we've mentioned, he'd visited

Ryton several times and made regular references to HDRA in his broadcasts. Thanks to the power of television, he was Britain's best-known organic gardener, respected and loved by millions, and his tragic death was widely felt throughout the country. Many members had written to us suggesting that we should mark his life and remarkable contribution to organic gardening in a special way. We had been thinking exactly the same thing, and so shortly after returning from Yalding we began to plan a new garden at Ryton that would be a living memorial to him.

Bob Sherman recommended two young landscape designers, Gabriella Pape and Isabella Van Groeningen, to design what was to become the Paradise Garden, named after his last television series, which had only just finished. It had been a sublime piece of filming and in my view Geoff's best, featuring gardens that embodied beauty and tranquillity. He'd also constructed two paradise gardens of his own at Barnsdale, one suitable for a town setting, the other for the country. This gave Isabella and Gabriella their idea for the design. Where it faced into the grounds, the garden would be essentially formal, with paved areas, a smart glasshouse, and a pergola leading to a pavilion. At the rear, the planting would be much more naturalistic, with a pond, wildflower meadow and informal flower arrangements, in keeping with the nearby conservation areas. The garden would also pick up on aspects of recycling that had been dear to Geoff's heart, including the use of reconstituted polystyrene as a timber substitute, a complete avoidance of peat, and rainwater collection. And the planting would find a place for the rose, sweet pea and penstemmon that had all been named after him.

Jackie had no problem in finding financial support for the project, with offers of assistance pouring in as soon as we announced it. For example, Alitex, the quality greenhouse manufacturer, donated a handsome Victorian-style greenhouse, and another company supplied all the bricks and stone for the walls and paving. The very realistic-looking grey shingle tiles covering the pavilion were supplied free of charge by Timbaplus, a company that specialized in timber substitutes made from recycled plastics, and a decorative wrought-iron gate that had originally hung at Barnsdale was donated by Geoff's widow, Lynda. HDRA members also responded magnificently to Jackie's appeal and the balance was made up, appropriately enough, by a generous gift from BBC *Gardeners' World* magazine, courtesy of its Editor, Adam Pasco.

We could never have imagined having to construct a garden under such adverse circumstances. From the moment the earthmover arrived in November 1998 until the following May, the site was awash with mud, as torrential rain lashed the grounds day after day. It was a small miracle that anything was planted at all. Even on the big day in June when the Paradise Garden opened, it was against a soundtrack of distant thunder and the steady drip-drip of relentless rain. Nevertheless, a lot of ordinary people came to show their respect, joined by a glittering array of gardening personalities, including Roy Lancaster, Stefan Buczacki and Gay Search. The atmosphere was tense with emotion when Lynda performed the opening ceremony.

I hope that these descriptions of the various attractive, beautifully designed ornamental gardens that HDRA created throughout the 1990s illustrates that organic growing doesn't only apply to fruit and vegetables. And we didn't stop there ...

Chapter Fifteen

✦

FOOD YOU CAN TRUST

FACING THE SHIMMERING grasses and colourful drifts of flowers in the 'new perennial' display was our brand new Cook's Garden, purposefully situated on land adjacent to the restaurant kitchen. It had been Jackie's idea and she'd found money to create it in the form of sponsorship from *The Mail on Sunday*. Kathleen Askew, the Deputy Head Gardener, had designed it to Jackie's brief, with the entire plot conceived as a stunning but fully edible garden. This was completely unlike a potager, where ornamentals mingle freely with vegetables and herbs. Even in the famous garden at the French chateau of Villandry on the River Loire, where intricate geometric designs of vegetables form the main feature, some plants are merely ornamental. The Cook's Garden, as far as we knew, would be unique. The plants would be used by the Ryton chefs in the restaurant to complement the more commonly grown vegetables that they normally obtained elsewhere in the gardens or from commercial organic growers. Kathleen therefore chose plants like the Japanese raisin tree (*Hovenia dulcis*), the Madeira vine (*Anredera cordifolia*) and Babbington's leek (*Allium babbingtonii*), along with scores of equally obscure edible ornamental plants. Even the circular, brick-edged pool, with its solar-powered fountain, was filled with flowering aquatic plants you could eat. It had taken Kathleen the best part of the previous winter and all of the spring to complete it, fitting it in between her other duties. The result was acknowledged by everyone – including Sophie Grigson, the celebrity chef who opened it in August 1998 – to be a triumph.

Nothing could be fresher than the plants picked from the Cook's Garden first thing in the morning and used in the day's recipes. This was all of a piece with Jackie's desire that the chefs should only cook with fresh, organic ingredients. In this she was carrying on the traditions of Cherry Hills and Sir Robert McCarrison, who were both passionately convinced that fresh, unprocessed organic wholefoods were essential for good health.

One big problem Jackie had faced back then, as I've said before, was the cost of organic produce, which was, and still is, more expensive than its conventionally grown equivalent. This is the chief reason more people don't buy organic food. The majority of shoppers say they'd prefer to eat it (80 per cent is the figure quoted in most consumer surveys), but only if the price came down. As it happens, around three out of four British households do buy some organic products from time to time, generating total retail sales of just under £2 billion in 2007. This may sound a lot, but it still only amounts to 2 per cent of the total spent on food and drink in Britain. It's a similar story in the United States, where the equivalent figure is 3 per cent, as it also is in Germany and Italy. Most other European countries record sales of less than 2 per cent (notable exceptions include Denmark (4.5 per cent) and Switzerland (6 per cent)).

Whenever I give public talks on organic gardening I can guarantee that someone in the audience will ask me about the cost of organic food. This makes sense, I suppose, when you consider that gardeners who elect to be organic probably try to buy organic food for the same reason. But just why does organic food cost more? I usually reply that it's certainly not the case that organic producers are greedier than their conventional counterparts. They are bound by the high environmental, conservation and ethical standards under which they've chosen to operate, and so they're producing food that's superior in quality – after all, no one would expect to buy a Rolls Royce for the price of a Mini, would they? I defy anyone who has compared the taste of an organic, free-range chicken with the bland offering of a mass-produced, factory-farmed bird, to say that there is no difference between them. But, apart from the question of taste, the main reason for the price discrepancy is that organic agriculture usually has a higher labour cost and a lower output, and it therefore costs more to produce. For example, the given number of animals that a farmer can keep (the so-called 'stocking density') on an organic farm is less than on a conventionally managed farm. Intensive livestock units ('factory farms'), where animals are crammed together as cheaply as possible, are forbidden altogether under organic standards.

Part of the problem, of course, is that we have all come to expect food to be cheap. According to the Expenditure and Food Survey carried out by the Office of National Statistics in 2008, the proportion of the average UK household budget that is spent on food has more than halved, from 33 per cent in 1957, to just 15 per cent today. And while some shoppers think nothing of spending £100 on a new pair of trainers, they baulk at the thought of paying £10 for an organic chicken. It could be that we've just got our priorities wrong! And in any case it's still possible to eat a cheap, tasty, nutritionally balanced meal made from organic ingredients.

As I point out in my talks, when a shopper buys, say, a bunch of conventionally grown carrots, the price doesn't reflect the environmental and other external costs that were incurred by the modern intensive farming methods used to produce it. That comes later when, for example, they receive a water bill, which includes a proportion of money to cover the water authority's costs for getting rid of the agro-chemicals that pollute all our drinking water supplies. Professor Jules Pretty at Essex University has calculated this alone to be about £20 million annually. In 2000 he estimated the total cost to the British economy of all the external environmental factors that could reasonably be attributed to conventional agriculture, and it came to a staggering £1.51 billion. So much for cheap food! In contrast, if British agriculture was run on entirely organic lines, the equivalent figure would be £385 million, a saving of £1.13 billion.

Cost is important, sure enough, but it's not everything. How do you even begin to put a price on the hundreds of thousands of miles of hedges that have been ripped out or the ancient woodlands that have been grubbed up or the countless acres of wildflower-rich meadows that have disappeared in the chemical revolution that has gripped British agriculture and horticulture for the past 60 years? Huge quantities of chemical fertilizers, which have increased more than 30-fold, have found their way into streams, rivers and lakes, causing unsightly algal blooms and the death of huge numbers of fish and other aquatic life. Nitrate-contaminated water percolates down through the soil to the deep aquifers below, which will contaminate water supplies for decades to come. Pesticides have done untold harm to wildlife, driving some species close to extinction. And, in all truth, we have little idea of the harm they may be doing to us.

We know, for example, from regular government monitoring, that 40 per cent of fruit and vegetables on sale in the European Union are contaminated by pesticide residues and that approximately one food in thirty contains levels that are above the legal limit. No one in authority appears to be unduly bothered about this. Britain's food watchdog, the Food Standards Agency (FSA), merely says that all pesticides have to pass stringent tests before they can be approved for sale, and residues are tiny in any case, so there is nothing to worry about. If this is so, why are pesticides being continually banned or withdrawn from the market? Forty have disappeared from sale during the past decade alone, in response to fresh evidence of their toxicity. It is simply wrong to say that a chemical has no effect just because it occurs at low levels. And the safety procedures used to test pesticides, although rigorous, only examine how these compounds behave individually. However, it's well known that two or more different pesticides can frequently be found in the same foodstuff and that our bodies can contain any number of pesticides from the totality of contaminated food that we eat. The combined toxicity of this melange of toxins can be magnified many-fold, in a synergistic reaction known as the 'cocktail effect'. Our systems are being bombarded by many thousands of man-made chemicals that they have never encountered before. We simply cannot predict the long-term health effects of eating pesticide-contaminated food over a lifetime. You could say that we are guinea pigs in a global, long-running experiment, the results of which may not be known until it's too late. As an example, a number of scientists have put forward the theory that chemical pesticides that harm or imitate human hormones may be responsible for the dramatic decline in male sperm count and the corresponding rise in the incidence of cancers of the reproductive organs observed in recent years.

Latterly, another worrying consequence of chemical-based growing has come to the fore – namely its planetary impact on global warming. Nobody can be in any doubt that the world is getting warmer. The 20th century was the warmest century in human history, the 1990s was the warmest decade and the three years from 2002 to 2004 were the hottest ever. Potent images of collapsing glaciers and polar bears helplessly marooned on ice floes are a stark reminder that something is going badly wrong with the world's climate. Almost all environmental scientists now agree that the burning of fossil fuels is the root cause of the rapidly increasing amounts of carbon dioxide and other so-called 'greenhouse gases' in the atmosphere, and that these are responsible for global rises in temperature. The level of carbon dioxide (CO_2) in the atmosphere has gone up from around 300ppm (parts per million) at the end of the 19th century to 386ppm today. It's expected to reach 500ppm by the year 2050. No-one can predict accurately what this will mean for the environment – we are in uncharted territory here – but we should expect rising sea levels leading to permanent coastal flooding, fiercer and more frequent extreme weather events, such as drought, flash floods and hurricanes, and far hotter temperatures, especially in the tropics.

James Lovelock, the scientist who originated the Gaia Theory, which explains the self-regulating global mechanisms that make life on Earth possible, believes that we have already passed the point of no return and that, apart from a meagre patch of land at the Arctic, most of the planet will be too hot to sustain human existence by the end of the 21st century. Others, incuding the authors of the 1970s study *The Limits to Growth*, who issued an update in 2005, believe that there is still time to turn things around. For the sake of our children and grandchildren, we must pray that they, and not Lovelock, are right.

It has been estimated that each UK citizen is responsible for the emission of around twelve tons of greenhouse gases into the atmosphere each year. Two tons of this is spent in getting food onto our plates, which is a greater amount than that emitted as a result of all our personal car use and electricity consumption combined. Of this food-related sum, by far the largest proportion involves the manufacture and use of fertilizers and pesticides. Making nitrogen fertilizers is a highly energy-intensive process, requiring huge quantities of natural gas, with nearly seven tons of CO_2-equivalent being given off for every ton of product. Then, when the fertilizers are spread onto the land, they are broken down by bacteria in the soil – a process that releases nitrous oxide into the atmosphere. Nitrous oxide is a far more powerful greenhouse gas than CO_2 – some 300 times more damaging, in fact.

And there's a double whammy here, for as I've already suggested (see page 11), soil organic matter breaks down when farmers use artificial fertilizers, releasing even more carbon back into the atmosphere. In summary, the manufacture and use of chemical fertilizers is responsible for 28 per cent of all greenhouse gas emissions associated with the UK food supply chain, compared with 4 per cent emitted by tractors and other farm machinery. Even road haulage and air freight combined are only responsible for 12 per cent of the two tons of 'food' emissions. By comparison, organic farming involves the emission of considerably fewer greenhouse gases.

Organic farming also uses approximately a third less energy than chemical-based agriculture, although this didn't impact on conventional farmers until relatively recently because oil prices were less than $50 a barrel. Organic food production was always going to lose out in this particular struggle because of its greater use of labour, which is far costlier than fuel. But as oil prices spiral ever upwards, the greater energy efficiency of organic horticulture and agriculture will start to win through, and it will be inorganic farming that will be seen as inefficient. In the past year alone fertilizer prices have tripled. So, in the same way that people are switching to smaller, more fuel-efficient cars, farmers in the future will come to appreciate the economic advantages of farming without chemicals.

But there are other unfortunate consequences associated with the use of chemical fertilizers, which affect our food directly. The past half-century has witnessed an incredible decline in the mineral and trace element content of fruit and vegetables. David Thomas, a former geologist, has tracked this downwards trend, using government data taken from a book called *The Composition of Foods*, written by two UK food scientists, Professor McCance and Dr Widdowson, which first appeared in 1940. They subsequently revised and periodically reissued it throughout the following decades. Over a period of 51 years, fruit and vegetables lost more than half their copper, iron and zinc. To illustrate the practical consequences of this you would need to have eaten ten tomatoes in 1991 to obtain the same copper intake as from one tomato in 1940. Astonishing isn't it?

A similar phenomenon has also occurred in the USA, according to Donald Davis, a researcher at the University of Texas. He discovered that between 1950 and 1999 the amounts of protein, calcium, iron, phosphorus and a number of vitamins in food dropped alarmingly.

Both Thomas and Davis are convinced that modern methods of agriculture are mostly to blame. High-yielding plant varieties that grow bigger and faster but don't take up nutrients at the same rate, and artificial fertilizers, which suppress the soil micro-organisms that make minerals and other micro-nutrients available, are just two of the contributory factors – although longer storage times and greater travelling distances from farm to supermarket or processing plant also have an adverse effect. As we saw in chapter five, the over-use of artificial fertilizers can 'lock up' minerals in the soil, preventing plants from absorbing them. Phosphate fertilizers, for example, have been responsible for zinc deficiency through the formation of zinc phosphate, which is insoluble in water. Critics of Thomas and Davis say that falling vitamin and mineral content in fruit and vegetables is of little consequence because they can be obtained from other foods, such as liver, which contains iron, or vitamin C-rich oranges. But they are surely missing the point. There is something drastically wrong in an agricultural system that produces such a pronounced degradation in the quality of the food we eat.

But what evidence is there to show that organic food is actually healthier? In January 2007, the then Environment Secretary David Milliband commented that organic food is merely a 'lifestyle choice that people can make', and the FSA is on record as saying that there is no nutritional difference between organic and conventionally produced food.

Well, as we have seen already, pesticides are not allowed in organic growing, apart from the small number of products referred to in chapter six. Artificial colourings, flavourings and preservatives are also banned from organic food products, other than for an extremely restricted range of natural substances. For these reasons alone organic food has got to be better for us.

When it comes to scientifically proving nutritional superiority, however, the evidence is not clear-cut. Studies comparing food from organic and non-organic farming systems are costly because they are complex and time-consuming, and the organic movement has never had sufficient resources to allocate to research. Even then it is also logistically difficult to find matched pairs of organic and conventionally run farms where the soil type is similar and where the crop variety, time of sowing, and all the other variables that can influence nutritional content, can be carefully controlled. It's not surprising, then, that such research is thin on the ground. Many experiments, particularly those from the last century, failed to give clear-cut results, which is how the FSA is able to take the line it does. Nevertheless, a consistent strand does run through the modest amount of research that has been done, in that the majority of results show that organic food contains higher amounts of essential minerals, especially iron, magnesium, phosphorus and zinc, and greater levels of vitamins, especially vitamin C. Also, organic food has around 15 per cent more dry-matter content than conventionally grown food, which is perhaps not surprising, since the higher crop yields associated with artificial fertilizers are partly due to their ability to boost a plant's water uptake. It's a sobering thought that when you buy conventionally grown food you are paying for expensively packaged water!

During the last few years additional evidence has started to emerge of how organic fruit and vegetables might help in the fight against cancer and heart disease because they contain significantly higher levels of phytochemicals (where phyto means 'produced by plants'), including 'anti-oxidants' – the compounds that help to protect us from disease by bolstering the body's immune system. Vitamin C is one such, as are glucosinolates in broccoli and other green vegetables, flavonoids in onions, garlic and blackcurrants, and lycopene in tomatoes. These anti-oxidants that are so useful to us are produced by plants to defend themselves against bacteria, viruses and fungi. However, when pesticides are used on a crop, the plants produce fewer phytochemicals – so if we eat conventionally grown produce we consume less disease-preventing anti-oxidants.

In 2008 a £12 million, four-year study at Newcastle University, funded by the European Union (EU) and involving a team of international researchers, reported that organically grown carrots, apples and peaches contained up to 40 per cent more anti-oxidants and higher levels of iron and zinc than those grown on conventional farms. Its co-ordinator, Professor Carlo Leifert, said that the health benefits were so striking that switching to organic food was equivalent to eating an extra portion of fruit and vegetables every day.

Another ten-year study by researchers at the University of California, Davis, which ended in 2006, found that the quantity of flavonoids in organic tomatoes was double that of tomatoes that had been grown conventionally. Other scientists at the same institution have separately recorded greater mineral content and enhanced levels of vitamin C and other anti-oxidants in organically grown kiwi fruits.

It appears that the early organic pioneers in the 1940s and 1950s were right in believing strongly that there was something in organic food – a special factor – that was essential to maintaining human health. It was for this reason, as I've said before, that Sir Albert Howard was so passionate about compost-grown crops, which appeared to be able to shrug off the diseases that struck down plants grown with chemical fertilizers; or his organically fed livestock, which could withstand infection from even the most contagious conditions, such as foot and mouth disease. No one was sure exactly what this factor was and it was therefore given the somewhat mystical name of the 'life force'. Could phytochemicals, which have a protective action against disease, be this special 'force', or could there be some other factor that we have not yet discovered? One problem in trying to identify it is that conventional tests require food samples to be dissolved in acid, which is hardly conducive to discovering what might be a vital living element. Radical new types of analysis are needed. Among the more promising is a scientific method that works on the principle that all living matter emits tiny, but detectable amounts of light energy. Examination has revealed clear differences between emissions from eggs laid by free-range hens and those produced by hens living in batteries. Likewise, between crops grown with or without chemicals. Another method involves a technique in which extracts of food are applied to an absorbent surface that has been treated with a weak solution of copper chloride. After a while a 'picture' emerges, not dissimilar from the designs that can appear when ice crystals form on a window pane. Patterns differ markedly according to the origin of the sample and occur with such regularity that researchers are able to correctly distinguish, in 99 cases out of a 100, whether the food sample is organic or not. It's almost as if the food has its own 'fingerprint'. What exactly is being measured, however, and whether it has any impact on human health, remains a mystery at this point in time.

At a conference hosted by Elm Farm Research Centre in November 2004, Professor Angelika Meier-Ploeger of Kassel University, Germany, summed up the current state of knowledge of these various unorthodox analytical methods as follows:

> More work needs to be done to correlate data from chemical analysis with holistic methods, and many more studies will need to be undertaken, before it is known how much information they give us beyond nutrient status. It is likely to be some time before we know if these 'pictures/structures/forces/energy' are important for animal and human health. But they do already show us that there is indeed an extra dimension or quality to organic food.

Over the coming years we can expect a greater flow of scientific evidence that confirms the value to our health of eating organic food. In this chapter I have touched mainly upon some of the environmental and health problems brought about by the use of artificial fertilizers and pesticides. It's hard to see how current methods of food production will be able to continue to feed the world's existing population, let alone the estimated nine billion souls who will inhabit the Earth by the middle of the century. Many now believe that chemical-based agriculture exerts too great a cost on the environment and our health, whether it is through destruction of the land, the pollution and depletion of water resources, pesticide contamination in food, or in heightened greenhouse gas emissions.

Globally, we scraped by in the 20th century by moving on from worked-out soils into virgin territory, as if there were no limits. This is no longer an option: forests are too precious as regulators of the global climate to be sacrificed in this way. Nor should we expect GM technology to come to our aid, despite the fact that siren voices in the media and biotech industry put forward genetic modification as a panacea for all our food problems. The fact is that none of the GM crops that have so far been developed have made the slightest impact on crop yields. And in any case, gene technology merely perpetuates the same discredited industrialized model of agriculture that has wreaked such damage in the past.

If we are to feed ourselves and future generations without destroying the environment a radical change of direction is needed, and Jackie and I, along with many other scientists, farmers, gardeners and consumers believe that the organic model is the way to go if we are to stand any chance of having a sustainable future.

Chapter Sixteen

BLOSSOMING OUT

ORGANIC GARDENING IS the most sustainable way to grow. That is the main reason we worked so hard at HDRA to promote it and to provide practical information about it. By the latter half of the 1990s organic gardening had indeed become more popular, but there were no grounds for complacency. We were well aware, for example, that only a handful of children had access to a school vegetable plot and that the majority of city dwellers hardly grew anything at all. It was also apparent that head gardeners at most of the country's stately homes still used modern chemicals, even though the houses themselves were restored and maintained in a historically authentic way, down to the last curtain thread. In 1998, in order to keep the momentum going, Jackie launched an ambitious national campaign called 'Grow Your Own Organic Fruit and Vegetables' to try and get everybody involved, whoever they were and wherever and however they lived.

We got off to a good start when English Heritage, the official body responsible for the nation's historic buildings, invited us to take over the running of the walled kitchen garden at Audley End, its flagship property outside the quaint market town of Saffron Walden in Essex. The house was built in the early 1600s by Sir Thomas Howard, Lord Treasurer to James I, and is thought by many to be one of the finest

Jacobean mansions in the country. When Jackie and I rounded the bend of what used to be the main London to Norwich road and saw Audley End for the first time, its beauty took our breath away. Not so the walled garden, which had been run as a commercial nursery on a tenanted basis for the previous 40 years and by then was in urgent need of some tender loving care.

Nick Hill, the friendly, enthusiastic project coordinator showed us round. In spite of its uncared-for appearance, the garden was actually in a fair state. Best of all, there was a 200-year-old greenhouse running the length of the end wall, with almost all of its glass still intact, which only required a lick of paint. We could easily imagine the garden as it would have appeared in its Victorian heyday and realized at once that, if restored, it would be the perfect place to set off the historic vegetable varieties in our Heritage Seed Library (HSL). It would also demonstrate to other stately home owners that it's possible to cultivate grand gardens organically and that it's a great way to bring their own walled kitchen gardens back to life.

After that first meeting early in 1998 we spent many months thrashing out an agreement with English Heritage, finally reaching a successful conclusion in December, when HDRA was given full responsibility to manage the land. Having spent so long working out the details we were keen to get started. Perhaps somewhat rashly, we set ourselves the ambitious target of being up and running by Easter, even though that gave us little more than three months to lick the garden into shape. Of course we didn't expect to have completely finished the restoration by then. The garden would be presented to visitors as 'work in progress', which in itself would be of interest. Everything depended on getting the right head gardener – someone with an in-depth knowledge of horticulture who was organically minded and could inspire and motivate the new team of gardeners and volunteers. Fortunately we found just the man in Mike Thurlow, a gently spoken Welshman, who had spent most of his working life as a professional gardener. So, while the staff of English Heritage refurbished the glasshouse, repaired loose masonry and re-laid the paths, Mike and his helpers set about clearing the land of rubbish and digging it over in preparation for planting hundreds of fruit trees and bushes. Meanwhile, Bob Sherman, whom I had recently promoted to the post of HDRA's Head of Horticulture, got on with the job of selecting which varieties to grow. Bob is passionate about fruit, and the thought of the hundreds of yards of tall brick walls against which Mike could train trees into fans, espaliers and other elaborate shapes, filled him with joy. And there was another exciting challenge waiting for him in the glasshouse, where two extremely gnarled and venerable grape-vines, just a couple of decades short of their 200th birthday, were ready to be coaxed back into life.

Working every day of the week to make up for the limited winter daylight, Mike and his team did their utmost to ensure that the garden would be ready on time. A hundred tons of green-waste compost was ordered from a nearby local authority to spread over the soil in an attempt to kick-start its micro-organisms into activity. Eight thousand young box plants were then transplanted along each side of every path – enough to create a mile of tightly clipped dwarf hedging.

By the time April arrived, the garden had been thoroughly trans-formed, ready for the first of the 100,000 people who would visit Audley End that year. It would take many more seasons of hard work and dedication to fully restore the fertility of the land, but even then the visitors could see that walled kitchen gardens could be productive powerhouses. A great start was made in that very first spring and summer of 1999 and both Jackie and I were extremely proud of what Bob, Mike and the rest of the team had achieved.

Audley End was not the only newly restored walled kitchen garden that the public could visit at the time. Heligan in Cornwall – which had been imaginatively brought back to life by Tim Smit during the early 1990s – and West Dean Gardens in West Sussex were two other notable examples. Audley, however, was by far the largest and the only one that was fully organic. Unfortunately, due to the massive costs involved in restoration and maintenance, most walled gardens in the UK either lay derelict and unloved at the time or were grassed over for car parking. This is understandable when you think that in Victorian and Edwardian times, 20 or 30 gardeners would have been needed to keep these intensively cultivated plots in full production. Who could afford this nowadays? As we had seen at Audley, a great deal could be achieved using volunteers, but not even the National Trust – the country's largest custodian of historic properties with millions of members – was making the best use of the walled gardens in its care. It would take until 2001, when Fiona Reynolds took over as Director General, to radically change the Trust's policy.

The country's stately homes were not the only target for Jackie's 'Grow Your Own Organic Fruit and Vegetables' campaign. She was also passionately interested in helping people living in towns and cities, where gardens were practically non-existent. So many had never even thought about growing their own food or believed that it was possible. She was also keen for HDRA to show them just how much food you can produce in a small space, because the figures were truly staggering. According to an American called Mel Bartholomew, an area just four foot by four foot was enough to supply a person with all the salad vegetables they needed during the five main months of the growing season. In his book *Square Foot Gardening*, published in 1981, his four-foot-square raised bed, edged with timber, was divided, by string, into 16 one-foot squares. A different sort of vegetable was grown on each square – carrots on one, lettuces on another, tomatoes on a third, and so on. The plants were spaced closely together, as with conventional bed growing, and no sooner was one crop finished than it was replaced by another. Good soil, he reckoned, is essential if such an intensive method of growing is to succeed, and for this reason Bartholomew recommended bringing in compost. Unfortunately, he also advocated the use of artificial fertilizers, but an HDRA member called Colin Shaw tried the technique using organic methods, and it had been just as productive.

It seemed to us, then, that the 'square-foot' method would be an excellent way of introducing people to vegetable growing. It shouldn't take up much time, the cost of tools, seeds and compost was minimal and hardly any space was required. You didn't even need a garden. If you wanted to, you could 'square-foot garden' on a balcony!

Jackie got down to work with Pauline Pears and her staff in HDRA's

Information and Education Department to write and produce a series of leaflets, posters and other campaign materials for distribution. Pauline dealt with the gardening information in the publications and Jackie designed them, making full use of the graphics department she had set up in-house. This saved HDRA a great deal of money because as well as working with mainstream publishers, HDRA had always self-published. During the 1960s Lawrence had started the trend with snappily titled booklets such as *War on Weeds* and *Perfumes against Pests*. They had been knocked out on an old Gestetner duplicator in those days, but Jackie thought that the look of them didn't do justice to the content, so she strove to improve the design.

Much of the advice that went into the handbooks came from the wealth of information and experience that HDRA had accumulated over many years of experimental work. As well as making this available through its magazine, which was sent to the members four times a year, the organization's advisory department had also written a comprehensive set of fact sheets and step-by-step guides, covering every aspect of organic gardening. As part of the new campaign Jackie decided to give them a fresh look, to update and reissue them. We already knew they were popular because Pauline's staff had sent out more than 40,000 fact sheets in response to enquiries in 1997. She and her team had also answered telephone gardening queries from over 4,000 members during the year. In the conference centre, her department's practical gardening courses were also proving to be extremely popular – especially 'Vegetable Growing for the Terrified', which was aimed at virgin vegetable growers. It meant a lot of extra work for the Information and Education Department, but they were a dedicated and hard-working team and reacted to demands from the public for advice with their usual professionalism.

As well as all this, they also produced comprehensive books on specific topics, which were published by Search Press and would serve us well in the new campaign. We had a good working relationship with the company's owner, Countess Charlotte de la Bedoyere (Lottie to her friends), who was husky-voiced, very good company and never went anywhere without her Alsatian dog! She had approached Jackie and me in 1990 with an offer to publish a series of full-colour, practical organic handbooks. The first two (*How to Make Your Garden Fertile,* and *Pests: How to control them on fruit and vegetables*), both written by Pauline, with Lottie taking the photographs, had come out that same year. Three more titles followed in 1991: one on diseases, which Pauline co-wrote with Bob; another on weeds; and a third on soil care – the last two titles were written by Jo Readman, a college lecturer and television researcher who had worked with us on *Loads More Muck and Magic.* Lottie again supplied the pictures. By 1998 we had produced eight titles and were sure that our new audience would find them extremely useful.

Jackie also persuaded our local HDRA groups to get involved in the campaign in a big way, and they attended shows and events in their area, and opened their gardens to the public using colourful display materials on loan from Ryton. We also sent information to other like-minded organizations such as the Soil Association, the Federation of City Farms and Community Gardens, and Greenpeace, which, conveniently, was running a 'True Food Campaign' at the time to encourage people to grow and eat organic food as an alternative to eating food that may contain genetically modified organisms. This all tied in well.

Leaving no stone unturned, Jackie then targeted community gardens, to encourage them to start growing organic vegetables. Faced with an acute shortage of allotments, and hence long waiting lists, people had already begun to take matters into their own hands by reclaiming plots of forgotten and derelict land and turning them into communal gardens. The result of all their efforts had begun to appear across the towns and cities of Britain during the late-1960s and were now rapidly expanding. Many of the people involved in the movement were enthusiastic novices who lacked practical experience, so they snapped up large quantities of our posters and leaflets. Titles like *Budget Gardening and Starting an Allotment* proved to be extremely popular. *The Cook's Garden Planner,* which we had produced thanks to support from *The Mail on Sunday,* also went down a storm, with two and a half million copies distributed.

Keri Schofield, an HDRA member from Cardiff, told us about her project at Fairwater Community Garden, which was based around the needs of students with learning difficulties. She wanted to expand the fruit and vegetable growing part of the garden and was keen to work with us. In Sheffield, Carol and Kevin Hall formed a pressure group to reclaim a disused two-acre allotment site and they soon had 15 committed families involved. 'The allotments are bringing people together in this community who never would have met otherwise,' Kevin said. 'They're all keen to go down there, get mucky, and have a laugh.'

If you watch the television these days you might be led into thinking that such initiatives are new, but they are in reality following a groundswell of developments over many years. And community gardens are not just confined to Britain. There are many to be found in other countries, including the United States (where they are especially strong in the northeast), Canada, Australia and New Zealand. Unlike our individual allotments here in Britain, which in most cases are a standard 90 feet by 30 feet, American community gardens come in all shapes and sizes, and the plots are usually a lot smaller – 10- and 20-feet-square versions being particularly common. The American Community Gardening Association, a non-profit coalition acting for community gardeners in North America, estimates that there are currently around 5,000 groups in the US alone; the comparable figure for the UK is thought to be around a fifth of that.

North America also has its Victory Gardens, which began during the last World War, when more than 20 million people 'dug for victory' and in so doing, produced over 40 per cent of the nation's vegetables. 'Plant more in '44' was the stirring slogan back home, as US troops stormed across the beaches of Normandy on D-Day. Some, like the Dowling Community Garden in Minneapolis, Minnesota, have been in continuous production ever since. There is also a grassroots movement currently trying to revive the idea for the 21st century. Prior to the US elections in 2008, for example, one audacious group called 'Eat the View' was attempting to persuade Barack Obama to convert one of the lawns at the White House into a vegetable plot should he become President! The campaign was a resounding success – just weeks after the Obamas took up residence in the famous building,

Michelle Obama, a keen advocate of fresh vegetables, was photo-graphed in her gardening gloves planting herbs and other seedlings in the South Lawn.

Around the same time that we were running the 'Grow Your Own Organic Fruit and Vegetables' campaign, we were also in discussions with local authorities throughout Britain urging them to support home composting initiatives. It was certainly in their interests to do this, with an ever-increasing amount of household rubbish chasing an ever-shrinking number of holes in which to dump it. An American scheme called 'Master Composters' had caught our eye – it involved enthusiastic volunteers acting as personal mentors, guiding individuals and groups through the nuts and bolts of making compost. The scheme had been operating successfully in the United States and Canada for about ten years, and in 1999 we introduced it to Britain. Each new Master Composter mentor received a two-day intensive training course led by HDRA members of staff, and then he or she undertook to spend 30 hours – some did many more – encouraging people in their neighbourhood to start making compost. This could take the form of giving compost-making demonstrations to allotment holders or hands-on workshops for teachers and children at a nearby school; a letter writing campaign to local newspapers and parish and community magazines; or perhaps talks to the district gardening and horticultural societies; anything, in fact, that would spread awareness of the value of compost and how to make it. On completing their mentoring duties, each volunteer would 'graduate' as a fully fledged 'Master Composter'. Cambridgeshire was one of the earliest counties to sign up and at one time had over 150 volunteers travelling the county, passing on their passion about the joys of making compost! Since then the idea has spread rapidly throughout the UK and at the time of writing there are more than 20 Master Composters schemes in operation.

Persuading adults to grow fruit and vegetables was important, but we also wanted to reach out to youngsters. In the past, HDRA's involvement with children had been fairly minimal, apart from the occasional school parties that visited Ryton and Yalding (where there were charming little Children's Gardens). Jo Readman, who collaborated with Pauline on the Search Press series of booklets, had written a book for children called *Muck and Magic*, but that was about the extent of it. Things improved when the bubbly ex-teacher Maggi Brown joined Pauline's team of advisors and started to make contacts with schools in the area. In 1996 she had also written a useful book called *Growing Naturally: A Teacher's Guide to Organic Gardening*, to show primary school teachers how they could successfully dovetail the subject into the National Curriculum.

That same year the government announced that it wanted schools to become more 'green', which was shorthand for saying that it wanted them to plant more trees and shrubs. This showed a singular lack of ambition as far as we were concerned. To us, the term 'green school' meant, at the very least, managing the grounds organically. So we contacted the Department of the Environment (DOE) and suggested that they commission HDRA to investigate how this might be achieved. Out of this came a three-year nationwide project with pilot schools called 'Go Organic in School Grounds', which looked at how schools currently maintained their premises and how things could be improved.

We were shocked by what we discovered. Schools no longer, apparently, employed their own staff to trim the grass on the playing fields, or keep the flowerbeds neat and tidy. They relied on outside contractors to do the work instead. In order to make life easier for themselves, and to speed up the job, the contractors invariably used large quantities of herbicides to clear mowing strips around clumps of shrubs and to keep flower beds weed-free. At one school near Oxford, for example, pupils found it impossible to germinate seeds because of toxic residues in the soil. Herbicides were also sprayed liberally onto playing fields, to eliminate dandelions, docks and other broad-leaved weeds, but nobody seemed to have thought about the potential risk to the pupils' health from the pesticide-contaminated turf that they played on, or sat on to eat their picnic lunches.

At many of the schools, grass trimmings, hedge prunings and other garden wastes, which could have been composted quite easily on site, were taken away and dumped, and the irresponsible use of strimmers was commonplace, leading to the death, through ring-barking, of newly planted trees. All these problems were entirely avoidable and we stated in our report at the end of the project that they could, and should, be replaced by environmentally friendly, fully organic methods of managing school grounds. We emphasized that this could result in considerable financial savings for the school.

What also came out during the project was a strong desire on behalf of many of the teachers involved to set up school gardens. This was exactly what we'd been hoping for, and we did all we could to encourage them to set aside land where students could learn how to grow fruit and vegetables for themselves. Unfortunately, when the project came to an end in 1998, the funding ended too, and without a dedicated full-time member of staff, it was difficult to see how we could carry on working with children proactively. Then, in the winter of 1999, as a result of discussions with someone from one of the Sainsbury Family Charitable Trusts, Jackie was offered three years' worth of funding to continue our involvement with schools. It marked a major turning point, setting in train what would become an important strand of HDRA's activities. The new project was called HDRA's 'Organic Network for Schools'.

Inevitably it took time to get going, as Maggi and Bridgette Barrett, the teacher who had been appointed to coordinate the project, prepared material for the posters, worksheets and other classroom materials for the schools that 'signed up' to the Network. They also organized training sessions at Ryton so that teachers could share experiences and pick up ideas from the gardens; they produced a regular newsletter and in collaboration with Simon Levermore, HDRA's talented Webmaster, set up a dedicated website. By the end of the first year a grand total of 36 schools had signed up. Like a snowball rolling downhill, the number grew exponentially and three years later the website was receiving 17,000 'hits' a month, with over 200 schools involved.

All of our organic gardening information for schools linked in with the National Curriculum, so the teachers were able to introduce it in all sorts of different ways. At Grovelands County Primary School in East Sussex, for example, pupils studied history by way of vegetable varieties that would have been grown during the wartime 'Dig for Victory' campaign. Students and staff at Minterne Junior School in Kent tipped soil into an abandoned swimming pool at the rear of the school and transformed it into a productive vegetable garden. Even schools where every square inch was covered with tarmac got involved – like New Hinksey School in Oxford, for example, where Maggi was able to suggest compact varieties of vegetables that were suitable for container-growing. By January 2003 we had used all our funding from the J J Charitable Trust and we were sorry to say goodbye to Mark Woodruff, our contact there, who had been incredibly supportive. Mark had sat on all the working group meetings, chaired by Jackie, and we had built up an extraordinary rapport with him during the previous three years. We were very worried at this point that we might have to let this good work go, so when Jackie's successful meeting with Duchy Originals – the company set up by The Prince of Wales to market the food produced at Highgrove and other organic farms – led to a sponsorship deal, it was a huge relief all round. Since that time the expansion of the Duchy Originals Garden Organic for Schools project has been astonishing and by 2008 the number of participating schools had swelled to more than 5,000.

Although I wasn't personally involved in any of the work with schools, Jackie kept me up-to-date with progress through her regular working-group meetings. I can remember being astonished to learn how little most children knew about vegetables and where they come from. Their knowledge of even basic crops, like carrots, peas and potatoes, was dreadful, and most ten-year-olds, if shown pictures of a celeriac root, an asparagus tip or a parsnip, were incapable of identifying them correctly. Indeed, they couldn't even make the connection between a packet of frozen peas and a freshly picked pea pod, or a plate of chips and a field of potatoes. Let's face it, most children don't even eat vegetables regularly, let alone know how they are cultivated. Incredibly, some of the teachers were almost as clueless as their charges, and only the keen gardeners among them were aware of the astonishing diversity in vegetables that existed – the hundreds of different varieties of carrots, onions and beans, and so on – that HDRA had made such an effort to protect. Helping schools to set up gardens, where kids could grow their own food and get their hands dirty, would undoubtedly be a big step in filling this gap in their knowledge of vegetables, and it might even stimulate them into eating more! We couldn't help thinking, though, that we should be going all out to increase awareness of one of the most essential elements of a healthy diet.

Jackie came up with an ambitious plan for how this might be achieved. She wanted to build a brand new visitor centre that combined the practical seed conservation activities of the Heritage Seed Library with HDRA's educational work, which would give children and adults alike a sense of the rich diversity, history and importance of the vegetable kingdom. Just as importantly it would convey knowledge about the value of vegetables in our diets and their role in maintaining good health. She knew that it would be a costly project and was also aware that HDRA would not be able to afford it from its own resources. It seemed to her that this was just the sort of project that the Heritage Lottery Fund ought to be supporting, so she wrote off for an application form, displaying her usual optimism and determination.

HDRA's Heritage Seed Library (HSL) had grown rapidly during the past few years, and in 1998 Jackie had won a government grant for work we wanted to do in searching for old vegetable varieties, which she called HDRA's 'Back Garden Biodiversity Project'. The plan was to ask gardeners to participate in the 'Seed Search' by giving us seeds from forgotten varieties of vegetables they were growing. In the past they had just contacted HSL by chance. We didn't have a clue whether our quest would bring in ten varieties or a thousand, but whatever the number, looking after them was going to put additional pressure on our already stretched facilities. There was also a good chance that some of these as yet undiscovered seeds would come with fascinating tales attached that deserved to be told to a wider audience – like the medieval 'Martock' bean sent in by the Bishop of Bath and Wells, or the 'Cherokee Trail of Tears' bean, already mentioned.

In charge of the Seed Search project was Sue Stickland, Ryton's previous Head Gardener. Sue had recently completed a book on heritage vegetables and was as excited as we were about the prospect of rediscovering varieties that had been dropped from the *UK National List* or that had never been registered because they had been saved at home, by keen gardeners. The press picked up on the story in a big way, appealing to their readers to send us their seeds and, before long, packets of every shape and size were winging their way to Ryton – 160 different varieties in the first year alone. Just as we'd expected, there were some spectacular finds, including Mr Bound's 'Bean' pea – a huge pea that looks and tastes like a broad bean – and 'Ryder's Midday Sun' tomato, which had originally been sold by a small local seed firm called Ryder's in St Albans, Hertfordshire, before it was swallowed up in the massive wave of seed company takeovers during the 1970s. Fortunately, Mrs Cullen, one of the company's loyal customers, had been so impressed by the taste of that tomato that she'd saved seeds from it ever since.

But the most amazing discovery of all was a tall garden pea provided by Mr Feltham from Gloucestershire, which had first been grown at a large country estate in Dorset. If the story can be believed, the pea had originally been found by Lord Caernarvon inside the tomb of Tutankhamen, when he had opened it in 1922, and he had subsequently given it to his friend, Lord Portman, the owner of the estate. Were they really the seeds of the pharaoh? Who knows? We like to think so!

Sue's extensive trawl of the nation's seed savers came to an end in 2001, by which time she had received more than 250 samples, all of which were consigned to the safety of the HSL so that they could be enjoyed by everyone in the future. We were truly thrilled that the extra seeds had pushed the total number of varieties in the collection up to 800, with demand increasing every year.

But individual gardeners weren't the only ones to appreciate vintage varieties of vegetables. The owners of historic houses had now begun to realize the importance of growing period-correct varieties, and they also turned to us at this time. When Fiona Reynolds became the new head of the National Trust she made the Trust's gardens a priority and, before long, their previously unused walled gardens were on the receiving end of a makeover. In 2002 they launched a 'Plot to Plate' project at the Chelsea Flower Show, and we supplied many of the heritage vegetable seeds they used. As part of the new initiative they grew heirloom varieties of vegetables at their properties and put them on the menu in the Trust's cafés and restaurants. They started with Clumber Park in Nottinghamshire, but within five years the Trust had increased its number of working and ornamental kitchen gardens to twenty-five. This was just what Jackie and I had been banging on about for years, so we couldn't have been more pleased.

Back at Ryton, Jackie's dream, our new visitor attraction, which she called the 'Vegetable Kingdom', was about to be realized, after two years of intensive planning and fundraising. The Heritage Lottery Fund had offered one million pounds towards the cost, but only if we could find matching finance. So Jackie had approached a small number of long-standing HDRA benefactors, including Charlotte Albuquerque and Amy Goldman, the Chair of Seed Savers Exchange in the USA. They had contributed handsomely, and The Prince of Wales had shown his support too, by hosting a highly successful fundraising event at Highgrove. Even Brussels had chipped in, in a manner of speaking, with a grant from its Regional Development Fund. This was ironic, when you come to think about it, because if it hadn't been for the EU's idiotic seed regulations, which were to blame for the demise of countless vegetable varieties, the HSL would never have come into being in the first place! Still, at least they were making up for it now.

Jackie, who had had her own clear vision of what the Vegetable Kingdom would look like, and the story it would tell, had also worked closely with the architects and Pauline, Bob and other staff, on its development. She had wanted a 'green' visitor centre in every sense of the word, making the maximum use of recycled materials and energy conservation.

Now it was complete. In the main exhibition area interactive displays and life-size models, constructed from papier-mâché and non-toxic glue, told of the importance of vegetables, their origins and history, and the science behind the seeds. Computer game stations,

vegetable cartoon characters and a play kitchen for younger children brought the subject alive. Outside, in two new, visually exciting,
wholly vegetable gardens, an enormous range of crops was growing.
Most important of all, we had designed in space and facilities to com-
fortably hold our existing seed collection, including an allowance for
substantial growth in future years. What's more, visitors could observe
members of HSL staff going about their day-to-day work through
large, plate-glass windows. If anything was going to inspire people to
start growing and eating organic vegetables, this was it, we hoped. The
Vegetable Kingdom would also turn Ryton Gardens into a year-round
visitor attraction and, if it was well publicized in the future, it would
increase the number of HDRA members and raise revenue through
the attractively refurbished and enlarged shop. The extra funds would
go towards the HSL and the organization's many projects to get the
public growing.

On 26 June 2003, HDRA's Patron The Prince of Wales came to Ryton
to perform the official opening ceremony in the Vegetable Kingdom
foyer, after paying a brief visit to the Conference Centre to look at a
wonderful bronze sculpture of himself on display there, created by
artist Nicola Kyle. His Royal Highness seemed to thoroughly enjoy
his tour of the Vegetable Kingdom and his speech was full of praise
for what HDRA had achieved in the fight to preserve and promote
Britain's vegetable heritage. Hopefully, I thought, with this amazing
new facility, we would be able to do even more in the future.

Chapter Seventeen

AN ORGANIC FUTURE

Standing in the bright and airy reception area of the Vegetable Kingdom when the speeches were over and the Prince was chatting to guests, I couldn't help thinking about how HDRA had developed over the last 30 years. A gathering like this, with such eminent guests and all the press, would have been inconceivable when we began working for Lawrence Hills in the 1970s – at that time hardly anybody had heard about organic gardening, let alone believed that it had a future.

Jackie and I had been Lawrence's first full-time employees, with the operation running to just half a dozen prefabricated buildings on a couple of acres of land in Essex and a membership of 3,000. Even our fears about oil running out, global environmental pollution and future food crises – the main reasons we'd decided to work there – were dismissed as nonsense by most people. Likewise, any attempt on our part to talk about the role that organic wholefoods play in maintaining good health was usually greeted with polite yawns.

Throughout the 1970s and early-1980s, as we kept plugging the organic message, our motto became 'KBO!' – 'Keep Buggering On!' – borrowing Sir Winston Churchill's famous phrase. Things improved when the organization moved to Ryton Gardens in 1985 because many thousands of visitors were then able to see for themselves that organic methods work, and the publicity we generated ensured that organic gardening became a talking point nationally. But it would take the Channel 4 television series *All Muck and Magic?* to change public consciousness and persuade the gardening public to grow organically in any sort of numbers.

HDRA continued to expand its influence in the 1990s, reaching out to millions of gardeners and consumers, thanks in no small way to thousands of press articles, and television and radio interviews about its work. Ryton Gardens was seen as the premier organic gardening demonstration centre in Europe, arguably in the world, with outlying sites at Audley End in Essex and Yalding in Kent. HDRA's greatest asset, however, was its staff – professional, knowledgeable and dedicated individuals, with a formidable reputation. At one time, for example, our team of 30-strong researchers was engaged on more organic horticultural research projects at home, and in the developing world, than any other comparable research institution in the UK; the organization's acclaimed Heritage Seed Library (HSL) was an inspiration to seed savers everywhere; and our Information and Education Department was the place of choice for tens of thousands of gardeners wanting accurate information and advice about organic growing. HDRA had also published many hundreds of leaflets, booklets, scientific papers and books on the subject, including a recently completed *Encyclopaedia of Organic Gardening*. Ryton Gardens restaurant had gained a reputation as the place to eat fine organic food, while the award-winning shop at Ryton stocked one of the widest selections of organic gardening products and organic food in Britain. Now we had the Vegetable Kingdom – a unique visitor centre that celebrated the important role vegetables play in our lives, and a superb new home for our HSL collection.

Brought out of my reverie with a start when Jackie tugged my arm, I looked around at our smiling guests, and the Prince, who was still chatting away. It dawned on me that all the hard work and dedication that the staff had put in for so many years – combined with the Prince's endorsement – had finally brought about the sea change in the perception of the general public towards organic growing that Jackie and I had been fighting for.

Of course, Jackie and I were well aware that HDRA would never have been able to do what it did without help from all the outside supporters who approved of our aims, like our good friend, actress and keen organic gardener Thelma Barlow, comedian Jasper Carrott and the actress Susan Hampshire. We had also had fantastic support from 'celebrity' chefs, including Raymond Blanc, with his impressive organic garden at Le Manoir aux Quat' Saisons, Shaun Hill and lovely Sophie Grigson, the well-known food writer who gave cookery demonstrations at Ryton on so many special occasions.

Lots of national companies had also been sympathetic to our aims, helping to push organic gardening by sponsoring HDRA events and campaigns – the supermarket chains Safeway and Waitrose, *The Mail on Sunday*, Severn Trent, and many others, including friendly firms that had given us 'gifts in kind'. All these, along with the long list of charitable trusts and individuals, responded to Jackie's good-natured badgering by lending their support in a myriad of ways.

The Prince of Wales, who had done so much for the organization over the years, then left Ryton to go on to his next appointment. I think it was a Prince's Trust event, where he would undoubtedly show the same kindly interest in the budding young entrepreneurs who had benefited from the scheme that he had shown to our guests. Later that evening, tired out, Jackie and I looked back on the day over a glass of wine, and we ended up reminiscing well into the night about all the people who had contributed to the uptake of organic cultivation and the surge of interest in growing fruit and vegetables.

As time had gone on, more and more professional horticulturalists and writers had made their particular contributions too. During the 1980s Joy Larkcom was one of the few gardening writers to openly side with the organic camp. Joy is rightly credited with having revolution-ized salad growing in the UK, and she had been gardening organically ever since 1977, when she returned from a year-long 'Grand Vegetable Tour' around continental Europe collecting seeds. Fabulously ornate lettuces, colourful chicories and endives had been just some of the spectacular fruits of that first trip; these are taken for granted by gardeners nowadays, but back then they caused a sensation. Nor did she stop there, and in subsequent visits to China and the Far East, and to Chinese immigrant communities in North America, she brought back numerous 'oriental vegetables' to add to the salad repertoire. Her books on salads, and Chinese and Japanese vegetables, are a must for any keen vegetable grower, and they are organic through and through. Her masterful *Grow Your Own Vegetables*, for example, is a book I couldn't bear to be without.

Over the years we had also become firm friends with Peter Surridge, who had a syndicated gardening column in several regional newspapers, and who was similarly sympathetic to organic growing and what HDRA had being trying to achieve. Likewise gardening writer Barbara Segall and food writer Lynda Brown, who both regularly supported events at Ryton.

Back in 1988, another friend of ours, ex-*Financial Times* journalist Basil Caplan, started *Organic Gardening* magazine – the first wholly organic journal to appear on British newsstands since the UK version of Rodale's *Organic Gardening and Farming* (which had collapsed ignominiously in September 1972 after only a few issues). This was Basil's first publishing venture and a brave move on his part, for it was by no means certain that there was a big enough market to sustain a regular monthly publication. But as he explained to me at Ryton, when he came to discuss his plans, the runaway success of *All Muck and Magic?* had given him the confidence to give it a go. And in spite of a few rocky moments along the way, the publication held its own. You can still find it on the shelves today, although Basil retired many years ago.

After 1986, the professionalism that was apparent in all the public areas of Ryton Gardens, and the reliability of its educational and research output, played a strong part in overcoming the 'cranky' image that organic gardening had been labelled with previously. This was helped even more when Geoff Hamilton, with his resolutely down-to-earth approach to gardening, reinforced what we had been saying on *All Muck and Magic?* by taking a far more pro-organic line on the BBC. His shocking and tragic death in 1996 was felt keenly by his family, friends and millions of viewers, who had come to regard him as a much-loved friend. But it was also a loss for organic gardening, and at HDRA we were concerned that whoever took over as the lead pre-senter of BBC's *Gardeners' World* might return to the bad old days of chemical growing. However, Alan Titchmarsh, Geoff's successor, carried on where Geoff had left off, being equally convinced that the organic approach was the best way to garden. In an interview in 2001 for HDRA's members' magazine, *The Organic Way*, Alan, by then one of Britain's best known gardeners, summed up his gardening credo as follows:

> Over the years I've become even more aware of the need to treat soil with respect, and to promote the activity of beneficial soil bacteria. Only organic fertilizers do this, and so for many years now I've been using them instead of inorganic chemicals, which offer a 'quick fix' but do little to contribute to long-term fertility. More recently – in the past five years – I've stopped using pesticides. I feel quite passionately that we cannot treat gardens and the countryside thoughtlessly. We need to have an eye to the future, and organic gardening makes that future assured.

Alan Titchmarsh, as popular as ever, stood down from *Gardeners' World* in 2002. His place was taken by Monty Don, who had spent the previous 14 years as a gardening writer and broadcaster and ran a two-acre garden at his home in Herefordshire on completely organic lines. Monty had visited Ryton not long after it had opened and had also filmed a piece there with Jackie for cable television in the early-1990s. His BBC appointment was an inspired choice as far as we were concerned because he was a tireless and spirited crusader for organic growing, and we were in no doubt that he would inspire millions of gardeners with his warm and generous approach to life and his obvious knowledge and experience. Over the next six years he would create the programme's new garden at Berryfields, which was both productive and stylish – a real testament to organic cultivation.

Back in 2003, though, after the Prince's visit, Jackie and I talked about our future. We would be retiring from HDRA that autumn, after almost 30 years with the organization, the last 17 years of which we had been at the helm. In part, this was because we felt that our job at

HDRA had been done. Organic gardening had become mainstream, so the battle was largely won. And we had never seen ourselves working for the organization well into old age, as Lawrence had done.

Other factors in our decision to leave then were that we were thoroughly fed up with having to deal with the endless flow of Brussels-inspired legislation that every organization has to endure nowadays, and we'd also had enough of the externally driven, mind-numbing culture of box ticking that had crept stealthily upon the country, pervading every aspect of work. We abhorred the associated tide of mindless modern management jargon, such as the ubiquitous 'thinking outside the box', 'transparency', 'accountability' and 'blue-sky thinking' – clichéd buzzwords that are often devoid of meaning. All of this was displacing individual responsibility and plain speaking, but its worst feature was that it prevented working people everywhere from getting on with the job, and this was costing the country a fortune. We objected to it on principle.

Mind you, Jackie wished that she'd had more time to spend on the nutritional side of our work (the whole ethos of organic wholefoods as the foundation of good health), but it was always going to take second place to our raison d'être – organic growing. She'd been able to put the philosophy into action through the shop, and the café at Ryton, with its simple wholefood dishes and then, when that expanded, through the restaurant's more elaborate cuisine. Likewise, events like the Organic Food and Wine Fairs, and the books she had co-written, such as *Thorson's Organic Consumer Guide* and its companion volume on wine, helped to win converts to organic food, but she was nevertheless worried that huge numbers of the population were eating badly and that this would result in massive health problems in the future.

HDRA's Chairman Bill Blyth had been very surprised, two years before, when we'd told him we were thinking of retiring early, but there were no hard feelings on his part. I think he was at least thankful that we had given the Council sufficient time to look for someone else to run the organization.

The staff had been shocked when we eventually informed them of our decision to go. It was a task we had not been looking forward to because we knew that the uncertainty about who would take over would be unsettling for them. Leaving them – many of whom were old friends – and the sheer buzz of the place were the downsides to our decision, but we really did want to get back to grassroots and were keen to spend more time in the garden and on our new allotment in Norfolk, where we had decided to live. Perhaps the greatest benefit of all would be the fact that we would be able to walk along the beach every single day and enjoy the sight and sound of the 30,000-strong skeins of pink-footed geese that fly low over our chosen village each and every winter's morning and evening – an experience that had taken our breath away on many weekend breaks in the area.

The next few months at Ryton before we left were exceptionally busy as we prepared to hand over the organization. The budget that Jackie and I had planned together each year for the past two decades was predicted to show a surplus at the end of the year and Jackie had already been promised a substantial legacy, which would more than absorb any costs associated with the changeover. The Vegetable King-dom, if marketed well, would also increase visitor numbers and attract new members, providing extra revenue on both fronts. All in all, we thought, HDRA was in good shape, and we were looking forward to setting up our own small consultancy company, doing interesting organic work too. In fact, as soon as we moved, in October 2003, Raymond Blanc asked us to help in organizing a tri-nation conference at Le Manoir on the future of farming and of gastronomy involving Britain, France and the USA. This was just up our street because organic farming and food were high on the agenda, so we really enjoyed our first project. Then we produced a master plan for a well-known charitable horticultural organization and went on to create educational materials with an environmental theme for a charitable trust. Following that, we carried out a feasibility study on setting up an organic nursery for yet another charity. And so it's gone on. It's all interesting work, and it suits us down to the ground.

Of course we've followed HDRA's progress too. After a rocky cash-flow situation in her first year (two substantial sources of income that had been promised were late in coming in, and there was an administrative oversight in the accounts office, which resulted in an overspend on the new office building), Susan Kay-Williams, the new Chief Executive, settled in and recruited extra senior staff to cover Jackie's fundraising, publicity, marketing and commercial functions. She also changed the name from HDRA to Garden Organic, which gives a clearer idea of what the organization is all about. A number of staff have left, but Pauline, Bob and Margi are still there, and are still acknowledged as three of the UK's leading organic horticulture experts.

The *Gardeners' World* TV programmes also continued to inspire the gardening public with indispensable organic information from Monty Don. In the autumn of 2004 they screened a five-part television series with him called *Growing out of Trouble*, which focused on a gardening project he had started on a smallholding in the West Midlands, working exclusively with a small number of young offenders, all of them drug addicts. At first it was obvious that Monty had his work cut out, but as the weeks passed by, with his patience and enthusiasm, these young people gradually gained confidence and motivation as they began to connect with the earth and experience the healing power of nature. It was a powerful alternative model of treatment, which hopefully will be taken up elsewhere. For Monty and his young charges, organic gardening was simply the right thing to do. We realized that this was a view that was by now being echoed by just about every other gardening presenter on television – Carol Klein, Sarah Raven and Joe Swift are just a few names that spring immediately to mind; while on radio, the indomitable Bob Flowerdew still dispenses sound organic advice on *Gardener's Question Time*.

In 2007 Susan Kay-Williams herself left Garden Organic and was replaced by Myles Bremner, a highly competent young man who will undoubtedly steer the organization through this current global downturn, just as Jackie and I saw HDRA safely through two recessions. Dr Bill Blyth retired as Chairman in 2004 after twelve years of sterling work and unstinting support, and Dr Bill Bourne, his deputy, took over, to be followed by Dr Sally Bucknall in 2007. Lord Kitchener stepped down as President in 2008, after 35 years of loyal service, and Tim Lang, Professor of Food Policy at City University, London, has replaced him.

In the world at large, two major issues have made Garden Organic's work even more relevant. One is the country's current health crisis, and the other is the looming energy and food shortage – both of which Lawrence, Jackie and I foresaw, but the authorities ignored. Now they are being forced to come to terms with them.

Because of the vast amount of junk food being eaten in Britain today, we have the fastest growing rate of obesity in the developed world, which, if unchecked, will affect a third of all women and half of all men by the middle of the century. By that time, obesity-related diseases – Type 2 diabetes, heart disease, stroke and cancers linked to the digestive and reproductive systems, along with a host of lesser complaints – will be at epidemic levels. And this is a global issue, affecting not only developed Western nations, but newly developing countries too. Since industrialization, China has adopted similar food- and lifestyles to our own and with exactly the same response in terms of obesity and the catastrophic rise in associated health problems – a million new cases of diabetes are diagnosed each year, an astonishing statistic, given that the disease was practically unheard of there as little as 20 years ago.

When Jamie Oliver began his televised campaign to improve the quality of school dinners, he discovered that huge numbers of children are being brought up on high-fat, high-salt junk food, epitomized by the ubiquitous 'turkey twizzler and fries'. *Jamie's School Dinners* appeared on Channel 4 in the summer of 2005 and was watched by huge audiences. As well as highlighting the abysmal state of school catering, it actually showed that many kids also eat rubbish at home – microwaved meals, takeaway TV dinners or, worse still, just chips, crisps, chocolate and fizzy drinks. Sadly, many parents these days have forgotten, or never learned, how to cook, even if they had wanted to. One reason for this is that practical cookery lessons were dropped from school classrooms during the 1980s when 'domestic science' was replaced by 'food technology', which taught kids how to design a pizza topping, or fashion elaborate icing patterns on a cake, but not how to boil an egg.

Jamie's programmes caused a national outcry, and within months the government had promised to give £280 million towards the cost of improving the quality of school meals, and it pledged to re-introduce the lost art of cooking with fresh ingredients. This pressure for change was kept up by voluntary groups, including those taking part in healthy eating initiatives such as the 'Food for Life Partnership', which was set up in 2007. Led by the Soil Association, with Garden Organic as one of the three other partners, its objective was to persuade schools to source seasonal, local and organic food, some of which would be grown in school gardens. In January 2008 things moved forward when the Secretary of State for Children, Schools and Families, Ed Balls, announced that cookery lessons would be compulsory from September for all 11 to 14 year-olds, commenting, 'Leaving school able to cook healthy dishes from scratch is an essential everyday skill all young people should have … it is at the heart of tackling obesity.' Sense at last!

The government has finally cottoned on to the dietary relevance of fresh fruit and vegetables – hence its campaign to get us all to eat five items a day and its caution against over-indulging in foods that are high in fat, sugar and salt. But it has far less to say about the importance of wholefoods, and nothing at all to say about the significance of food being organic. Many celebrity chefs now demand vegetables and other fresh ingredients that are sourced locally and grown organically and they urge us to cook from scratch, rather than buy processed food; but none of them insists on using ingredients made from wholegrain cereals in their recipes. Then there's the medical profession, which does advise us to eat wholegrain cereals and other foods that contain plenty of roughage, but, like the Department of Health, is silent on the subject of organic food. To their credit, most of the supermarkets stock some organic vegetables and unpolished rice, wholemeal flour and wholewheat pasta, although there are not always organically grown versions on offer – you have to find a good wholefood store for that.

There are now many sources of dietary advice, some of it different, some of it overlapping, some of it conflicting and nobody at all seems to be pulling it all together into one simple message – that a diet containing lots of organic fruit and vegetables, as freshly picked as possible, and unprocessed organic wholefoods, promotes good health.

As usual, many ordinary people throughout the world have been way ahead of governments in recognizing what's actually going wrong and they are changing the way they eat. Their reaction to global warming has been to try to reduce their own personal 'carbon footprint'. In Britain this has resulted in a massive increase in organic fruit and vegetable growing – an activity that is acknowledged to be more environmentally friendly. Sales of vegetable seeds in 2007 topped £36 million, exceeding those of flowers for the first time since the Second World War. Unwins, the UK's largest seed supplier to the amateur market, announced that vegetable seeds now accounted for nearly three-quarters of its business, up from just over a third five years ago. The Horticultural Trades Association, the body that represents the garden industry, also reported that in the same year, herb sales were up 18 per cent on the previous year, while sales of fruit trees grew by a massive 36 per cent, despite 2007 having been one of the wettest years on record. These figures would have been even greater if all the people who had wanted to grow their own fruit and vegetables had not been prevented from doing it by the fact that over half of all local authorities in England had long waiting lists for allotments: more than 4,000 in London alone.

Another reason that more people than ever are growing organic fruit and vegetables is the rising cost of food. During 2007 the price of many foodstuffs went up by three times the annual rate of inflation. Poor harvests were partly to blame – the exceptionally wet summer caused severe shortages of potatoes and other vegetables, for example. This may just be the start of more serious, long-term factors coming in to play, signalling that the days of cheap food are gone forever. Chief among these factors is that the world's food supply is not keeping pace with the growth in human populations, which rise by 79 million every year. In 1949, when Jackie and I were born, there were 2.5 billion people, now there are over 6.7 billion, and this is expected to reach 9 billion by 2050.

All these initiatives to grow food at home have to be a good thing. In September 2008 Tim Lang commented in *The Daily Telegraph* that, 'A global food crisis is looming. This crisis can be solved by the democratisation of gardening – opening up and encouraging everyone to grow their own produce where possible in their own back garden or local community – changing thinking from food miles to food metres. Ultimately people have to take more control of their food systems.'

It's a message endorsed by Hugh Fearnley-Whittingstall, Britain's current self-sufficiency guru (following in the footsteps of John Seymour), whose *River Cottage* television programmes extol the virtues of the 'good life' to a new generation. In 2007, under his watchful eye, a group of people from Bristol who had never gardened before took over a patch of overgrown wasteland owned by Bristol Council and turned it into a productive vegetable plot, and the following year they even introduced pigs and chickens. His latest initiative is to tackle the problem of an acute shortage of allotments by bringing would-be gardeners and land owners with spare land together via a website – www.landshare.net – launched earlier this year.

This has echoes of the anarchic attempts by my late friend Tony Wigens, back in the 1970s, to commandeer unused and derelict land and bring it back into production – a story he told, most entertainingly, in his book *Clandestine Farm*. And it is evident in the well-known exploits of Liz Christy and friends, who founded the Green Guerrillas group in New York in 1973. They began by planting vegetables on disused building sites and vacant lots – anywhere, in fact, where land was going begging – and ended up pioneering the community gardening movement in the USA.

In Britain today, an estimated 215,000 tons of fresh produce is grown on just 300,000 allotment plots. That works out at a massive 12 tons an acre. And this is achieved by people working the land for as little as two or three hours a week, and who range from outright beginners to experienced gardeners. Most will grow at least two and sometimes even three different crops on the same piece of land each year – as soon as one is harvested, another is planted.

And as for commercial organic growing, you only have to look back 100 years to see how productive professional gardeners can be. During the second half of the 19th century most of the large cities in Europe were supplied with fresh produce from smallholdings located out in the suburbs. What is now the practice field at Lord's Cricket Ground in St John's Wood, London, used to be just such a market garden, with an enviable reputation for growing some of the finest pineapples in the capital. Across the English Channel in Paris, around 5,000 *maraîchers* (market gardeners) fed a population of two million on just 2,125 acres of land. These skilled growers extracted between 50 and 100 tons of fresh fruit and vegetables, on average, from a single acre of land – and all of it was grown organically. If we have the will to do it, there is nothing to prevent us from establishing similar market gardens once again. And if the same sorts of yields were achieved – and they could be – the population of Britain could rise to as much as 90 million without people going hungry.

The rediscovered joys of producing home-grown fruit and vegetables have gone hand in hand with an appreciation of the principles of organic gardening. This is due largely to the fact that most newly published gardening books adopt an organic approach. As a result, Garden Organic's website now receives over a million 'hits' a month from gardeners the world over who are thirsty for practical knowledge. Even the much-respected Royal Horticultural Society (RHS) has accepted that organic gardening has come of age and has cut chemical use in its show gardens at Wisley in Surrey by more than half, in a drive to minimize its environmental impact. The RHS also discovered from a readership survey conducted in its in-house journal, *The Garden*, in April 2009 that, 'More than 80 per cent of readers said they already garden organically – or are considering doing so.' An indication of this dramatic change in horticultural practice came as early as 2006, when the RHS awarded Jackie and me Honorary Fellowships, stating at the award ceremony: 'Alan and Jackie Gear have helped organic gardening develop from being a fringe activity into what is now the major influence on 21st-century gardens and gardening.' We accepted the fellowships very much on behalf of HDRA as a whole.

Growing food organically is now a major influence the world over. It is one good way to ensure that we can feed ourselves and our families far into the future. Unlike alternative energy, it doesn't require any technical breakthroughs. It's something we can all do now, especially when expert help is at hand from organizations such as Garden Organic and from television and radio gardeners and other experts the world over. There is a massive base of experience out there that novice growers can draw on. Whether in fields, allotments, community gardens, back yards, or even in pots on window sills, we can thoroughly enjoy ourselves producing fresh, tasty, home produce. The preceding 60 years have been but a prelude to a truly sustainable organic future.

LIST OF ACRONYMS

The following acronyms have been used in the book:

BAA: Biodynamic Agricultural Association
BOSC: British Organic Standards Committee
BSE: Bovine Spongiform Encephalopathy
CAT: Centre for Alternative Technology
CJD: Creutzfeldt-Jakob disease
DDT: Dichloro-diphenyl-trichloroethane
DEFRA: Department for Environment, Food and Rural Affairs
EFRC: Elm Farm Research Centre
EU: European Union
FAFS: Farm and Food Society
FiBL: Forschungsinstitut für Biologischen Landbau (Institute of Biological Husbandry)
FSA: Food Standards Agency
GGA: Good Gardeners' Association
GOAN: Ghana Organic Agriculture Network
HDRA: Henry Doubleday Research Association
HSL: Heritage Seed Library
IFOAM: International Federation of Organic Agricultural Movements
IIBH: International Institute of Biological Husbandry
IWS: International Wool Secretariat
MAFF: Ministry of Agriculture, Fisheries and Food
MSC: Manpower Services Commission
NIAB: National Institute for Agricultural Botany
NPK: Nitrogen, phosphorus, potassium
OF&G: Organic Farmers & Growers Ltd
OGA: formerly Organic Growers Association; now Organic Growers Alliance
RHS: Royal Horticultural Society
SSE: Seed Savers Exchange
UKROFS: United Kingdom Register of Organic Food Standards
UNEP: United Nations Environment Programme
WWOOF: formerly Working Weekends on Organic Farms; now World Wide Opportunities on Organic Farms

GLOSSARY

Agroforestry: a system of agriculture that combines growing crops and/or rearing livestock in close association with trees.

Eutrophication: the excessive growth of aquatic plant life in rivers, lakes and other bodies of water, brought about by an over-abundance of nutrients, especially phosphate, usually as a result of agricultural pollution or sewage discharge.

F1 hybrid vegetable seed: the offspring resulting from crossing two different varieties of the same plant species (the first filial generation); frequently out-performs either of the parents in vigour. Seeds saved from F1 varieties don't breed true.

Green Revolution: an agricultural approach, first introduced in Mexico in 1943 and still employed in the Third World, based on the use of high-yielding cultivars of wheat, rice and other crops, high fertilizer and pesticide applications and the widespread use of irrigation. While crop yields have undoubtedly increased, this has frequently been achieved at considerable environmental and social cost.

Green manure: certain plants that are sown to improve the fertility of the soil and minimize nutrient loss. They are usually dug into the soil before the plants reach maturity but can also be harvested and composted, then added later. Commonly used green manures include various clovers (which 'capture' atmospheric nitrogen), grazing rye, mustard and *Phacelia*.

Haulm: the stems, shoots and leaves of plants such as peas, beans, tomatoes, potatoes and chrysanthemums.

Humus: the organic component of soil, produced by the decomposition of fallen leaves and other plant and animal 'waste' material by micro-organisms and other soil-dwelling creatures.

Leach out: the process by which soluble chemicals are washed out of the soil by the action of rainwater.

Leafmould: material made from dead and decaying leaves, which gardeners add to the soil to improve its structure and use as an ingredient in growing media.

Mulch: materials, usually of plant or animal origin, such as compost, bark or well-rotted animal manure, that are spread onto the soil surface and around plants to suppress weeds, feed the soil and reduce water lost by evaporation.

Paviour: term used by manufacturers of paving slabs for the coloured concrete blocks that resemble bricks. The blocks are laid on a bed of sand without a cement base and are then compacted with a vibrating plate machine to give a tight fit.

Permaculture: food-growing systems that are largely based around the use of tree crops and other perennial plants. The word is a synthesis of the term 'permanent agriculture'.

Polytunnel: an elongated, walk-in structure made from semi-circular metal hoops covered with clear polythene sheeting in which out-of-season and delicate crops are grown.

Ring barking: damage to a tree, usually caused by rabbits, squirrels or deer that nibble the bark away in a complete ring, such that the cells along which nutrients and water are carried are damaged irreparably, often resulting in the tree's death.

Sustainable farming: agriculture that avoids depletion of natural resources and minimizes chemical inputs, such that it can maintain food production indefinitely.

Transpiration: the process by which plants emit water vapour (via evaporation) into the atmosphere through openings on the surface of their leaves called stomata.

Windrow: a long row of waste plant or animal material, approximately four feet wide and tall, which breaks down to form compost.

SELECT BIBLIOGRAPHY

The bibliography that follows is by no means a complete record of all the works we have consulted throughout our many years in organic gardening, farming and food. However, it does list some of the major titles that have contributed, in one way or another, to the production of this book as well as to the formulation of some of our fundamental ideas and principles. It also acts as an excellent source of reference for those who wish to pursue the subject in more depth.

Chapter 1: Origins

Balfour, Lady Eve, *The Living Soil and the Haughley Experiment* (Faber and Faber, London, 1975; first published as *The Living Soil*, 1943)

Bruce, Maye E., *Commonsense Compost Making* (Faber and Faber, London, 1945)

Cobbett, William, *Rural Rides* (Penguin, London 1967; first published 1830)

Easey, Ben, *Practical Organic Gardening* (Faber and Faber, London, 1955)

Howard, Sir Albert, *The Waste Products of Agriculture: Their Utilization as Humus* (Oxford University Press, London, 1931)

Howard, Sir Albert, *An Agricultural Testament* (Oxford University Press, London, 1940)

—— *Farming and Gardening for Health or Disease* (Faber and Faber, London, 1945)

Jacks, G.V., and R.O. Whyte, *The Rape of the Earth* (Faber and Faber, London, 1939)

King, E.H., *Farmers of Forty Centuries* (Cape, London, 1926)

King, F.C., *Gardening with Compost* (Faber and Faber, London, 1940)

—— *The Compost Gardener* (Titus Wilson, Kendal, Cumbria, UK, 1943)

Newman Turner, Frank, *Fertility Farming* (Faber and Faber, London, 1951)

Pfeiffer, Ehrenfried, *The Earth's Face* (Faber and Faber, London, 1947)

Roberts, Jonathan, *Cabbages & Kings* (Harper Collins, London, 2001)

Rodale, Jerome Irving, *Pay Dirt: Farming and Gardening with Composts* (Devin Adair, New York, 1945)

—— *The Organic Front* (Rodale Press, Emmaus, PA, USA, 1948)

—— *Organic Gardening: How to Grow Healthy Vegetables, Fruit and Flowers Using Nature's Own Methods* (Rodale Press, Emmaus, PA, USA, 1955)

Shewell-Cooper, Dr W.E., *The Complete Vegetable Grower* (Faber and Faber, London, 1955)

Sykes, Friend, *Humus and the Farmer* (Faber and Faber, London, 1946)

Tudge, Colin, *Neanderthals, Bandits and Farmers* (Weidenfeld & Nicolson, London, 1998; Yale University Press, New Haven, 1999)

—— *So Shall We Reap* (Penguin, London, 2003)

Chapter 2: Philosophy into Practice

Hills, Lawrence D., *The Propagation of Alpines* (Faber and Faber, London, 1950)
—— *Russian Comfrey* (Faber and Faber, London, 1953)
—— *Down to Earth Fruit and Vegetable Growing* (Faber and Faber, London, 1960)
—— *Grow Your Own Fruit and Vegetables* (Faber and Faber, London, 1971)
—— *Fighting Like the Flowers* (Green Books, Bideford, Devon, 1989)

Chapter 3: New Roots

Meadows, Donella, et al, *The Limits to Growth* (Universe Books, New York, 1972)

Chapter 4: The Good Life

Grant, Doris, *Your Daily Bread* (Faber and Faber, London, 1943)
McCarrison, Robert, *Nutrition and Health* (Faber and Faber, London, 1953)
Nearing, Scott and Helen, *Living the Good Life* (Schocken Books, New York, 1954)
—— *Continuing the Good Life* (Schocken Books, New York, 1979)
Seymour, John, *The Fat of the Land* (Faber and Faber, London, 1961)
—— *Self Sufficiency* (Faber and Faber, London, 1970)

Chapter 5: Fertility without Fertilizers

Appelhof, Mary, *Worms Eat My Garbage* (Flower Press, Kalamazoo, Michigan, USA, 1982)
Duddington, Dr C.L., *The Friendly Fungi* (Faber and Faber, London, 1957)
Kitto, Dick, *Composting* (Thorsons, Wellingborough, Northants, UK, 1988)
Lampkin, Nicolas, *Organic Farming* (Old Pond Publishing, Ipswich, Suffolk, UK, 1982)

Chapter 6: Poison-free Pest Control

Carson, Rachel, *Silent Spring* (Houghton Mifflin, Boston, 1962; Hamish Hamilton, London, 1963)
Hills, Lawrence D., *Pest Control without Poisons* (HDRA, Bocking, Essex, UK, 1964)
—— *Operation Tiggywinkle* (HDRA, Bocking, Essex, UK, 1970)
Philbrick, Helen, and Richard Gregg, *Companion Plants and How to Use Them* (Devin Adair, New York, 1966; Robinson and Watkins, London, 1967)
Van Den Bosch, Robert, *The Pesticide Conspiracy* (Doubleday & Co, New York, 1978; Prism Press, Dorchester, UK, 1980)

Chapter 7: Branching Out

Jeavons, John, *How to Grow More Vegetables than you ever thought possible on less land than you can imagine* (Ten Speed Press, Berkeley, California, USA, 1974)
Rodale, Robert, and Glenn F. Johns, *The Basic Book of Organic Gardening* (Ballantine, New York, 1971)

Chapter 8: Seeing is Believing

Guest, A., *Gardening without Digging* (1949; reprinted by Marshalls Seeds, Cambridge, UK, in association with the Good Gardeners Association, 1999)
King, F.C., *Is Digging Necessary?* (Levens Gardens, Kendal, Westmoreland, UK, 1946)
Ratcliffe, Dr Derek, *Objectives and Strategy for Nature Conservation in Great Britain* (Nature Conservancy Council, London, 1983)
Stout, Ruth, *How to Have a Green Thumb without an Aching Back: A New Method of Mulch Gardening* (Exposition Press, New York, 1955)

Chapter 9: All Muck and Magic?

Coleman, Eliot, *The New Organic Grower* (Chelsea Green Publishing, Vermont, USA, 1989)
—— *Four-Season Harvest* (Chelsea Green Publishing, Vermont, USA, 1992)
Flowerdew, Bob, *The Organic Gardener* (Hamlyn, London, 1993)
—— *Bob Flowerdew's Organic Bible* (Kyle Kathie, London, 1998)
—— *Grow Your Own, Eat Your Own* (Kyle Kathie, London, 2008)
Merrill, Richard (ed), *Radical Agriculture* (New York University Press, New York, 1976)

Chapter 10: Enter the Prince

HRH The Prince of Wales and Charles Clover, *Highgrove: Portrait of an Estate* (Chapmans, London, 1993)
HRH The Prince of Wales with Stephanie Donaldson, *The Elements of Organic Gardening* (Weidenfeld & Nicolson, London, 2007)
HRH The Prince of Wales and Candida Lycett Green, *The Garden at Highgrove* (Weidenfeld & Nicolson, London, 2000)

Chapter 11: Food Champions

Davies, Gareth, and Margi Lennartsson (eds), *Organic Vegetable Production* (The Crowood Press, Marlborough, Wiltshire, UK, 2005)
Schlosser, Eric, *Fast Food Nation* (Penguin Books, London, 2002)

Chapter 12: Third World Growing

International Assessment of Agricultural Knowledge, Science and Technology for Development (IAASTD) *Executive Summary* (Johannesburg, South Africa, April 2008)

Parrott, Nicholas, and Terry Marsden, *The Real Green Revolution: Organic and Agroecological Farming in the South* (Greenpeace Environmental Trust, London, 2002)

Pearse, Andrew, *Seeds of Plenty, Seeds of Want: Social and Economic Implications of the Green Revolution* (Oxford University Press, London and New York, 1980)

Pretty, Jules, *Agri-Culture: Reconnecting People, Land and Nature* (Earthscan, London, 2002)

UNEP-UNCTAD, *Organic Agriculture and Food Security in Africa* (UN, Geneva, 2008)

Chapter 13: Vanishing Vegetables

Brac de la Perrière, Robert Ali, and Franck Seuret, *Brave New Seeds: the Threat of GM Crops to Farmers* (Zed Books, London, 2000)

Cherfas, Jeremy, and Michel and Jude Fanton, *The Seed Savers' Handbook* (Grover Books, UK, 1996)

Fowler, Cary, and Pat Mooney, *The Threatened Gene* (The Lutterworth Press, Cambridge, UK, 1990; University of Arizona Press, USA, 1990)

Guillet, Dominique, *The Seeds of Kokopelli* (Kokopelli Seed Foundation, Boston, MA, USA, 2004)

Romans, Alan, *The Potato Book* (Frances Lincoln, London, 2005)

Shiva, Vandan, *Stolen Harvest: The Hijacking of the Global Food Supply* (Zed Books, London, 2000)

Vellvé, Renée, *Saving the Seed: Genetic Diversity and European Agriculture* (Earthscan, London, 1992)

Wilson, Alan, *The Story of the Potato* (self-published, 1993; ISBN 0 9520973 1 1)

Chapter 14: Designed to be Green

Cobbett, William, *Cottage Economy* (Landsmans Bookshop, Hereford, 1975 – facsimile of 1821 edition)

Hamilton, Geoff, *Organic Gardening* (Dorling Kindersley, London, 1987)

—— *Geoff Hamilton's Paradise Gardens* (BBC Books, London, 1997)

Hart, Robert, *Forest Gardening: Cultivating an Edible Landscape* (Green Books, 1991)

Kingsbury, Noel, *The New Perennial Garden* (Frances Lincoln, London, 1996)

Mollison, Bill, C., and David Holmgren, *Permaculture 1: A Perennial Agricultural System for Human Settlements* (Environmental Psychology, University of Tasmania, Australia, 1978)

Oudolf, Piet, and Noel Kingsbury, *Designing with Plants* (Conran Octopus, London, 1999; Timber Press, Portland, Oregon, USA, 1999)

Traegar, Tessa, and Patrick Kinmonth, *A Gardener's Labyrinth: Portraits of People, Plants and Places* (Booth-Clibborn Editions, London, 2003)

Whitefield, Patrick, *How to Make a Forest Garden* (Permanent Publications, East Meon, Hants, UK, 1996)

Chapter 15: Food You Can Trust

Davis, Donald R., 'Trade-Offs in Agriculture and Nutrition', *Food Technology*, Vol. 59, No. 3, March 2005

Goodall, Chris, *How to Live a Low-Carbon Life* (Earthscan, London; Sterling, VA, USA, 2007)

Heaton, Shane, *Organic Farming, Food Quality and Human Health: A Review of the Evidence* (The Soil Association, Bristol, UK, 2002)

Ho, Mae-Wan, and Lim Li Ching, *The Case for a GM-Free Sustainable World* (Institute of Science in Society, London, 2003; Third World Network, Penang, Malaysia, 2003)

Jones, Andy, *Eating Oil: Food Supply in a Changing Climate* (Sustain / Elm Farm Research Centre, London / Newbury, Berks, UK, 2001)

Lovelock, James, *Gaia: A New Look at Life on Earth* (Oxford University Press, Oxford; New York, 1979)

—— *The Revenge of Gaia* (Allen Lane, London, 2006)

McCance, R.A., and E. M. Widdowson, *The Composition of Foods* (Royal Society of Chemistry, 6th revised ed, 2002)

Meadows, Donella, Jorgen Randers and Dennis Meadows, *Limits to Growth: the 30-Year Update* (Earthscan, London, 2005)

Meier-Ploeger, Angelika, 'Does Organic Food have an Extra Quality?' (Elm Farm Research Centre, *Food Quality & Organic Food and Faming Conference*, 23 November, 2004)

Pretty, J.N., A.S. Ball, T. Lang and J.L. Morison, 'Food miles and farm costs: the full cost of the British food basket', *Food Policy* (Vol. 30(1), pp.1–20, 2005)

Roberts, Paul, *The End of Oil* (Bloomsbury, London, 2004)

Thomas, David, *The Mineral Depletion of Foods Available to Us as a Nation (1940–1991)* (Mineral Resources International, Forest Row, East Sussex, UK, 2004)

Chapter 16: Blossoming Out

Bartholomew, Mel, *Square Foot Gardening* (Rodale Press, Emmaus, PA, USA, 1981)

Brown, Maggi, *Growing Naturally: A Teacher's Guide to Organic Gardening* (Southgate Publishers, Crediton, Devon, UK, 1996)

Campbell, Susan, *A History of Kitchen Gardening* (Frances Lincoln, London, 2005)

Davis, Jennifer, *The Victorian Kitchen Garden* (BBC Books, London, 1987)

Search Press titles on organic gardening (Tunbridge Wells, Kent, UK)

Stickland, Sue, *Heritage Vegetables: The Gardener's Guide to Cultivating Diversity* (Gaia Books, London, 1998)

Chapter 17: An Organic Future

Conford, Philip (ed), *A Future for the Land* (Green Books, Bideford, Devon, UK, 1992)

Don, Monty, *Growing Out of Trouble* (Hodder and Stoughton, London, 2006)

Kropotkin, Peter, *Fields, Factories and Workshops Tomorrow* (Freedom Press, London, 1974; first published 1899)

Larkcom, Joy, *Grow Your Own Vegetables* (Frances Lincoln, London, 2002)

—— *The Organic Salad Garden* (Frances Lincoln, London, 2003)

—— *Oriental Vegetables* (Frances Lincoln, London, 2007)

Oliver, Jamie, *Jamie's Dinners* (Penguin, London, 2006)

Pears, Pauline, and Sue Stickland, *Organic Gardening* (Mitchell Beazley, London, 1999)

Pears, Pauline Pears (ed.), *Encyclopaedia of Organic Gardening* (Dorling Kindersley, London, 2001)

Rodale's New Encyclopaedia of Organic Gardening: The Indispensable Resource for Every Gardener (Rodale Press, Emmaus, PA, USA, 1999)

Titchmarsh, Alan, *The Kitchen Gardener: Grow Your Own Fruit & Veg* (BBC Books, London, 2008)

Wigens, Anthony, *Clandestine Farm* (Paladin, 1981)

USEFUL ADDRESSES

AUSTRALIA

Organizations

Bio-Dynamic Gardeners Association Incorporated
Tel: +61 (0)3 9842 8137
www.demeter.org.au

Biological Farmers of Australia
Tel: +61 (0)7 3350 5716
www.bfa.com.au

Henry Doubleday Research Association of Australia
www.hdra.org.au

Organic Federation of Australia
www.ofa.org.au

Organic Guide
www.organicguide.com

Suppliers

Eden Seeds
Tel: +61 (0)7 5533 1107
www.edenseeds.com.au

Green Harvest
Tel: +61 (0)7 5435 2699
www.greenharvest.com.au

Seed Savers Network
Tel +61 (0)2 6685 6624
www.seedsavers.net

AUSTRIA

Arche Noah
Tel: +43 (0)2734 8626
www.arche-noah.at

FRANCE

Association Kokopelli
www.kokopelli-seeds.com

Terre Vivante
Tel: +33 (0)4 76 34 80 80
www.terrevivante.org

GERMANY

International Federation of Organic Agriculture Movements
Tel: +49 (0)228 926 50-10
www.ifoam.org

HONG KONG

Handmade Projects
www.journeytoforever.org

IRELAND

The Organic Centre
Tel: +353 (0)71 985 4343
www.theorganiccentre.ie

NEW ZEALAND

Organizations

Biodynamic Farming and Gardening Association of New Zealand
Tel: +64 (0)4 589 5366
www.biodynamic.org.nz

Organics Aotearoa New Zealand
Tel: +64 (0)4 890 3769
www.oanz.org.nz

Soil and Health Association of New Zealand
Tel: +64 (0)9 419 4536
www.organicnz.org

Suppliers

Koanga Institute
Tel: +64 (0)9 431 2732
www.koanga.org.nz

SWITZERLAND

FiBL
Tel: +41 62 865 72 72
www.fibl.org

ProSpecieRara
Tel: +41 (0)22 418 52 25
www.prospecierara.ch

UNITED KINGDOM

Organizations

Brogdale Farm
Tel: +44 (0)1795 536250
www.brogdalecollections.co.uk

Biodynamic Agricultural Association
Tel: +44 (0)1453 759501
www.biodynamic.org.uk

Centre for Alternative Technology
Tel: +44 (0)1654 705950
www.cat.org.uk

English Heritage
Tel: +44 (0)870 333 1181
www.english-heritage.org.uk

Federation of City Farms and Community Gardens
Tel: +44 (0)117 923 1800
www.farmgarden.org.uk

Garden Organic (formerly HDRA)
Tel: +44 (0)24 7630 3517
www.gardenorganic.co.uk

Landshare
www.landshare.net

National Trust
Tel: +44 (0)844 800 1895
www.nationaltrust.org.uk

The Organic Research Centre
(formerly Elm Farm Research Centre)
Tel: +44 (0)1488 658298
www.organicresearchcentre.com

The Soil Association
Tel: +44 (0)117 314 5000
www.soilassociation.org

Permaculture Association
Tel: +44 (0)113 230 7461
www.permaculture.org.uk

Pesticides Action Network UK
Tel: +44 (0)20 7065 0905
www.pan-uk.org

World Wide Opportunities on Organic Farms
www.wwoof.org.uk

Suppliers

Alanromans.com
Tel: +44 (0)1337 831060
www.alanromans.com

Green Gardener
Tel: +44 (0)1603 715096
www.greengardener.co.uk

Kings Seeds
Tel: +44 (0)1376 570000
www.kingsseeds.com

The Organic Gardening Catalogue
Tel: +44 (0)845 130 1304
www.organiccatalogue.com

The Real Seed Catalogue
Tel: +44 (0)1239 821107
www.realseeds.co.uk

Thomas Etty Esq
Tel: +44 (0)1460 57934
www.thomasetty.co.uk

Tuckers Seeds
Tel: +44 (0)1364 652233
www.tuckers-seeds.co.uk

USA & CANADA

Organizations

American Community Gardening Association
Tel: +1 877 275 2242
www.communitygarden.org

*Biodynamic Farming and Gardening
Association*
Tel: +1 888 516 7797
www.biodynamics.com

Canadian Organic Growers
Tel: +1 613 216 0741
www.cog.au

Kokopelli Seed Foundation
www.kokopelli-seed-foundation.com

Rodale Institute
Tel: +1 610 683 1400
www.rodaleinstitute.org

Suppliers

Agrestal Organic Heritage Seeds
www.agrestalseeds.com

Buglogical Control Systems
Tel: +1 520 298 4400
www.buglogical.com
www.gardeninsects.com

Ecogenesis
Tel: +1 877 836 3693

Gardens Alive
Tel: +1 513 354 1482
www.gardensalive.com

Heritage Harvest Seed
Tel: +1 204 745 6489

Johnny's Selected Seeds
Tel: +1 877 564 6697
www.johnnyseeds.com

Redwood City Seed Company
Tel: +1 650 325 7333
www.ecoseeds.com

Seeds of Change
Tel: +1 888 762 7333
www.seedsofchange.com

Seeds of Diversity
Tel: +1 866 509 7333
www.seeds.ca

Seed Savers Exchange
Tel: +1 563 382 5990
www.seedsavers.org

INDEX